Pentecostal Migration in Secular Sweden

Pentecostal Migration in Secular Sweden

Multi-disciplinary Perspectives on a
New Religious Cosmopolitan Landscape

Edited by
Victoria Enkvist and Katarina Westerlund

SHEFFIELD uk   BRISTOL ct

Published by Equinox Publishing Ltd.

UK: Office 415, The Workstation, 15 Paternoster Row, Sheffield, South Yorkshire S1 2BX

USA: ISD, 70 Enterprise Drive, Bristol, CT 06010

www.equinoxpub.com

Earlier versions of Chapters 2, 3, 4 and 5 were first published in volume 22.1 of the journal *PentecoStudies*, © Equinox Publishing Ltd 2024
Chapters 1, 6, 7 and 8 are previously unpublished

© Victoria Enkvist, Katarina Westerlund and contributors 2025

All rights reserved. No part of this publication may be reproduced or transmitted in any form or by any means, electronic or mechanical, including photocopying, recording or any information storage or retrieval system, without prior permission in writing from the publishers.

ISBN-13 978 1 80050 641 1 (hardback)
         978 1 80050 642 8 (paperback)
         978 1 80050 643 5 (ePDF)
         978 1 80050 707 4 (ePub)

British Library Cataloguing-in-Publication Data
A catalogue record for this book is available from the British Library.

Library of Congress Cataloging-in-Publication Data
Names: Enkvist, Victoria editor | Westerlund, Katarina, 1962- editor
Title: Pentecostal migration in secular Sweden : multi-disciplinary perspectives on a new religious cosmopolitan landscape / edited by Victoria Enkvist and Katarina Westerlund.
Description: Sheffield, South Yorkshire ; Bristol : Equinox Publishing Ltd., [2025] | Includes bibliographical references and index. | Summary: "Around the globe, migrant communities are being established in modern, Western societies where they are creating new, vital Pentecostal churches, worship groups, and religious communities. This book analyzes this global phenomenon from different disciplinary perspectives, with the Swedish capital Stockholm as an example"—Provided by publisher.
Identifiers: LCCN 2025028423 (print) | LCCN 2025028424 (ebook) | ISBN 9781800506411 hardback | ISBN 9781800506428 paperback | ISBN 9781800506435 pdf | ISBN 9781800507074 epub
Subjects: LCSH: Pentecostal churches—Sweden—Stockholm—History | Stockholm (Sweden)—Church history
Classification: LCC BX8762.A45 S865 2025 (print) | LCC BX8762.A45 (ebook)
LC record available at https://lccn.loc.gov/2025028423
LC ebook record available at https://lccn.loc.gov/2025028424

Typeset by JS Typesetting, Porthcawl, Mid Glamorgan

Contents

Foreword by Grace Davie — vii

1. International Pentecostalism in Sweden: Researching a New Cosmopolitan Landscape — 1
   Victoria Enkvist and Katarina Westerlund

2. Desecularization of Stockholm? Changes in Numbers of Churches and International Pentecostalism 1980–2020 — 15
   Magdalena Nordin and Torbjörn Aronson

3. Ecclesiology with Unintended Consequences: Pingströrelsen and the Integration of International Pentecostal Churches in Stockholm 1980–2020 — 37
   Torbjörn Aronson

4. "Living Theology": Everyday Life, Challenges and Resources among International Pentecostals in Stockholm — 60
   Katarina Westerlund

5. Suburbia and the Subway: Pentecostalism and Migration in Stockholm — 78
   Émir Mahieddin

6. Legal Regulation of Religious Minorities in Sweden: The Example of International Pentecostals — 96
   Victoria Enkvist

7. International Pentecostals in Metropolitan Stockholm: Rethinking Relations between Voluntary and State Religion in Urban Sweden — 117
   Anders Bäckström

8. Broadening the Perspectives: An International Outlook — 139
   Allan H. Anderson, Simon Coleman, Kim Knibbe and Pamela Slotte Russo

Index — 158

Foreword

Grace Davie

I am more than pleased to recommend this volume, which looks in detail at three groups of Pentecostal Christians who have settled in the Stockholm area; each group comes from a different part of the world. The questions that the authors raise are the following. What role does Pentecostalism play among migrants in Sweden? What challenges do they face in terms of their religious lives, and what challenges do they pose to Swedish society? Conversely how does this society, and more importantly the Swedish state react to their presence? How, in other words, does it handle religious minorities whose values as well as lifestyles deviate from the secular views of the great majority of Swedish people? The answers unfold in the following pages.

The significance of this work needs to be placed in context, first in terms of its provenance and second in terms of its wider implications. With respect to the former, it is a welcome addition to the growing list of publications emerging from the Religion and Society Research Centre (CRS) at Uppsala University in Sweden. Regarding the latter, it adds substantially to the literature concerning religion in Europe, and in particular the corpus of work that brings together the ongoing secularization in this part of the world on the one hand, and growing religious diversity on the other – a combination that needs close and careful scrutiny.

The Uppsala Religion and Society Research Centre has been in existence for more than twenty years (see www.uu.se/en/centre/crs for more about the Centre's structure, development, research programmes and publications). An early focus on the separation of church and state in Sweden in the year 2000 led in turn to a series of comparative studies on religion and welfare across Europe. The second of these, "Welfare and Values in Europe" (WaVE), funded by the European Commission's 6th Framework Programme, ran from 2006-09. WaVE was primarily concerned with values and the role of religion in promoting solidarity and cohesion, or – conversely – tension and exclusion in this part of the world. To examine these alternatives, the research team paid increasing attention to the growing ethnic and religious diversity in the countries under review, asking in particular how the increasing numbers of newcomers arriving in Europe were to be integrated into their host societies, not least their welfare systems? What might be the role of the churches and other religious organizations in this process and how might this vary in different European societies? At stake were crucial – and largely unresolved – questions about accommodating difference and avoiding conflict, questions that continue to resonate.

A subsequent – and pivotal – step in the evolution of the CRS can be found in the programme entitled "The Impact of Religion – Challenges for Society, Law and Democracy" (IMPACT). This was an interdisciplinary initiative funded by the Swedish Research Council that ran over a ten-year period (2008-18); its purpose was to clarify the significance of religion in economic, social, political, cultural and legal questions both in Sweden and its Nordic neighbours. It brought together a wide variety of projects involving some 60 researchers from six different faculties at Uppsala University, including ten or so representatives from the Faculty of Law. Its outputs were many and varied. An important follow-up found its focus in a Horizon 2020 project known as RESPOND, which addressed the "Multilevel Governance of Mass Migration in Europe and Beyond", and looked in particular at the reactions of European states to the so-called refugee crisis of 2015. RESPOND compared the border management, reception and integration strategies in eleven countries along the entire Balkan route, from the Middle East to the Balkans and, eventually, the destination countries in northern Europe.

Turning now to the project described in this book, we find continuing attention to immigration in Northern Europe and a similar range of skillsets, with the addition of a welcome French voice. But as already indicated, the migrants in question are Pentecostal Christians who have come from different global regions – principally Latin America, sub-Saharan Africa and the Arab world – and are living in and around Stockholm. The detailed descriptions of their respective communities represent the core of the project. The focus on Pentecostalism may be new for the CRS but the expertise honed over two decades is clearly visible: there is the same emphasis on careful empirical research, rigorous theorizing and effective multi-disciplinarity, including a developed legal perspective. Equally present are the insights of theologians and church historians keeping in mind that the presence of Pentecostal churches is hardly new in Sweden. Indeed, the interactions between what might be termed "old" and "new" Pentecostals constitutes an important thread in the chapters that follow.

As a hinge to the more general questions that conclude this Foreword, it is worth looking in more detail at the situation in Stockholm. It comes as something of a surprise to outsiders to learn that, in 2021, people with a foreign background made up circa 25 per cent of the Swedish population, a figure that rises to 34 per cent in Stockholm. Sweden remains, nonetheless, one of the most secular countries in Europe, keeping in mind a persistent Nordic pattern displayed in relatively high levels of church membership alongside (very) low levels of practice and belief. It follows that the Nordic countries find themselves at the forefront of an increasingly urgent debate: how can such markedly secular nations accommodate the ethnic and religious diversity that comes with high levels of immigration? Hence the research questions outlined above that drive this project.

The Pentecostals portrayed in the following chapters are particularly interesting in this respect in that they are indeed a minority, or – more accurately – a cluster of minorities who (for the most part) come from outside Sweden. Globally speaking, however, Pentecostalism is a central and rapidly growing part of the Christian tradition rather than an other-faith community. It follows that the questions raised in this enquiry are distinctive. And if the questions raised are distinctive, it is likely that the answers will be too. It is for this reason that the project not only adds a new dimension to the work of the CRS, but to an increasingly significant research field.

The wider debate concerning religion in Europe has moved in stages. The contours themselves have already been outlined: Europe – and in particular Western Europe – is noticeably secular in global terms; at the same time, it is becoming markedly more diverse. Clearly the movement of people lies at the core of these changes, but it is important to note an associated shift in academic thinking. In the second half of the twentieth century (beginning in the 1950s), new arrivals in Europe were very largely categorized in terms of their race or ethnicity, generating significant – but *secular* – discussions about racial, ethnic and national issues. Towards the end of the century, however, the debate turned increasingly to questions of religion – a shift that discomfited many of Europe's secularists and the professions of which they were part. New questions arose: how were European societies to accommodate religious rather than ethnic differences and how were legal scholars, secular social scientists, politicians and policy-makers to address both the theoretical and practical questions that followed?

In short, an unexpected reversal was taking place. Scholars accustomed to talking in terms of the privatization of religion – seeing this, correctly, as the consequence of secularization – were increasingly obliged to note the rising profile of religion in *public* debate, despite the falling indicators of religious activity. Also reversed were expectations about urban and rural religion; religion was growing in the former rather than persisting in the latter. Put differently, more than one thing was happening at once: continuing and undisputed secularization alongside insistent, and at times heated, exchanges about the place of religion in late modern societies, especially Europe's larger cities. Even more difficult was the growing awareness that the protracted secularization was eroding the knowledge, vocabulary and sensitivities demanded by the increasingly visible presence of religion in the public sphere. What was to be done?

This, very briefly, is the overall picture. The significance of the work carried out by the CRS, displayed – among many other places – in the following chapters, lies in addressing the detail as scholars from a variety of disciplines attempt both to understand and to resolve the demanding questions that arise in relation to the management of particular religious traditions, taking into account the distinctive history, confessional background and characteristics of the Swedish case. These questions are clearly laid out in the introduction to this volume which not only sets out the steps in the argument, but pays careful attention to the definitions deployed in the project; the detailed analyses follow. The book concludes with a series of interesting reflections from Pentecostal scholars from other fields, and from different parts of the world.

I will end with a personal comment: as a British scholar, I am particularly pleased to see the parallels drawn with the relatively recent account of religion in London set out in *The Desecularisation of the City: London's Churches, 1980 to the Present*, edited by David Goodhew and Anthony-Paul Cooper (Routledge, 2019). I was privileged to contribute to the London volume and am delighted to recommend a Swedish sequel.

Grace Davie is an emeritus professor of sociology at the University of Exeter, UK and a lay canon of the Anglican Diocese in Europe. She is a past-president of the Association for the Sociology of Religion (2003) and the International Sociological Association RC 22 (Sociology of Religion) Research Committee (2002–2006). Recent publications include *Religion in Britain: A Persistent Paradox* (Wiley-Blackwell, 2015) and *The Oxford Handbook of Religion and Europe* (co-edited with Lucian Leustean; Oxford University Press, 2021).

Chapter 1

International Pentecostalism in Sweden: Researching a New Cosmopolitan Landscape

Victoria Enkvist and Katarina Westerlund

Introduction

One usually thinks that Sweden is becoming more and more secularized. That persons and organizations become less and less orientated towards religious beliefs and religious ways of living. However, simultaneously with this process, a religious revival is taking place right in front of us. This revival is linked to globalization and migration. Migration is one of the main political and social conflict issues in Sweden today.

The composition of the population in Sweden has changed significantly during the last couple of decades. In 2021, people with a foreign background make up about 25 per cent of the Swedish population, and in Stockholm, 34 per cent have a foreign background.[1] Among these are people who identify with different religions as well as those who have no religious affiliation.[2] The population change not only means that religion appears in new ways but also that there is a growing group of individuals without religious affiliation. This may be linked to an issue of identity and perception: migrants may no longer associate themselves primarily with their culture of origin but are still perceived as belonging to a particular ethnic and religious tradition. Nevertheless, migration has made religion significantly more visible in the secular Swedish society. But while Muslim, Catholic, and Orthodox migration have captured research attention, "Pentecostal migration" has previously been overlooked.

This book is a result of a research project on international Pentecostal groups in Sweden. The growth of Pentecostal churches and network-based environments in the Swedish capital Stockholm has been extensive during the last decade. A similar development is taking place in other large cities in Sweden and above all in European cities such as London and Paris.[3] This ongoing religious and social change, and its significance for the policy-making area, is the background to a multidisciplinary research project named "Pentecostal Migrants in Secular Sweden: Influences and Challenges". The project was financed by the Swedish Research Council for the years 2019–2022.[4]

In this introductory chapter, we will provide an overview of the research project, including some overarching results and the different disciplinary perspectives employed in the project. Furthermore, we will try to position Sweden and give a picture of the complex religious and legal landscape that affects and is affected by international Pentecostals. The choice of the term "international" will thus be clarified, alongside an outline of the volume. Finally, we will provide some overarching reflections on the results and indicate the need for further research.

The Research Project

The aim of the "Pentecostal Migrants in Secular Sweden: Impact and Challenges?" research project was to investigate what role Pentecostalism played among migrants in Sweden, what challenges they faced about secular Swedish society, and what challenges they posed to the society. The project focused both on the life situation of individuals and on the social and religious interaction of these migrants in a new Swedish context, but also on how the Swedish society or the Swedish state handle religious minorities with values that deviate from the secular context of the majority.

The research results presented in this volume build on two types of material. Firstly, a quantitative, geographical, and demographic study of Pentecostal growth and a broader mapping of the religious landscape in Greater Stockholm, done by the church historian Torbjörn Aronson, and sociologist of religion Magdalena Nordin. Most of the International Pentecostal churches in the Greater Stockholm area came to be after the year 2000. There are both independent churches and churches connected to Swedish Pentecostal churches. The municipalities in the Greater Stockholm area show different patterns and frequencies of international Pentecostal churches. The number is larger in the Southern part than in the inner parts of Stockholm and Western parts. Number of people with foreign background, ethnic origins, and languages, public transportation, and access to public meeting rooms are affecting the localization of the International Pentecostal churches in the Greater Stockholm area.[5]

The significance of Pentecostalism in the migrants' daily lives and relation to their integration into local and regional Swedish society was investigated through ethnographic field studies in three Pentecostal migrant churches. These three Pentecostal churches are located in the Greater Stockholm area and represent differences in national background, culture, and language, as well as when they were established. The first, Iglesia Nueva Creatión (Latin American, Spanish/Portuguese language), is located in Sollentuna municipality. It was established before 2000 and its members are mainly second or third-generation migrants. People visiting the church have their backgrounds in different Latin American countries, but there are also visitors from Mozambique, Syria, and Sweden. Iglesia Nueva Creatión could be categorized as a classical Pentecostal church, independent of the national Pentecost–Free Churches in Cooperation.[6]

The second church, City Church International (African, English or African languages) is located in Greater Stockholm and was established after the year 2000. City Church International is part of a Swedish classical Pentecostal church but has also developed neo-charismatic traits. People visiting this church have roots in different African countries, like Kenya, Uganda, and Tanzania, but one also find visitors from India, Singapore, and Sweden. Furthermore, City Church International is connected to Kensington Temple in the UK and has a sister church in Kampala, Uganda.

The Arabic church, the third studied church (mostly Arabic language), is located in the Sundbyberg municipality and was also established after the year 2000. This church is also a part of a Swedish Pentecostal church, of a classical type. Visitors typically have their background in countries like Syria, Iraq, Lebanon, and Egypt, but there are also some Muslim converts from the northern parts of Africa. The Arab church has many international contacts and is part of an international network for Arabic Pentecostal churches.

The fieldwork was done by the anthropologist Emir Mahieddin, the practical theologian Katarina Westerlund, the church historian Torbjörn Aronsson, and the sociologist of religion Magdalena Nordin.

The three churches studied have their particular features, history, and organizational characteristics. Moreover, their activities and the lives of their members are multifaceted and fluid. There are services, everyday activities and groups for different ages and purposes, internal- and external charities, as well as Internet, TV, and music broadcasting. Church members come from many different countries and their occupational, educational, and social backgrounds varies widely. Many have been on the move for some time: between countries, occupations, educational opportunities, and churches within Stockholm and Sweden.

Multidisciplinary

The authors of the various chapters have different disciplinary backgrounds: sociology of religion, anthropology, practical theology, church history, and law. This multi-disciplinary approach has provided both depth and width to the research. The project's also multi-disciplinary reference group has furthermore challenged disciplinarity, as well as national blind spots, and controversies. The scholarly disciplines of anthropology and practical theology have, through their respective disciplinary methods, enabled meetings with people in different congregations within the Pentecostal groups. In combination with church history, these encounters bring knowledge of new and old religious contexts, practices, and experiences that individuals have made and are making. Church history also provides knowledge about the development of these groups and the growth and change of the Pentecostal movement over time, which has also enabled comparisons. Furthermore, theological and ecclesiological logics that shape and justify the activities of international Pentecostal groups are revealed, by practical theology and church history.

No religious practice takes place in a vacuum. Contexts shape both the position and understanding of the scholar and the meaning and scope of the religion studied. An important part of the societal context is the state apparatus and the legal system(s) and policies that govern society and affect individuals and groups in different ways. Constitutional law and the sociology of religion provide a broader picture of the social and cultural context in which the Pentecostal groups operate and must relate to, as well as an analysis of the role and meaning of social and legal systems for the groups studied.

Migrant or International

In the title of this book the word migration is used, as well as in the title of the project. At the start of the research project, we had several multi-disciplinary discussions about concepts and their meaning. Migration turned out to be a concept that was hard to use cross-disciplinary, and therefore not productive from all disciplinary perspectives given the purpose of the project. In the multi-disciplinary discussion and analysis of the material, we agreed to replace the concept of migration with "international" to describe the groups studied more accurately.

Furthermore, migration is usually understood as the movement of individuals from one country to another and the Pentecostals studied, move between different countries and belong to global religious networks. Migration has today a negative connotation, while mobility and international have a more positive connotation. A reason for using the term international is thus a desire to avoid stereotyping.

In the reach project we have, therefore, chosen to apply the label international Pentecostalism instead. This refers to faith and worship communities connected with some historical branch of Pentecostalism which consist mainly of people born outside of Sweden and where activities are mainly conducted in a language other than Swedish. Pentecostal and Pentecostalism are mainly academic concepts that in the volume are used as generic terms for the charismatic branch of Christianity, understood from its historical development.[7] As suggested by Allan H. Anderson, we can among these churches find "family resemblances" in that they all emphasize an experience of the Holy Spirit and the exercise of spiritual gifts.[8]

To place the results and the volume we then turn to an overview of the context of the research and for the international Pentecostal groups studied.[9]

The Complex Swedish Religious and Legal Landscape

New religious groups are part of complex religious and legal patterns in Swedish society. The so-called religious complexity in contemporary Swedish and other Nordic societies refers to the presence of several, and sometimes contradictory religious trends.[10] From an overarching and global perspective, Swedish citizens place less emphasis on religion, traditional family values, and authority, together with a strong orientation towards freedom, self-realization, and quality of life, prioritizing environmental protection, growing tolerance of foreigners, gender and lesbian equality, and high demands on participation in public decision-making.[11] This significant secularization and individualization depicted during decades by the World Values Survey has shaped a cultural narrative of Sweden as exceptional. But this picture is more complex and in need of nuance.

One way of deepening the understanding the role of religion, and highlighting some characteristics, in Swedish society, is to use ideal types that identify typical expectations and modes of regulations that will constrain or encourage religious action.[12] In Sweden, there is a long Christian tradition and history that has shaped an *established* religious tradition, that also has given authority to a specific church. Swedish society is still organized around Christian holidays, and more than half of the population belongs to the former state church, the Lutheran Church of Sweden, which still retains some legal privileges.[13] This heritage shapes Christian religious normality, where religion is supposed to be private, primarily defined by a set of cognitive beliefs, and preferably to be found inside religious organizations. Religiosity in public spaces will in such a context oppose the norm.

This heritage thus comes across as an *institutional* ideal, meaning that religion is supposed to happen in specific places, and not others, and that has its organization, activities, and rules. There are also specialized forms of religious knowledge and expertise within religious organizations, other than what is labeled secular. In the Swedish culture and society religion and religious practices is thus supposed to be found in churches and other religious communities, and perhaps in private life. Other spheres are to be ruled by secular logic.[14]

However, the commitment and formal affiliation to institutionalized and organized religion, especially to Christian churches, are in decline in Sweden.[15] There is a gradual decrease in the number of people who report a belief in God or regularly engage in some sort of religious activity. This pattern is thus modified when focusing on migrants. Behind a general decline in religious beliefs and practices, there are growing groups where the religious activity is well and thriving.[16] This points toward, a seemingly contradictory trend: on the one hand, a growing secularization in the population; on the other, increasingly religious and ethnic pluralism and diversity of which international Pentecostalism is a vital force.[17]

Legally, the former National Lutheran Church of Sweden is regulated by a specific law. This law is accompanied by one law on religious communities, and one law on financial support to religious communities. Furthermore, the responsibility for the state's financial support to religious communities is handled by a government agency, the Swedish Agency for Support for Faith Communities. In Swedish law, a religious community is defined as a religious body that performs worship. The Swedish Agency for Support for Faith Communities is furthermore assigned to stipulate how religious communities should work for democracy, democratic values, and prevent non-democratic and extremism.[18] In this way, these laws reinforce or shape institutionalized religion in Sweden, as embodied in specific organizations that perform worship. Recognition as a faith community by the state will thus depend on the religious group's adherence to these specific values, and the religious groups willingness to apply for this status.

More generally the legal *system,* or in some cases the legal *systems* that set the framework for how society is organized, will affect individual and collective religion. Virtually everything a person does is governed by some form of rules. Knowledge of the existence of these rules and knowledge of how these rules can, and in some cases should, be understood can be crucial to an individual's ability to operate in different ways. Both the right to have a religion and the right to manifest one's faith in various ways are regulated by legal systems. In these systems complex considerations are made on how to view different religious groups and how society may or may not support different religious groups. Regulations also affect, for instance, which school children will attend and the framework and conditions of the Swedish school system about religion.

Furthermore, the constitutional protection of freedom of religion and, to a certain extent, freedom of expression, and national rules concerning state support for religious communities in Sweden becomes important for international Pentecostals. Do the various regulations take into account the specificity of religious minorities, should the regulations do so, and what are the consequences if the rules are not understood by those to whom they are directed?

In this respect Swedish society is modern, with rational systems of authority, divided into separate systems, logics, and specific experts, shaping religion as institutional, governed by legal systems. The modern diversified Swedish society is thus characterized by bureaucratic, rationalistic, and economic practices which shape a growing number of Western societies.[19]

On an individual level, people in Sweden are becoming less religious, and remain unconnected with faith or worldview communities, and in everyday conversations, religion, God, and the meaning of life are rarely discussed.[20] As a result of widespread secularization and declining participation in church activities, knowledge about religion and spirituality is generally low in Sweden. To be active in a church and to practise organized religion is rare, and might be regarded as somewhat awkward or even stupid.[21] Religious authorities and organizations are thus weak, and religious practices, if or where it is present, are individualized, fluid, and diffuse. Non-institutional settings like "nature", and other spaces created to foster a sense of connection to a higher or universal reality are instead places for "religious" activities in Sweden.[22] In this kind of context, one can choose and change religious traditions depending on desire or need. Religious traditions are thus not life-long or identity-defining. This freedom of choice and cast a side of religious traditions fit neatly with the global neoliberal order. Furthermore, religious justifications for moral positions lose their place in a secular public life.[23] Sweden could therefore be described as an *interstitial* religious context. On an individual level this decrease in traditional faith, practice, and membership in established churches, is coupled with an interest in other forms of "non-religious" spirituality and with what has been described as a subjective turn.[24] This religious complexity furthermore, displays heightened visibility of religion on a societal level, with the increase of other religions displaying a religious plurality and market.

Sweden could still be characterized as a Christian country, but this Christian identity is like a "cultural figure" displayed materially in numerous church buildings, names, and holiday seasons. But also, in rhetoric references to Christian values such as solidarity, equality, and trust, which are interpreted in line with the Swedish liberal welfare state, a welfare state that has its specific culturally shaped laws and regulations. It is not difficult to understand that people from other countries, expect something else when depicting Sweden as a Christian country, and have a hard time decoding the Swedish religious and legal landscape.

Outline of the Volume

This introductory chapter is followed by "Desecularization of Stockholm? Changes in Numbers of Churches and International Pentecostalism 1980–2020" (Chapter 2). In this chapter sociologist of religion Magdalena Nordin and church historian Torbjörn Aronson lay the ground by taking an overarching social perspective on the contemporary religious landscape in the Swedish capital Stockholm. The desecularization of Stockholm is depicted. Against the backdrop of a similar process in London, the authors explore the general changes in the numbers of local churches and their adherents in the Greater Stockholm area, with a special focus on Pentecostal churches. The chapter highlights that although there is a general secularization in Sweden, we see a growing number of Churches in Stockholm since 1980. This 40 per cent growth, is found among international Pentecostal churches together with Orthodox and Catholic churches. But at the same time, there has been a decline in several churches and adherents of the former National Church of Sweden and Classical Swedish free churches. Like in London, this change is probably partly related to immigration. Immigration in turn leads to increased religious diversity, and some of the immigrants show a higher degree of religiosity. Thus, the growing religious diversity and some migrants' heightened religiosity plays an important role in the desecularization of Stockholm.

In Chapter 3, "Ecclesiology with Unintended Consequences: Pingströrelsen and the Integration of International Pentecostal Churches in Stockholm 1980–2020", the church historian Torbjörn Aronson explores how the growth of international Pentecostal local churches has influenced the native Classical Pentecostal movement in Sweden, Pingströrelsen. The overarching question in chapter 3 concerns how Pingströrelsen has interacted with the growing number of international Pentecostal churches in Stockholm during the four last decades. The chapter shows how Pingströrelsen has become a more diversified movement at the same time as its organizational and legal structures have been strengthened and modified while the original congregationalism of the movement is still the operating ecclesiological principle. This means that the integration of new local international Pentecostal churches that have taken place in Stockholm 1980–2020 has been facilitated through the congregationalist ecclesiology and some additional changes of the ecclesial structures of *Pingströrelsen* in the twenty-first century. Still, the number of international churches integrated into the movement has been limited in comparison with the overall figure of local international Pentecostal churches in the Stockholm Region.

In Chapter 4, entitled "'Living Theology': Everyday Life, Challenges and Resources among International Pentecostals in Stockholm", challenges and resources among international Pentecostals living in Stockholm are explored by the practical theologian Katarina Westerlund. Using interviews and fieldwork, the meaning of religious belonging and spiritual practices in contemporary Sweden is highlighted. In the chapter lived religion works as theoretical framework, showing the importance of religion as embodied in specific material practices and places, combined with the expression of both positive and negative emotions, moral judgments, and narrative structuring. The spiritual dimension of lived religion is found foundational for the international Pentecostals, and this dimension is also transcribed as theology in the chapter. The lived dimensions and the strong spirituality among international Pentecostals is thus shown to be at odds with the secular logic of Sweden and its specific institutional religious context.

In Chapter 5, named "Suburbia and the Subway: Pentecostalism and Migration in Stockholm", the anthropologist Émir Mahieddin uses extensive fieldwork to explore Pentecostals' interpretations of the city, with a special focus on the city outskirts. He highlights the fluidity of the contemporary logic of religious belonging in urban settings in the Swedish society, and discusses how the category of "suburbia" is imagined as a place peopled by "immigrants". Pentecostals living and worshipping in the suburbs of Stockholm are fitted into this imagination and by occupying the peripheries of the city, which could be called "counter-places", their otherness or difference are manifested. Furthermore, the chapter explores how the margins of the city, the suburbs, and also the subway, become missionary hotspots. The affinity between the mission and social margins thus becomes important for the Pentecostal churches' activities. In the outskirts of Stockholm, as well as in London, Paris, or Amsterdam, the mission is been carried out by Pentecostals, by "marginalized immigrants", which could be viewed as a force to (re)christianize secularized Sweden or Europe.

In Chapter 6, "Legal Regulation of Religious Minorities in Sweden: The Example of International Pentecostals", Victoria Enkvist (a researcher in public and constitutional law) explores the legal frameworks that and are of importance and in various ways affect religious individuals and groups in Sweden. The legal regulations discussed in the chapter are based on results from the field studies in the project. In the chapter she discusses how legal rules concerning human rights and freedoms such as freedom of religion and freedom of expression can affect international Pentecostals, as these rules stipulate the right to possess and manifest religiously. The conditions under which these rights may be restricted are further addressed. Although these rights are of great importance for both individuals and groups, other legal rules may affect religious people in different ways. The provisions in the Act Lag (1999:932) about support to faith communities, and Regulation (1999:974) on state funding for faith communities that regulate state aid to religious communities, will affect the ability of religious groups to operate in Swedish secular society. How these rules are formulated may also affect the internal organizational life of religious communities. A number of the interviewees mention the issue of their children's schooling, where the choice between religious independent schools and municipal schools is central. What this freedom of choice means is highlighted in the Enkvist chapter. This chapter differs from the other chapter because legal rules concerning religion in Swedish are largely based on a secular system where little if any consideration is given to the content of different religions. The chapter therefore contains a general overview of the most important legal rules that may affect religious individuals who, for various reasons, come to Sweden to live and work, even if only temporarily.

Chapter 7, "International Pentecostals in Metropolitan Stockholm: Rethinking Relations between Voluntary and State Religion in Urban Sweden", has a theoretical take. With the use of Pentecostals as a good example of the flow of people entering Sweden, sociologist of religion Anders Bäckström argues that there has been a turn towards the social dimensions of religion which challenges traditional forms of secularization, and state policies. He notes that Pentecostalism is a growing global phenomenon that creates links between host and home countries through new communications, stimulates the economy in both host and home countries through market competition, influences the landscape of the host society, through mission, but is also influenced by the egalitarian ethos of secular Sweden.

Finally, Chapter 8, "Broadening the Perspectives: An International Outlook", consists of comments from four members of the research project's international reference group. First, Allan H. Anderson, professor emeritus of mission and Pentecostal studies at the University of Birmingham, UK, reflects on difficulties in delimiting and defining Pentecostalism and "migrant" churches. He discusses the complex meeting between the "host culture" and Pentecostal churches in different settings and proposes that Sweden may need to work out its definitions and categories of Pentecostalism. Swedish culture, mode of secularization, language, and the specific ecclesiology in the national Pentecostal movement, among other things will shape Pentecostalism differently than in for instance the UK. In this process, there is much to learn about the distinct and persistent identity and expressions of the "migrant" Pentecostal churches, as part of globalization and migration.

Second, Simon Coleman, Chancellor Jackman professor at the Department for the Study of Religion, University of Toronto, Canada, reflects upon what he calls Pentecosmopolitan cities and whether we might see Stockholm as one, comparable to other cities on the globe where Pentecostalism is in the rise. From an anthropological perspective, he advocates a general alertness to varieties of religious expressions, shifting temporarily and culturally, not least to religious complexity.

Third, Kim Knibbe, associate professor of sociology and anthropology of religion at the University of Groningen, Netherlands, discusses the meaning of globalization and secularization for the growth of Pentecostalism and points to significant differences between regional cultural contexts and conditions. Thus, she concludes with asking for more research on "lived religion" but also "lived secularities" exploring cultural encounters between different Christian expressions, and secular organizations and practices.

Finally, Pamela Slotte Russo, professor of religion and law at the Åbo Akademi University and vice-director of the Centre of Excellence in Law, Identity and the European Narratives at the University of Helsinki, Finland, notes how Swedish legislation on religion approaches religion in different ways and the historical links still influence the legal approach today. She highlights that the Pentecostal "form" does not fit well into traditional Swedish legal patterns regarding religion and its organization. Eventually, she stressed the risk of religion becoming a primary maker of identity at the expense of other categories – "religification" of minority positions – and calls for further research.

Concluding Remarks

The complex cosmopolitan religious world in Stockholm is mainly the result of immigration which has led to increased religious diversity. The religious change taking place is part of an increasing religious pluralism, most prominent in larger cities but also visible in the rest of the country. The rise of International Pentecostal churches, in 2020 there were about one hundred in the Greater Stockholm area, is significantly changing the scene, especially the city outskirts. Simultaneously, the International Pentecostal churches have a key role in the globalization of religion through their international networks and use of the Internet.

This volume aims to bring forth some pictures of the complex Swedish religious landscape in which international Pentecostal groups operate. The various chapters provide knowledge about how these groups have developed over time and thrive today, from both a societal and an individual perspective.

Of crucial importance is to enhance the understanding of the religious complexity at hand, which affects people's daily lives and contacts between the individual, organizations, and the state at different levels. Further research is thus important for understanding the transformation of what we understand as secular-religious or multiple secularities, as part of the globalization of religion, about different states and societies, for the people inhabiting this complex world.

As mentioned at the start of this chapter, the concept of migration needs to be problematized in a complex social context. The concept of migrants has certain negative connotations that one would like to avoid, and it is not accurate for the groups studied due to international Pentecostal's complex patterns of mobility. The purpose of mobility differs between individuals, groups, and within the various groups. Some end up staying in Sweden permanently, while others move between countries to different part of the world. Therefore, it is likely that there is a difference in motivation when it comes to familiarizing oneself with the complex Swedish system and learning the language.

In terms of language, Sweden might differ compared to countries like the UK or France. Thus, language is important for religious identity, in the Swedish context there is a strong desire to retain one's mother tongue and believers seek out churches that belong to their linguistic group. In an English- or French-speaking context this pattern of forming small language-based churches might not be that prominent. The meaning of language for both religious identities, and forming of churches cross-culturally requires further research.

The religious complexity is also visible concerning the organization of the state, not least regarding the norms of the legal system and expressed and unspoken values. The specific Swedish legal rules concerning freedom of religion and the institutional approach to religion in the public sphere, are adjusted to and shape religion as institutionalized and private. Growing ethnic and religious heterogeneity and mobility are thus changing the scene and pose new questions about religious freedom, and religious expression in the public arena. Is religiosity allowed to be expressed in ways that International Pentecostals might want and need? And what knowledge and ability to exercise these rights are held by whom in a complex religious context? Even more crucial, what knowledge and actions are found among governmental bodies and legal authorities about the new religious complexity? Further research into actual interactions or clashes between religiosity in the public and the legal systems is of high relevance.

Questions about religion and religiosity thus become even more complex and challenging, for both the state and society and for religious groups and individuals. There is a risk that religious expressions and experiences remain in the margins, both as private and as part of the outskirts of communities and cities. This kind of exclusion can be reinforced by legal systems, norms, and cultural patterns of interstitial religiosity. It is important to acknowledge these underlying tensions in the broader Swedish society, with its secular logic and sometimes lurking racism.

The tensions between a new more "hot" and embodied Christianity, found among International Pentecostals, are not only visible to the wider Swedish cultural and legal context, there are also tensions between this type of charismatic revival and institutionalized church structures, both with the classical Pentecostal movement and other Christian churches in Sweden. More research is thus needed to deepen the understanding of these tensions, not least in realtion to other growing churches such as the Orthodox and Catholic.

The international Pentecostals are thus building new communities in the Swedish society that gives support and stability for their living. Simultaneously, the outreach of these communities reshapes the city by inhabiting and exploring new places and providing sacred spaces for evangelization.

Victoria Enkvist is associate professor of constitutional law and senior lecturer in public law at the Faculty of Law at Uppsala University. Her research focuses mainly on rights and freedoms in different systems and how these rights are interpreted and applied in different situations. A main track in Enkvist's research is religious freedom and its legal framework. Enkvist is currently engaged in several different multidisciplinary research projects dealing with rights and subjects of rights.

Katarina Westerlund is professor in practical theology at the Department of Theology, Uppsala University, and project leader for the research project *Pentecostal Migration in Secular Sweden*. Her research interests include studies of worldview in contemporary society, with a focus on youth, family, and existential health, and practice, learning, and lived religion. Among recent publications we find "And the Word Was Made Flesh? - Exploring Young People's Situated Learning in Leadership and Spirituality in a Secular Context" in *Journal of Youth and Theology* (2021) and "Turning to Practice in Academic Theology and Religious Studies: Research Circles as an Example" in *Studia Theologica* (2021).

Notes

1. Foreign background here meant, by Statistics Sweden's definition, persons who were born abroad or persons born in Sweden who have two foreign-born parents.
2. Erik Willander, *The Religious Landscape of Sweden: Affinity, Affiliation, and Diversity in the 21st Century* (Stockholm: Swedish Agency for Support to Faith Communities, 2019), pp. 26ff.
3. Internationally, there is a corresponding growth of churches and congregations in large city areas. See David Goodhew and Anthony-Paul Cooper (eds), *The Desecularisation of the City: London's Churches, 1980 to the Present* (London: Routledge 2018); and David Garbin and Anna Strhan (eds), *Religion and the City* (London: Bloomsbury Academics, 2017). The situation in Sweden is described in Torbjörn Aronson, *A New Charismatic Landscape in Sweden* (Uppsala: Areopagus, 2016).
4. The project is located at the Center for Multidisciplinary Research on Religion and Society at Uppsala University (CRS). Torbjörn Aronson (associate professor in church history), Sven-Erik Brodd (professor emeritus in ecclesiology), Anders Bäckström (professor emeritus in sociology of religion), Victoria Enkvist (associate professor in constitutional law), Emir Mahieddin (fil. dr. in anthropology), Magdalena Nordin (professor in sociology of religion) and Katarina Westerlund (professor in practical theology) participated in the research project. See https://crs.uu.se/forskning/pentecostal--migrants-in-secular-sweden.
5. The analyses of these mappings are presented in Chapters 2 and 3 of this volume.
6. In Chapter 3 the national Swedish Pentecostal movement is further discussed as a backdrop to the inclusion of International Pentecostal churches. A report with further analysis of the different municipalities, types of international churches and locations is also available in Swedish: see Katarina Westerlund, (ed.). *Internationell Pentecostalism i Storstockholm: Tre församlingar i ett förändrat religiöst landskap*, CRS rapporter no. 1 (Uppsala: Uppsala universitet, 2021).
7. Pentecostalism can be understood and defined differently. Historically, it can be divided into four branches: classic Pentecostalism, independent Pentecostalism, charismatic revival movement, and neo-Pentecostal churches and networks. In Chapter 8 Allan H. Anderson discusses further classifications of Pentecostalism.
8. See also Chapters 3 and 8, especially the comment from Allan H. Anderson in the latter.
9. The social and legal context are discussed theoretically in Chapters 6 and 7 of this volume.
10. Inger Furseth (ed.), *Religious Complexity in the Public Sphere Comparing Nordic Countries* (New York: Springer, 2018).
11. See www.worldvaluessurvey.org/WVSNewsShow.jsp?ID=467
12. Nancy T. Ammerman, *Studying Lived Religion: Contexts and Practices* (New York: New York University Press, 2021), pp. 30–31. Ammerman established the ideal types *entangled*, *established*, *institutional* or *interstitial*, with *postcolonial* contexts as a hybrid.
13. The Lutheran Church of Sweden had been governed by the state until the year 2000. Despite the separation of church and state, the Church of Sweden still carries out certain official duties, such as managing funeral services and collecting specific taxes.
14. Ammerman, *Studying Lived Religion*, p. 40.
15. During recent decades, the number of people belonging to the Lutheran Church of Sweden has diminished gradually. In 2000, 83% of the Swedish population belonged to the Church of Sweden. These figures have continued to fall, being 70% and 58%

in 2010 and 2018 respectively. The numbers for church attendance, baptisms, church weddings, and confirmations show a similar declining trend. During the last three decades, the number of churchgoers has more than halved.

16 Willander, *The Religious Landscape of Sweden*; Magdalena Nordin, "Migration och ungdomars förhållningssätt till religion", in Maria Klingenberg and Mia Lövheim (eds), *Unga och religion – Troende ointresserade eller neutrala?* (Malmö: Gleerups, 2019).
17 Furseth, *Religious Complexity in the Public Sphere*, p. 17.
18 Linnea Lundgren, *A Risk or Resource? A Study of the Swedish State's Shifting Perception and Handling of Minority Religious Communities between 1952-2019* (Stockholm: Ersta Sköndal Bräcke University Collage, 2021). The Swedish Agency for Support for Faith Communities should also compile overviews of xenophobic acts against religious minorities, and reach out to groups with low electoral participation.
19 José Cassanova. "The Karel Dobbelaere Lecture: Divergent Global Roads to Secularization and Religious Pluralism", *Social Compass* 65(2) (2018), pp. 187–198, https://doi.org/10.1177/0037768618767961. We see a paradox in Sweden and other European countries: while religion is becoming more diverse and visible in the public sphere, secularization is growing at the individual level. See Grace Davie, *Religion in Britain: A Persistent Paradox* (Chichester: John Wiley and Sons, 2015); and Linda Woodhead and Rebecca Catto (eds), *Religion and Change in Modern Britain* (Abingdon: Routledge, 2012).
20 Phil Zuckerman, *Society without God: What the Least Religious Nations Can Tell Us about Contentment* (New York University Press, 2008), p. 70.
21 David Thurfjell, *Det gudlösa folket: de postkristna svenskarna och religionen* (Stockholm: Nordsteds förlag, 2015).
22 David Thurfjell, Cecilie Rubow, Atko Remmel and Henrik Ohlsson, "The Relocation of Transcendence: Using Schutz to Conceptualize the Nature Experiences of Secular People", *Nature and Culture* 14(2) (2019), pp. 190–214.
23 Ammerman, *Studying Lived Religion*, pp. 42–43.
24 Paul Heelas and Linda Woodhead, *The Spiritual Revolution: Why Religion Is Giving Way To Spirituality* (Oxford: Blackwell Publishing, 2005).

Bibliography

Ammerman, Nancy T. *Studying Lived Religion. Contexts and Practices*. New York: New York University Press, 2021.
Aronson, Torbjön. *A New Charismatic Landscape in Sweden*. Uppsala: Areopagus, 2016.
Cassanova, José. "The Karel Dobbelaere Lecture: Divergent Global Roads to Secularization and Religious Pluralism." *Social Compass* 65(2) (2018).
Davie, Grace. *Religion in Britain: A Persistent Paradox*. Chichester: John Wiley and Sons, 2015.
Furseth, Inger (ed.). *Religious Complexity in the Public Sphere Comparing Nordic Countries*. New York: Springer , 2018.
Garbin, David and Anna Strhan (eds). *Religion and the City*. London: Bloomsbury, 2017.
Goodhew, David and Anthony-Paul Cooper (eds). *The Desecularisation of the City London's Churches, 1980 to the Present*. London: Routledge, 2018.
Heelas, Paul and Linda Woodhead. *The Spiritual Revolution: Why Religion Is Giving Way To Spirituality*. Oxford: Blackwell Publishing, 2005.
Lundgren, Linnea. *A Risk or Resource? A Study of the Swedish State's Shifting Perception and Handling of Minority Religious Communities between 1952-2019*. Stockholm: Ersta Sköndal Bräcke University Collage, 2021.

Nordin, Magdalena. "Migration och ungdomars förhållningssätt till religion." In Maria Klingenberg and Mia Lövheim (eds), *Unga och religion – Troende ointresserade eller neutrala?* Malmö: Gleerups, 2019.

Thurfjell, David. *Det gudlösa folket: de postkristna svenskarna och religionen.* Stockholm: Nordsteds förlag, 2015.

Thurfjell, David, Cecilie Rubow, Atko Remmel and Henrik Ohlsson 2019. "The Relocation of Transcendence: Using Schutz to Conceptualize the Nature Experiences of Secular People." In *Nature and Culture* 14(2), pp. 190–214.

Westerlund, Katarina (ed.). *Internationell Pentecostalism i Storstockholm: Tre församlingar i ett förändrat religiöst landskap.* CRS rapporter no. 1. Uppsala: Uppsala universitet, 2021. www.uu.se/download/18.300bef8f18f0f87bbe9ab06/1714063783038/c_981614-l_3-k_internationell-pentekostalism-i-storstockholm--21-12-01-.pdf

Willander, Erik. *The Religious Landscape of Sweden: Affinity, Affiliation, and Diversity in the 21st Century.* Stockholm: Swedish Agency for Support to Faith Communities, 2019.

Woodhead, Linda and Rebecca Catto (eds). 2012. *Religion and Change in Modern Britain.* Abingdon: Routledge, 2012.

Zuckerman, Phil. *Society without God: What the Least Religious Nations Can Tell Us about Contentment.* New York: New York University Press, 2008.

Chapter 2

Desecularization of Stockholm? Changes in Numbers of Churches and International Pentecostalism 1980–2020

Magdalena Nordin and Torbjörn Aronson

Introduction

Sweden, known to be among the most secularized countries in the world, has in recent decades become a religiously diverse society. Today we find various Muslim, Hindu and Buddhist denominations in Sweden. Moreover, the Christian landscape has become more diverse with the establishment of various international Pentecostal and Orthodox churches. However, it is not known whether this diversity may lead to an increase of religion in Sweden, that is, to processes of desecularization. The majority church in Sweden, the Evangelical Lutheran Church of Sweden, has seen a decrease in membership and closed entire parish churches, but it is not certain whether this decrease in religion on a congregational (i.e. meso) level has been outweighed by the growth of other religious denominations and their members.

Research into religious changes in cities in Europe, Australia, and the USA shows how religion still is important in shaping these cities, and despite consisting of "a messy set of contrary trends"[1], some of these changes can arguably be seen as tendencies of desecularization.[2] One example is London, where between 1970 and 2012 there was an increase in the number of local churches from 3400 to 4791, and there are in 2018 figures pointing to a 50 per cent increase in London local churches.[3] This could also be the case in Stockholm, Sweden, where we, for example, have seen a large increase in the number of local international Pentecostal churches in recent decades and also some increase in Orthodox churches.[4] Whether this increase outnumbers the decrease in other local churches will be tested here.

With inspiration from the book *The Desecularisation of the City: London's Churches, 1980 to the Present*, edited by David Goodhew and Anthony-Paul Cooper[5] we will explore the general changes in the number of local churches and their adherents in Stockholm Region between 1980 and 2020.

Aim and Research Questions

In conversation with ideas about processes of desecularization, the chapter explores the trajectories of local churches in Stockholm Region between 1980 and 2020, focusing on the role of international Pentecostalism. This will provide an insight into the diverse ecclesial landscape of Stockholm, from the southern suburbs, to the city centre, and to the surrounding less densely populated municipalities in the north of the region, from Nigerian Pentecostals to Polish Catholics, from the parishes of the Church of Sweden to churches only recently established in Sweden. The aim of the chapter is to demonstrate, through focusing on the complex configurations of international Pentecostal churches, how the overall landscape of local churches in Stockholm Region changed over the studied period. Three overarching questions will guide us:

- What changes took place in Stockholm Region regarding the number of local churches between 1980 and 2020?
- What changes took place in Stockholm Region regarding adherence to local churches between 1980 and 2020?
- What is the place of international Pentecostalism in these changes, and where, and in what ways, was international Pentecostalism part of the changed ecclesial landscape?

The reason for choosing this period and the focus on international Pentecostalism is that there was only one local international Pentecostal church in 1980 (i.e. a Finnish-speaking church founded in 1972).[6] The situation has changed much since that time, with a significant growth in the number of local international Pentecostal churches.

The analysis will focus on changes in the number of different types of local churches. However, to complement the analysis of changes in the actual numbers of local churches, we will also, when possible, analyse the "size" of various local churches by taking account of their numbers of adherents. We know that the structures and sizes of local churches vary widely. Some of the older historical churches have fewer local churches, often defined by specific territories, with many nominal members but many fewer active adherents. In some local international Pentecostal churches the situation is the opposite, that is, there are many smaller local churches with considerably fewer nominal members but a higher percentage of active adherents.[7] Figures and facts related to this will be analysed when possible; however, due to the uncertainty of the numbers, they will not form the main angle of analysis.

State of the art

In Goodhew and Cooper's 2019 study of churches in London, processes of desecularization were scrutinized. To our knowledge, this is one of the few studies that not only explores the increase in religious plurality due to immigration, but also relates this to changes in religious plurality due to decreased number of local churches and adherence in majority and other established churches. Previous research into contemporary changes of religion in cities in Europe, Australia, and the USA mostly addresses religious changes due to immigration, at both congregational and individual levels.[8] These studies are often based on in-depth ethnographic research into some of the more newly established congregations; few studies address the changes at a more aggregated level and even fewer examine how the Christian landscape has become more diverse in general.[9]

The historical period examined by Goodhew and Cooper coincides with a general growth of the London population, primarily from international immigration. However, Goodhew and Cooper argue that it would be too simplistic to claim a causal relationship between immigration and the increase in the number of churches in the city – the situation is much more complex.

First, they contend that immigration to London during this period has meant greater ethnic diversity: today in London there is no ethnic majority, and with this follows an increase in religious diversity. Therefore, it is not immigration per se that has led to an increase in the number of churches; instead, the increase in religious diversity following from immigration is the cause. Second, while some immigrants display more religiosity than the average population, others are less religious. This means that it is not immigration per se that has led to an increase in the number of churches, but rather the religiosity of some immigrants. Goodhew and Cooper have showed how research from London indicates that some ethnic minorities bring with them an increase in churchgoing, others a decrease: some immigrants become less religious, others more religious, and among still others there is no change.[10]

Goodhew and Cooper also make us aware of how immigration is an ongoing process at the aggregated level but not the individual level. People have always moved, and who is or is not seen as an immigrant is fluid. This is also the case for churches: While the religious diversity seen in London is related to increased immigration in the last decade, can local churches established in the 1980s still be seen as immigrant churches, and not British churches? Another aspect to keep in mind when considering the ongoing changes is that demography is crucial, but not destiny.[11] It is too early to say whether demographic shifts in recent decades will lead to temporary or permanent changes of the religious landscape in London. Goodhew and Cooper ask whether, over time, the desecularization of London will revert to secularization, or will religion continue to grow? Is there a tipping point when it comes to these processes? They also argue that the increase can be explained by the agency of the local churches that have seen growth, and that one must be aware of gender differences when it comes to the establishment and maintenance of churches.[12] All of these considerations are also of interest when analysing changes in the Stockholm Region Christian landscape.

Theoretical and Methodological Considerations

Secularization and its Opposite

In the chapter we will use the idea of desecularization in Stockholm Region as an analytical tool to study. However, changes in the ecclesial landscape does not cover all the religious changes occurring in this area over the last forty years. First, it does not include changes related to religions other than Christianity. We are well aware that the religious landscape in Stockholm Region has also changed due to changes related to Islam, Buddhism, Hinduism, and other religious traditions, but the focus here is on Christianity.

The choice to study religious communities, that is, local churches, as the primary unit for mapping the ecclesial landscape of Stockholm was inspired by Karel Dobbelaere's analytical categories in investigating secularization and desecularization. Dobbelaere has suggested a three-tiered typology of secularization: (1) secularization in wider society (i.e. on a macro level); (2) secularization in terms of the decline of individual subscription to religious faith (i.e. on a micro level); and (3) secularization in terms of the shrinkage of local churches (i.e. on a meso level).[13]

The trajectory of local churches, rather than individual and societal religious behavior (i.e. the third category in the above secularization typology) is the focus of this study.[14] This is not to say that individuals and society do not matter; rather, the present focus expresses the centrality of church life to Christian life in general. Moreover, academic discussions of secularization have often taken church decline as a given, supporting their analysis with that assumption.[15] An interesting aspect of the above typology is that it allows for simultaneously occurring opposite developments: a city like Stockholm could move in a desecularizing direction at the congregational level, while continuing to develop along secularizing lines at the societal level.[16] Research into particular areas and groups has shown that local churches are capable of vigor.[17] However, we still find research claiming a general secularization in Sweden, as well as in the rest of the West.[18]

In sum, this study will not *test* the theory of desecularization in Stockholm. Instead, it will, in accordance with Goodhew and Cooper's study of changes in the church configuration in London, use the concept as an analytical tool to map out a particular trend within a broader landscape of religion in Sweden.

Definition of Concepts and Delimitations

To answer the research questions, definitions, and data quality merit consideration. In the chapter, "local church" refers to a group of believers who have a continuous liturgical and congregational life, a local leadership, and an official registration as either an association or a faith community. "Worship group" refers to a group of believers who are part of a local church but have their own worship services. "International local church" means, given this background, a public local *ecclesiâ* using a language in worship other than Swedish and/or having a mother church in another country.

When the chapter analyses the growth and decline in number of local churches, this refers to local churches that adhere to a Trinitarian theistic faith and are associated with any of the four major Christian traditions of the world today: the Orthodox, Catholic, Protestant, or Pentecostal traditions. This way of describing Christianity is common today, being based on well-known historical and ecclesial developments. The rationale for labelling Pentecostalism as an independent Christian tradition is its numerical growth and its unique theological emphasis on the Holy Spirit.[19] In the chapter, this fourfold differentiation will be used in comparative analysis to highlight the ecclesial changes in Stockholm Region. Faith communities such as Jehovah's Witnesses and the Church of Jesus Christ of Latter-day Saints (popularly called "Mormons") fall outside of this study because of their non-Trinitarian theism.

The statistical analysis of the number of local churches is also, when possible, complemented by another quantitative measure, that is, adherence, understood as both membership and affiliation. Membership is in this case to be understood as a legal term. In Sweden, most international local Pentecostal churches are registered as associations. Membership in associations entails democratic influence, such as the right to vote and speak in associational meetings, which is sometimes conditional on payment of a yearly membership fee. Membership in historic churches registered as officially recognized faith communities is mostly tied to baptism. Affiliation is a term used here in accordance with the definition of the Swedish Agency for Support for Faith Communities (SASFC),[20] that is, it should be a community for religious activity, which includes organizing worship, that contributes to maintaining and strengthening the fundamental values on which the society rests and that it is stable and has its own vitality.[21]

Another definition needed is what we mean by "Stockholm", which can be understood as the area defined by the government as "Greater Stockholm", that is, the administrative and political unit *Stockholm Region*. Stockholm Region consists of 26 municipalities with 2.3 million inhabitants in total. The largest of these is Stockholm Municipality, or Stockholm City, with approximately one million inhabitants. The other municipalities are more or less suburbs of Stockholm Municipality and are connected via a centralized and efficient transportation system. A few of these municipalities have a history of their own going back to Medieval times, such as Sigtuna and Södertälje, while others grew into independent municipalities during the era of urbanization in the twentieth century. There were 26 municipalities in Stockholm Region in 2020, up from 23 in 1980.[22]

Stockholm Region has grown into a very diverse place over the last four decades, and seven of the most diverse municipalities in Sweden can be found here. In Botkyrka, nearly 60 per cent of the population is of "foreign background" according to the Swedish Central Agency of Statistics, meaning that either these inhabitants or both their parents were born in another country. However, other municipalities in Stockholm Region have populations characterized by small proportions of such immigrant populations. Age, unemployment, and poverty likewise vary hugely between Stockholm Region municipalities (www.lansstyrelsen.se).

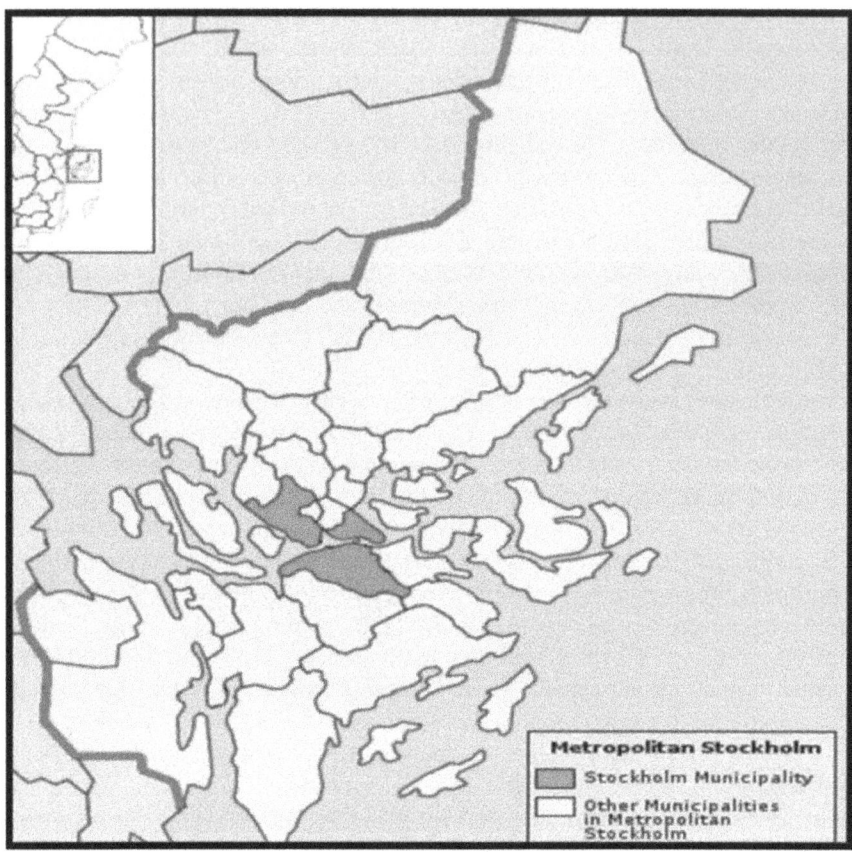

Figure 2.1. Stockholm region with municipalities.

The Church of Sweden is a territorial church with thirteen dioceses. Stockholm Region consists of the Diocese of Stockholm and parts of the dioceses of Uppsala and Strängnäs.[23] The borders of the municipalities generally coincide with borders of the parishes.

Sources and Methodology

The statistics in the chapter are based on:

- the registry of officially recognized faith communities, which is maintained by the Legal, Financial, and Administrative Services Agency (Kammarkollegiet) as well as municipal and commercial registries of associations;
- statistics from SASFC;

- public statistics of the Church of Sweden;
- a survey of the local churches of the Syriac Orthodox Church conducted in 2020 (see Nordin and Johnsén, 2023);
- the websites of local churches and denominations, e-mail and telephone communications with local churches, and books and unpublished articles about the history of local churches; and
- yearbooks published by the established free-church denominations.[24]

Since there are no official registers of religious communities or of religious affiliation in Sweden, it has been quite difficult to obtain information about more recently established churches in Sweden. Given the resources available for writing the chapter, conducting a total survey of the number of adherents of all Christian churches in Stockholm Region in 1980 and 2020 was impossible. For a number of Byzantine and Oriental Orthodox churches and Oriental Catholic churches, there were not even specific contemporary figures for the parishes in Stockholm Region. The adherents of international Pentecostal churches have been easier to estimate because of the wealth of published material about these churches available from websites and Facebook pages.[25] For most established free-church denominations, annual reports were made available.

In the cases in which we could not obtain exact information, we have made estimates; we rarely needed this for estimating the number of local churches, but did resort to this method more often for adherence, especially in 1980. Given both authors' in-depth knowledge of the topic, these estimates are most likely quite accurate.[26]

Changes in Numbers of Local Churches

Concerning the change in the number of local churches in Stockholm Region between 1980 and 2020, there were overall tendencies of both growth and decline. There was a total growth of 22 per cent from 354 local churches in 1980 to 433 in 2020 (Table 2.1). If Norrtälje Municipality is excluded, the total growth was from 287 local churches in 1980 to 401 in 2020 – an increase of 40 per cent.[27] However, the population of Stockholm Region grew by over 50 per cent between 1980 and 2020, from 1,528,200 to 2,368,269 inhabitants, which would apparently explain the growth of local churches, although this is not the case. What has also happened is that the population of Stockholm Region became more diverse in Christian adherence over this time. Adherence to the Church of Sweden was completely dominant in the 1980s, encompassing over 90 per cent of the population at that time; now, however, over thirty Christian traditions claim adherents, and many of these traditions are new on Swedish soil.

The growth in the number of local churches was only partially related to the growth of inhabitants during the studied period. In the following, we will examine the dynamics of these changes.

Table 2.1. Changes in number of local churches of different Christian churches and traditions in the Stockholm Region.

Churches	1980	2020	Change in number of churches	Change in %
Church of Sweden	145	98	−47	−32
Older Free Church	147	94	−53	−36
International Protestantism	13	19	+6	+46
Classical Pentecostalism	21	36	+15	+71
Other Pentecostalism	12	37	+25	+200
International Pentecostalism	0	83	+83	–
Catholic churches	5	23	+18	+360
Orthodox churches	12	49	+37	+300
Total	354	433	+79	+22

Church of Sweden

Regarding the Church of Sweden, the number of parishes in Stockholm Region has declined from 145 to 98 through mergers, representing a decrease of over a third (i.e. 32%). Small rural parishes, in particular, have been merged into larger units. The Church of Sweden is still bound by parliamentary legislation to have a local presence throughout Sweden. Because of their territorial nature, Church of Sweden parishes never, in a strict sense, cease to exist, but instead merge with other parishes into larger geographical units. Although this results in larger units, membership numbers declined in nearly all parishes of the Church of Sweden between 1980 and 2020.

Free Churches: Denominational Variations among the Local Churches

Most of the older Protestant free churches and Low Church movements in Sweden have their roots in nineteenth-century revivals. The Low Church movements organized their followers in associations within the parishes of the Church of Sweden, as *ecclesiola in ecclesia*, retaining its sacramental services while organizing independent communities with their own worship and congregational life. In this study, such associations are counted as local churches. In 1980, there were 147 local churches belonging to Classical Free Churches and Low Church movements, with the Swedish Mission Covenant Church (Svenska Missionsförbundet) having the largest number, with 60 local churches in Stockholm Region. Some of the other Free Churches and Low Church movements only had one local church each in Stockholm Region, having their principal following elsewhere in the country.

By 2020, several of the Classical Free Churches had merged, with some of them experiencing a downhill trajectory very much like the Church of Sweden. This applies especially to the Equmenia Church (Equmeniakyrkan), founded in 2011 as a result of a union between the Swedish Mission Covenant Church and two other free churches.[28] However, some smaller denominations with a conservative theological profile have experienced growth. For example, the Seventh Day Adventists and Swedish Mission Alliance (Svenska Alliansmissionen) have both benefited from immigration and started new local churches in which specific language groups are accommodated. The overall figure for the Classical Free Churches and Low Church movements was a drop from 147 to 94 (i.e. a decrease of 37 per cent).

Table 2.2. Changes in number of local churches in Stockholm Region belonging to Classical Free Church denominations or Low Church movements.

Denomination	1980	2020	Change in number of churches	Change in %
EFS (Evangelical Lutheran Inner Missions)	20	9	−11	−55
Equmeniakyrkan (Equmenia Church)	99	57	−42	−42
Frälsningsarmén (Salvation Army)	21	11	−10	−47
SAM (Swedish Mission Alliance)	1	6	+5	+500
SDA (Seventh-Day Adventists)	2	5	+3	+150
Other Swedish Protestant free churches	4	6	+2	+50
Total	147	94	−53	−37

Pentecostal Churches

Classical Pentecostalism in Stockholm

In the Pentecostal sphere, the classical Pentecostal denominations (Pingströrelsen) dominated in 1980 with 21 local churches.[29] Added to that were eleven local churches with backgrounds in different new Pentecostal movements in the 1960s and 1970s. These movements were inspired by the healing revival in the USA in the 1950s and the Charismatic renewal that began in Stockholm in the late 1960s. Some of these churches belonged to smaller denominations with their roots in the International Holiness Movement of the nineteenth century. In 1980, the total number of local Pentecostal churches was 33.[30] Only one of these, the Södertälje Finnish Pentecostal Church (Södertälje Finska Pingstförsamling), worshipped in a language other than Swedish.[31]

In 2020, the number of local Pentecostal churches with Swedish as their language of worship and/or their mother church in Sweden had more than doubled to 73. Thirty-six of these belonged to classical Pentecostal denominations and 20 belonged to a new Pentecostal church created in 1997, the Evangelical Free Church (Evangeliska Frikyrkan), through the union of three small holiness denominations. There were also several non-denominational churches with some kind of connection to the Word of Faith movement. As of 2020, both the classical Pentecostal denominations and the more newly established Evangelical Free Church had international Pentecostal churches affiliated with them, the classical Pentecostal denominations with 16 international churches and the Evangelical Free Church with nine churches. This development points to an increasing awareness and interest among Classical Free Churches to integrate newly formed local churches that are usually connected with immigrants. Clearly, both a process of internationalization and increasingly integrative policies are shaping Swedish Pentecostal free churches' relationships with immigrants. In 2020 we also find a small number of local international Pentecostal churches belonging to the Classical Free Churches and Low Church movements. The total number of local Pentecostal churches is then in fact a little higher than the number arrived at when adding the three categories of Pentecostalism in Table 2.1.

International Pentecostal Churches

Pentecostal migrants have influenced the ecclesial landscape of Stockholm Region in at least four ways. First, there are individuals of foreign background who are members of the historical classical Pentecostal churches. We have not estimated their numbers for the chapter, but we know from our research into some of these churches that many of them have such adherents. Second, there are worship groups within classical Pentecostal churches whose services and other congregational activities are conducted in languages other than Swedish. There are about 25 of these language-based worship groups among the classical Pentecostal churches in Stockholm Region. These groups have sometimes evolved into autonomous local churches, while in other cases they have been dissolved and the participants have instead joined in Swedish-speaking congregational activities. Third, there are local international Pentecostal churches that have become members of classical Pentecostal denominations. Fourth, we have local international Pentecostal churches that are either independent and non-denominational or have a mother church in another country. The fourth category grew from zero to 83 churches during the study period, and the third category from one church to 25. This means that in 2020 there were 108 local international Pentecostal churches in total in Stockholm Region. The local international Pentecostal churches have thus become the majority of the local Pentecostal churches and they constitute about 25 per cent of all local churches in Stockholm Region. The conclusion is that international Pentecostalism has become a major feature of the ecclesial landscape of the Swedish capital. The size of these local churches may differ, ranging from mega churches with over 2000 adherents to small local churches with 20 to

Table 2.3 Number of local international Pentecostal churches and worship groups.

Denomination	1980	2020	Change in number of churches
Local international Pentecostal churches being members of classical Pentecostal denominations	1	25	+24
Local international Pentecostal churches (independent, non-denominational, mother church in another country)	0	83	+83
Worship groups within classical Pentecostal churches services, other congregational activities in languages other than Swedish	11	25	+14
Total	12	133	+121

30, but in that respect, they do not differ from other local classical Pentecostal churches. Regarding national background, about 75 per cent of the churches have either an African or Latin American background.

"Immigrant-Based" Churches in Stockholm

International Protestant Churches

Since the eighteenth century there have been Protestant churches in Stockholm serving immigrant communities. Among these, the French and Dutch Reformed churches and the Church of England have the longest continuous histories in Stockholm. The Moravian Church, that is, the Herrnhuter Brüdergemeinde, obtained the right found a local church in 1755. The Church of Denmark and Church of Norway also have historic churches in Stockholm. During the Cold War, Protestant refugees from Estonia, Latvia, and Hungary started exile churches. After 1989, they reorganized their relations with churches in their home countries and remain active today. There were 13 international Protestant churches in Stockholm in 1980, growing to 19 by 2020. Some of these new churches are Evangelical churches with mother churches in the USA and a clear missionary purpose. There are also some Reformed churches with their mother churches in Africa or Asia, serving immigrant members of these churches in Sweden. Some of the international Protestant churches have quite large numbers of adherents. Although their level of activity may not be very high, they provide basic pastoral care for their respective communities.

Catholic Churches

The Post-Reformation Roman Catholic Church was allowed to worship and organize a church in Stockholm in 1783. In 1860, Swedish citizens were allowed to change their allegiance from the Church of Sweden to the Roman Catholic Church. During the nineteenth and twentieth centuries, the number of Roman Catholics in Stockholm grew mostly through immigration and new parishes were added. In 1953, the Catholic Diocese of Stockholm was organized, with all of Sweden under its jurisdiction. In 1980, there were five Roman Catholic parishes, that is, local churches, in Stockholm and the immigration of Oriental Catholics had only just begun. The four decades between 1980 and 2020 witnessed strong growth through extensive Catholic immigration to Sweden in general, and to Stockholm in particular. Today, a large part of the registered Catholic worshippers in Sweden is found in Stockholm and the number of parishes has quadrupled to 20. The number of adherents grew from fewer than 15,000 in 1980 to over 45,000 in 2020. Catholics from Latin America and Poland are major immigrant groups in the Roman Catholic parishes in Stockholm Region.

As of 2020, nine of these Catholic churches are Uniate Catholic churches with their roots in the Middle East, for example, the Maronite Church, the Chaldean Catholic Church, the Melkite Greek Catholic Church, the Syrian Catholic Church, and the Armenian Catholic Church. Among these, the Chaldean Catholic Church has the most adherents in Sweden. As far as we could determine, none of these churches was already established in 1980. There is uncertainty about how many adherents these churches had as of 2020, but probably in total about 30,000 Stockholm resident could be counted among their membership.

Orthodox Churches

The Orthodox tradition is divided into the Byzantine Orthodox churches, which are mostly in communion with one another, and the Oriental Orthodox churches, with their roots in the rejection of the Council of Chalcedon in 451. Also, among the Byzantine Orthodox churches we find some with a long history in Stockholm, beginning with the Russian Orthodox Church in the seventeenth century. Orthodox immigration to Sweden began to increase after the Second World War, and by 1980, there were 11 Orthodox parishes in Stockholm. Today we find nearly 50 Orthodox parishes in Stockholm Region, representing most of the major Orthodox churches and traditions. Among these, the largest growth has been seen in the Syriac Orthodox Church, which increased from two parishes in 1980 to 15 in 2020, and from about 1600 adherents in 1980 to over 22,000 in 2020.

Conclusion

Older churches mostly declined in Stockholm Region between 1980 and 2020. This especially applies to the Church of Sweden and the Classical Free Churches. In the case of the Church of Sweden, this decline has partly been due to mergers of parishes. Classical Pentecostalism has grown strongly and is increasingly

Table 2.4. Changes in number of local immigrant-based churches in the Stockholm Region.

Denomination	1980	2020	Change in number of churches
International Protestant churches	13	19	6
Roman Catholic churches	5	20	15
Orthodox churches	11	50	39
Total	29	89	+60

also trying to integrate new international Pentecostal churches in its respective denominations. As of 2020, international Pentecostal churches accounted for about a quarter of all local churches in Stockholm. The Catholic and Orthodox churches are largely international churches and have grown strongly. As a whole, the ecclesial landscape of Stockholm Region has become more diverse, but has also grown during this period, and international Pentecostal churches are a major part of this. The rise of international Pentecostalism in Stockholm thus is part of a broader trend of Christian internationalization in the city.

Adherents: Growth or Decline?

In 1980, the Church of Sweden had 7,690,636 members, representing 93 per cent of the total national population. In Stockholm Region, about 92 per cent of the total population belonged to the Church of Sweden, which amounted to 1,405,944 members.[32] By and large, Stockholm Region in 1980 had a homogeneous Protestant church population, that was, however, fairly disengaged from the practice of their faith, with a low degree of religious practice. Membership in the older Protestant free churches still mostly overlapped with membership in the Church of Sweden, due to the integration of church and state. All new-born children in Sweden automatically became members of the Church of Sweden if at least one of their parents was a member. In 1996, baptism became mandatory for membership in the Church of Sweden. This, together with a growing tendency to leave the Church of Sweden, has led to a decrease in membership. By 2020 the Church of Sweden membership in Stockholm Region had fallen to 1,085,166, meaning a decrease of 320,778 members. By then only 45 per cent of the population were members, well below the national average of 54 per cent, meaning that the Church of Sweden had become a minority church in Stockholm Region. In the municipalities south of Stockholm Municipality, where much of the immigrant population of Stockholm Region lives, the membership rate is as low as 28 per cent.

However, as mentioned previously, it is difficult to obtain information about how many people belong to the other churches in Stockholm, and this has been especially challenging when it comes to information about the situation in 1980.

Table 2.5 presents the number of adherents of the Church of Sweden, and the estimated numbers of adherents of the Protestant free church denominations (i.e. international Protestant churches, Classical Free Churches, and Low Church movements), Pentecostal churches (all types), the Roman Catholic Church, and the Syriac Orthodox Church.

One figure that is not included in Table 2.5 is the number *served* by Protestant free churches and Pentecostal churches. Infants do not become members through baptism in most of these churches, so they are excluded from the totals. There are also some churches with huge diaconal and educational outreach efforts, serving many young people and people on the margins of society. If these groups were added as "affiliated" or "served", it would probably mean an increase of about 50 per cent in the numbers for the Protestant free churches and Pentecostal churches. For example, the Church of St Clare in Stockholm City Centre is run by an evangelical association belonging to a Low Church movement with 374 members in 2020. The number of those "affiliated" or "served", however, was 6600 at that same church in 2020.[33] In Table 2.5, it is the membership of 374 in the evangelical association that has been counted.

Table 2.5. Changes in number of adherents of churches in Stockholm Region.

Denomination	1980	2020	Difference
Church of Sweden	1,405,944	1,085,166	−320,778
Protestant free churches	26,782	19,283	−7499
Pentecostal churches	13,560	32,368	+18,808
Roman Catholic Church	13,230	48,143	+34,913
Orthodox churches	~35,000	~100,000	~+65,000
Syriac Orthodox Church	1600	22,718	+21,118

Despite major growth in number of all types of local churches except for the Church of Sweden between 1980 and 2020, and even if the figures for all the Orthodox and Catholic churches were available and the figures for those "affiliated" with the Pentecostal and Protestant churches were added, it is unlikely that the combined total would make up for the staggering membership losses of the Church of Sweden. Table 2.1 clearly indicates that there was concurrent church growth and church decline in Stockholm Region between 1980 and 2020.

Conclusions

This chapter shows that, taking all local Christian churches together, the number of churches in Stockholm Region has grown since 1980. The total number of active and existing local churches was 22 per cent higher in 2020 than 40 years before, and local international Pentecostal churches, together with Orthodox and Catholic churches, contributed to this growth. If Norrtälje Municipality is omitted, the growth was considerable, reaching nearly 40 per cent, that is, a geographical shift of churches from northern to southern Stockholm is taking place.

Regarding the Church of Sweden, there has been a faster decline in membership in Stockholm Region than in the country in general. There was also a general decline in the number of parishes in Stockholm and in the number of members of these parishes, despite a 50 per cent increase in the region's population during the studied period. There was also a marked decline in the number of local parishes and their adherents in Classical Free Churches in Stockholm during the studied period. However, in terms of the number of local churches, this, together with the decline in the number of parishes in the Church of Sweden, has been outweighed by the expansion of other churches.

The changes in the ecclesial landscape of Stockholm are clearly related to the decline of older local churches, such as the Church of Sweden and Classical Free Churches, and the growth of local churches related to contemporary immigration, that is Pentecostal, Catholic, and Orthodox churches. An important part of this increase are the local international Pentecostal churches which in 1980 comprised only one such church, a Finnish-language church. Forty years later these churches have increased to 108, constituting one fourth of all local churches in Stockholm Region, thereby being an important aspect of the contemporary ecclesial landscape in the city.

Goodhew and Cooper's 2019 study of churches in London identifies similar processes, and the authors offer various and complex potential explanations to be aware of when considering these changes. One is that the increase in the number of churches is partly, or even mostly, related to immigration, which also must be related to a growth in religious diversity. That is, it is not immigration itself that leads to growth in local churches, but growth in religious *plurality* following from immigration, which is certainly the case in Stockholm.

A causal relationship between an increase in the number of local churches in Stockholm and immigration must also take account of the religiosity of the immigrants. As Goodhew and Cooper showed in London, there is great variation in this. In Sweden, some studies underscore this variation, but the general trend is for a decrease in religiosity among immigrants in Sweden, although the process is slow.[34] Whether this is the case in larger cites in Sweden, such as Stockholm, is not known. As Goodhew and Cooper argued, we must also remember that immigration is an ongoing process at an aggregated level but not at an individual or group level. Being an immigrant-based local church is a fluid identity.[35] The diversity of churches in Stockholm seen in this study is related to increased immigration in recent decades, but we must ask ourselves whether local churches established in the 1980s still can be seen as immigrant churches, and not as Swedish churches.

As Goodhew and Cooper put it, demography is crucial but not destiny.[36] They claim that it is too early to know whether the shifts in demography in recent decades will lead to temporary or permanent changes of the religious landscape in London. Could it be that, over time, the increase in numbers of churches, a possible sign of desecularization on a congregational (meso) level, in London and Stockholm will stop or even decrease, a sign of secularization, or will local churches continue to grow in number? Is there a tipping point when it comes to these processes? These matters merit further study.

The increase in numbers of churches can also be explained by the agency of the local churches that have seen growth.[37] The Pentecostal churches, which are the ones that explain a large partof the increase in the number of local churches in Stockholm, are also the ones with an active missionary agenda, and they do reach out to people with their active social undertakings. Research also shows that church belonging leads to improved wellbeing – relational as well as physical, mental, and economic.[38] So, in this case it may not be immigration alone that explains the increase in churches, but also the nature and benefits of belonging to these churches.

Magdalena Nordin is professor in sociology of religion at the Department of Literature, History of Ideas, and Religion at Gothenburg University. Her research focus has been about religion and migration focusing on change of religiosity among migrants, religious plurality and public institutions and interfaith dialogue. Among her recent publications we find *Migration and Religion*, IMISCOE Short Readers (2023); "Veiled Integration: The Use of Headscarves among a Christian Minority in Sweden, in *International Journal of Religion* (2023) and "Family and the Transmission of Traditions in the Syriac Orthodox Church in Sweden", in *Nordic Journal of Religion and Society* (2023).

Torbjörn Aronson is professor-at-large at Southeastern University (Lakeland), professor of church history at Scandinavian School of Theology (Uppsala) and associate professor in the same discipline at Uppsala University. He holds both a PhD in political science (University of Lund) and ThD in church history (Uppsala University). He has taught and conducted research at several universities during more than three decades. His main fields of research in political science are conservatism and nationalism, and in church history they are Lutheran ecclesiology, Pentecostalism, and the relationship between religion and migration.

Acknowledgement

This work was supported by the Swedish Research Council (no. VR 2018-01438).

Notes

1 Deborah Stevenson et al., "Religious Belief across 'Post-Secular' Sydney: The Multiple Trends in (De)secularisation", *Australian Geographer* 41(3) (2010), pp. 323–350.
2 David Goodhew and Anthony-Paul Cooper , *The Desecularisation of the City: London's Churches, 1980 to the Present* (Abingdon: Routledge, 2019); Scott Hanson, *City of Gods: Religious Freedom, Immigration, and Pluralism in Flushing, Queens* (New York: Fordham University Press, 2016); Paul D. Numrich and Elfriede Wedam, *Religion and Community in the New Urban America* (Oxford: Oxford University Press, 2015); Jane Garnett and Alana Harris (eds), *Rescripting Religion in the City: Migration and Religious Identity in the*

Modern Metropolis (Ashgate: Farnham, 2013); Lars Ahlin et al., "Religious Diversity and Pluralism: Empirical Data and Theoretical Reflections from the Danish Pluralism Project". *Journal of Contemporary Religion* 27(3) (2012), pp. 403-418, https://doi.org/10.1080/13537903.2012.722034; Mark Gornik, *Word Made Global: Stories of African Christianity in New York City* (Grand Rapids, MI: Eerdmans, 2011); Stevenson et al., "Religious Belief across 'Post-secular' Sydney"; Alex Stepick, Terry Ray and Sarah J. Mahler (eds), *Churches and Charity in the Immigrant Church: Religion, Immigration, and Civic Engagement in Miami* (New Brunswick, NJ: Rutgers University Press, 2009); Michael W. Foley and Dean R. Hoge (eds), *Religion and the New Immigrants: How Faith Communities Form Our Newest Citizens* (New York: Oxford University Press, 2007); Martin Baumann, "New Religious Plurality in Switzerland: Studying Lucerne's Religious Diversity", in Pratap Kumar (ed.), *Religious Pluralism in the Diaspora* (Leiden: Brill, 2006), pp. 353-370; Marianne Qvortrup Fibiger, *Religious Diversity: Mapping Religion and Spirituality in Aarhus* (Højbjerg: Systime, 2004); Marianne Qvortrup Fibiger, "The Danish Pluralism Project". *Religion* 39 (2009), pp. 169-175, https://doi.org/10.1016/j.religion.2009.01.004; Tuomas Martikainen, *Immigrant Religions in Local Society: Historical and Contemporary Perspectives in the City of Turku* (Åbo: Åbo Akademy UP, 2004); Nils Grübel and Stefan Rademacher (eds), *Religion in Berlin* (Berlin: Weissensee Verlag, 2003); Tony Carnes and Anna Karpathakis (eds), *New York Glory: Religions in the City* (New York: New York University Press, 2001); Helen Rose Ebaugh and Janet Saltzman Chafetz, *Religion and the New Immigrants: Continuities and Adaptations in Immigrant Congregations* (Walnut Creek, CA: Altamira, 2000); Lowell Livezey (ed.), *Public Religion and Urban Transformation: Faith in the City* (New York: New York University Press, 2000).

3   Goodhew and Cooper, *The Desecularisation of the City*, p, 7-8
4   Torbjörn Aronson, "Migration and Global Pentecostalism in the Greater Stockholm Area: A Mapping of the Growth of Local Migrant Churches in Stockholm", *Pentecostudies* 20(1), (2021), pp. 78-101, https://doi.org/10.1558/pent.41045; Thomas Arentzen, *Ortodoxa och österländska kyrkor i Sverige*. SST:s skriftserie nr 5 (Stockholm: Nämnden för statligt stöd till trossamfund, 2016); Magdalena Nordin, *Migration, religion och integration* [*Migration, Religion and Integration*], Kunskapsöversikt, 2023:2 (Delegationen för migrationsstudier, SOU Ju 2013:17. Delmi, 2023); Magdalena Nordin and Henrik Johnsén (eds), *Tradition och integration: Syrisk-ortodoxa kyrkan i Sverige* [*Tradition and Integration: The Syriac Orthodox Church in Sweden*] (Myndigheten för stöd till trossamfund (SST), 2023). In Norway the situation is similar, with growth in the number of Christian congregations related to immigrants. Up to 300 local immigrant churches can be found in Norway, of which international Pentecostal churches make up the majority; see Lemma Desta, *Faglig rapport om migrantmenigheter* (Oslo: Flerkulturelt kirkelig nettverk i Norges kristne råd, 2019); Lemma Desta, "Migrasjon og norsk kirkeliv: Afrikanske og asiatiske menigheter i Norge", in O. Tjørholm (ed.), *Kirkesamfunnene i Norge: Innføring i kirkekunnskap* (Oslo: Cappelen Damm Akademisk, 2018), pp. 295-312.
5   Goodhew and Cooper, *The Desecularization of the City*.
6   While there may have been earlier international Pentecostal churches, the historical record about them is not reliable.
7   Aronson, "Migration and Global Pentecostalism in the Greater Stockholm Area".
8   Hanson, *City of Gods*; Numrich and Wedam, *Religion and Community in the New Urban America*; Garnett and Harris, *Rescripting Religion in the City*; Ahlin et al., "Religious Diversity and Pluralism"; Gornik, *Word Made Global*; Stevenson et al., "Religious Belief across 'Post-secular' Sydney"; Stepick, Ray and Mahler, *Churches and Charity in the Immigrant Church*; Foley and Hoge, *Religion and the New Immigrants*; Baumann,

"New Religious Plurality in Switzerland"; Fibiger, "The Danish Pluralism Project"; Fibiger, *Religious Diversity*; Martikainen, *Immigrant Religions in Local Society*; Grübel and Rademacher, *Religion in Berlin*; Carnes and Karpathakis, *New York Glory*; Ebaugh and Chafetz, *Religion and the New Immigrants*; Livezey, *Public Religion and Urban Transformation*.
9   The exception for the former (on an aggregated level) is the study of Sydney, Australia, that focuses mostly on the religiosity of individuals, and not on congregations (Stevenson et al., "Religious Belief across 'Post-Secular' Sydney"); for the latter (the Christian perspective) the exceptions are a study of Miami in which the charity and civic engagement of these churches are examined (Stepick, Ray and Mahler, *Churches and Charity in the Immigrant Church*) and a study of African Christian churches in New York (Gornik, *Word Made Global*).
10 Goodhew and Cooper, *The Descularization of the City*, p. 16.
11 Ibid., p. 17.
12 Ibid., p. 19.
13 Karel Dobbelaere, *Secularization: An Analysis at Three Levels* (Brussels: Peter Lang, 2002); Goodhew and Cooper, *The Descularization of the City*, p. 4-5; Steve Bruce, *God is Dead: Secularisation in the West* (Oxford: Blackwell, 2002); Peter Berger (ed.), *The Desecularization of the World: Resurgent Religion and World Politics* (Grand Rapids, MI: Eerdmans, 1999).
14 Dobbelaere, *Secularization*.
15 Erika Willander, What Counts as Religion in Sociology? The Problem of Religiosity in Sociological Methodology, PhD thesis, Uppsala University, 2014; Gary Bouma, *Australian Soul: Religion and Spirituality in the Twenty-First Century* (Melbourne: Cambridge University Press, 2006); Bruce, *God is Dead*. See also Magdalena Nordin, "Vad vi vet och inte vet om kristna migranter i Sverige" ["What We Know and Do Not Know About Christian Migrants in Sweden"], in Anders Aschim et al. (eds), *Kristne migranter i Norden* [*Christian Migrants in the Nordic Countries*] (Oslo: Cappelen Damm, 2016), pp. 21-38.
16 For example, Goodhew and Cooper, *The Descularization of the City*, pp. 4-5.
17 Nordin and Johnsén, *Tradition och integration*; Magdalena Nordin and Jonas Otterbeck, *Migration and Religion*, IMISCOE Short Readers (London: Springer, 2023); Torbjörn Aronson, *Ett nytt karismatiskt landskap i Sverige* (Uppsala: Areopagos, 2016); Torbjörn Aronson, "Bilaga 1: Tabeller över internationella pentekostala församlingar i Storstockholm", in Katarina Westerlund (ed.), *Internationell pentekostalism i Storstockholm: Tre församlingar i ett förändrat religiöst landskap* (Uppsala: Uppsala University, 2021), pp. 117-126.
18 Per Pettersson and Annette Leis-Peters, "Religion i Sverige: kontinuitet och förändring", in Mia Lövheim and Magdalena Nordin (eds), *Sociologiska perspektiv på religion i Sverige* (Malmö: Gleerups förlag, 2022); David Thurfjell and Erika Willander, "Muslims by Ascription: On Post-Lutheran Secularity and Muslim Immigrants", *Numen* 68(4), pp. 307-335, https://doi.org/10.1163/15685276-12341626.
19 Douglas Jacobsen, *The Global Gospel: An Introduction to Christianity on Five Continents* (Grands Rapids, MI: Baker Academics, 2015); Douglas Jacobsen, *The World's Christians: Who They Are, Where They Are and How They Got There* (Oxford: Wiley Blackwell, 2021).
20 SASFC (Swedish: Myndigheten för stöd till trossamfund, SST), is a government agency under the Swedish Ministry of Culture and its mission is to promote dialogue between the government and faith communities in Sweden as well as to contribute to knowledge of religion. The agency is also responsible for grants to faith communities. These grants are distributed according to the number of people affiliated with each faith community, meaning those registered as regular participants in activities of the community. For further information on SASFC, see www.myndighetensst.se.

21 SFS 1998:1593, *Lag om Svenska kyrkan*; SFS 1999:932, *Lag om trossamfund*.
22 Three new and quite small municipalities were created between 1980 and 2020: Österåker (1983), Salem (1983) and Nykvarn (1999) (www.scb.se).
23 Four parishes (i.e. Nykvarn, Salem, Södertälje and Nynäshamn) belong to the Diocese of Strängnäs, but also to Stockholm Region. Six parishes (i.e. Bro, Kungsängen-Västra Ryd, Sigtuna, Märsta, Roslagens västra pastorat and Roslagens östra pastorat) belong to the Diocese of Uppsala, but also to Stockholm Region. Some of these parishes have several local churches.
24 For example at www.kammarkollegiet.se/engelska/start/about-us; www.bolagsfakta.se/bransch/stockholms-kommun; www.allabolag.se/verksamhet/verksamhet-i-religiosa-samfund; www.hitta.se. The public statistics of the Church of Sweden are available at: www.svenskakyrkan.se/statistik. Others are Arentzen, *Ortodoxa och österländska kyrkor i Sverige*; Hans Ljunggren (ed.), *Himmelska lador och jordiska tempel: Missionshus och församlingar anslutna till Svenska Missionsförbundet i skärgårdskommunerna från Södertörn till Roslagen* (SMF i Stockholms distrikt, Stockholm, 1985); and Süleyman Wannes, *Syrisk-ortodoxa kyrkan: bildandet, ankomsten och utvecklingen i Sverige* (Linköping: 2008). Two examples of local and denominational historical accounts. Two examples of yearbooks of free-church denominations are *Pingströrelsens årsbok* (1980, 2020) and *Svenska Alliansmissionens årsbok* (1980). The Roman Catholic and Eastern Catholic churches in communion with Rome have a website with extensive information about their local parishes: www.katolskakyrkan.se/forsamlingsliv. Most of the Orthodox churches have websites with information about their history in Sweden and their local parishes, for example: www.syriskortodoxakyrkan.se.
25 We are well aware of that Pentecostal churches tend to inflate their numbers because of their emphasis on numerical success, and have taken this into consideration.
26 Aronson, *Ett nytt karismatiskt landskap*; Aronson, "Bilaga 1"; Aronson, "Migration and Global Pentecostalism in the Greater Stockholm Area"; Magdalena Nordin, *Religiositet bland migranter: Sverige-chilenares förhållande till religion och samfund*, Lund Studies in Sociology of Religion (Lund: Lund University, 2004), https://lup.lub.lu.se/search/publication/21918; Nordin, *Religiositet bland migranter*; Nordin, "Vad vi vet och inte vet om kristna migranter i Sverige"; Nordin, *Migration, religion och integration*; Nordin and Johnsén, *Tradition och integration*; Nordin and Otterbeck, *Migration and Religion*.
27 Norrtälje, the northernmost tip of Stockholm Region, was densely populated countryside in the first half of the twentieth century, with parishes and local free churches in a large number of small villages. The total number of local churches was 67 in 1980. Many of those local churches and parishes had disappeared by 2020, when the total number of local churches was 31. The high number of local churches in Norrtälje in 1980 contributed to a much higher total number for the region in 1980, and consequently to a lower growth rate for 2020 than otherwise would have been the case.
28 The Methodist Church and the Swedish Baptist Association formed together with the Swedish Mission Covenant Church the Equmenia Church in 2011. In 2015–2016, the Swedish Salvation Army joined the Equmenia Church.
29 *Pingströrelsens årsbok 1981* (Stockholm: Förlaget Filadelfia, 1981), p. 83.
30 Torbjörn Aronson, "Ecclesiology with Unintended Consequences: Pingströrelsen and the Integration of International Pentecostal Congregations in Stockholm 1980–2020", *Pentecostudies* 22(1) (2023).
31 This local church was one of the first fully autonomous Finnish-based churches among the classical Pentecostal denominations and had its background in Finnish immigration after the Second World War.

32 *Statistisk årsbok 1982/83, Årgång 69* (Stockholm: Statistiska centralbyrån, 1983), p. 49.
33 The old parish of Church of St Clare had only around 700 parishioners (1980). It was a small inner-city parish with few people living within its confines, with most of the buildings in the parish housing expensive shops and offices. The high number of served people today is taken from the official yearbook of Evangeliska Fosterlands-Stiftelsen (the Evangelical Fatherland Foundation, a Low church-movement) and based on the rules for counting established by Swedish Agency for Support for Faith Communities (SASFC). From 1989 and onwards, the charismatic renewal has taken hold of the church. The high number of served people is due to the considerable charitable work among marginalized and impoverished people and drug addicts, many of whom live on the streets of Stockholm. On a typical Sunday around one thousand attendees gather in the main service and the regular weekly activities also see vivid attendance Most of the people who participate in the church activities and are served by the church are not members of Evangeliska Fosterlands-Stiftelsen and Church of St Clare is formally part of the Stockholm Cathedral Parish of Church of Sweden. But the Cathedral Parish has delegated the economic responsibility for the maintenance of the church and the church activities to Evangeliska Fosterlands-Stiftelsen and there is also a special partner association founded called the Friends of the Church of St Clare. The partner association helps with recruitment of donors, etc.
34 Eva Hamberg, *Livsåskådningar, religion och värderingar i en invandrargrupp: En studie av sverigeungrare* (Stockholm: CEIFO, 2000); Nordin, *Religiositet bland migranter*; Nordin, *Migration, religion, integration*; Maria Klingenberg and Magdalena Nordin, "Migration och ungdomars förhållningssätt till religion" ["Migration and Young People's Approach to Religion"], in Maria Klingenberg and Mia Lövheim (eds), *Unga och religion – Troende ointresserade eller neutrala? [Young People and Religion – Believers, Disinterested, or Neutral?]* (Malmö: Gleerups, 2019), pp. 109–126.
35 Ebaugh and Chafetz, *Religion and the New Immigrants*; Goodhew and Cooper, *The Descularization of the City*; Gornik, *Word Made Global*; Hanson, *City of Gods*; Martikainen, *Immigrant Religions in Local Society*; Nordin and Johnsén, *Tradition och integration*; Numrich and Wedam, *Religion and Community in the New Urban America*; Stepick et al, *Churches and Charity in the Immigrant Church*.
36 Goodhew and Cooper, *The Descularization of the City*, p. 17.
37 Ibid., pp. 17–19.
38 Ibid.; Luhrmann, *When God talks Back*; Gornik, *World Made Global.*

Bibliography

Ahlin, Lars, Jørn Borup, Marianne Fibiger Qvortrup, Lene Kühle, Viggo Mortensen and René Dybdak Pedersen. "Religious Diversity and Pluralism: Empirical Data and Theoretical Reflections from the Danish Pluralism Project." *Journal of Contemporary Religion* 27(3) (2012), pp. 403–418. https://doi.org/10.1080/13537903.2012.722034

Arentzen, Thomas. *Ortodoxa och österländska kyrkor i Sverige*. SST:s skriftserie no. 5. Stockholm: Nämnden för statligt stöd till trossamfund, 2016.

Aronson, Torbjörn. "Ecclesiology with Unintended Consequences: Pingströrelsen and the Integration of International Pentecostal Congregations in Stockholm 1980–2020." *Pentecostudies* 22(1) (2023).

Aronson, Torbjörn. "Bilaga 1: Tabeller över internationella pentekostala församlingar i Storstockholm." In Katarina Westerlund (ed.), *Internationell pentekostalism i*

Storstockholm: Tre församlingar i ett förändrat religiöst landskap, 117–126. Uppsala: Uppsala University, 2021a.

Aronson, Torbjörn. "Migration and Global Pentecostalism in the Greater Stockholm Area: A Mapping of the Growth of Local Migrant Churches in Stockholm." *Pentecostudies* 20(1) (2021b), pp. 78–101. https://doi.org/10.1558/pent.41045

Aronson, Torbjörn. *Ett nytt karismatiskt landskap i Sverige*. Uppsala: Areopagos, 2016.

Baumann, Martin. "New Religious Plurality in Switzerland: Studying Lucerne's Religious Diversity." In Pratap Kumar (ed.), *Religious Pluralism in the Diaspora*, 353–370. Leiden: Brill, 2006.

Berger, Peter (ed.). *The Desecularization of the World: Resurgent Religion and World Politics*. Grand Rapids, MI: Eerdmans, 1999.

Bouma, Gary. *Australian Soul: Religion and Spirituality in the Twenty-First Century*. Melbourne: Cambridge University Press, 2006.

Bruce, Steve. *God is Dead: Secularisation in the West*. Oxford: Blackwell, 2002.

Carnes, Tony and Anna Karpathakis (eds). *New York Glory: Religions in the City*. New York: New York University Press, 2001.

Desta, Lemma. *Faglig rapport om migrantmenigheter*. Oslo: Flerkulturelt kirkelig nettverk i Norges kristne råd, 2019.

Desta, Lemma. "Migrasjon og norsk kirkeliv: Afrikanske og asiatiske menigheter i Norge." In O. Tjørholm (ed.), *Kirkesamfunnene i Norge: Innføring i kirkekunnskap*, 295–312. Oslo: Cappelen Damm Akademisk, 2018.

Dobbelaere, Karel. *Secularization: An Analysis at Three Levels*. Brussels: Peter Lang, 2002.

Ebaugh, Helen Rose and Janet Saltzman Chafetz. *Religion and the New Immigrants: Continuities and Adaptations in Immigrant Congregations*. Walnut Creek, CA: Altamira, 2000.

Fibiger, Marianne Qvortrup. "The Danish Pluralism Project." *Religion* 39 (2009), pp. 169–175. https://doi.org/10.1016/j.religion.2009.01.004

Fibiger, Marianne Qvortrup. *Religious Diversity: Mapping Religion and Spirituality in Aarhus*. Højbjerg: Systime, 2004.

Foley, Michael W. and Dean R. Hoge (eds). *Religion and the New Immigrants: How Faith Communities Form Our Newest Citizens*. New York: Oxford University Press, 2007.

Garnett, Jane and Alana Harris (eds). *Rescripting Religion in the City: Migration and Religious Identity in the Modern Metropolis*. Ashgate: Farnham, 2013.

Goodhew, David and Anthony Paul Cooper. *The Desecularisation of the City: London's Churches, 1980 to the Present*. Abingdon: Routledge, 2019.

Gornik, Mark R. *Word Made Global: Stories of African Christianity in New York City*. Grand Rapids, MI: Eerdmans, 2011.

Grübel, Nils and Stefan Rademacher (eds). *Religion in Berlin*. Berlin: Weissensee Verlag, 2003.

Hamberg, Eva. *Livsåskådningar, religion och värderingar i en invandrargrupp: En studie av sverigeungrare*. Stockholm: CEIFO, 2000.

Hanson, Scott. *City of Gods: Religious Freedom, Immigration, and Pluralism in Flushing, Queens*. New York: Fordham University Press, 2016.

Jacobsen, Douglas. *The Global Gospel:. An Introduction to Christianity on Five Continents*. Grands Rapids, MI: Baker Academics, 2015.

Jacobsen, Douglas. *The World's Christians: Who They Are, Where They Are and How They Got There*. Oxford: Wiley Blackwell, 2021.

Klingenberg, Maria and Magdalena Nordin. "Migration och ungdomars förhållningssätt till religion" ["Migration and Young People's Approach to Religion"]. In Maria Klingenberg and Mia Lövheim (eds), *Unga och religion - Troende ointresserade eller neutrala? [Young People and Religion - Believers, Disinterested, or Neutral?]*, 109–126. Malmö: Gleerups, 2019.

Livezey, Lowell (ed.). *Public Religion and Urban Transformation: Faith in the City*. New York: New York University Press, 2000.
Ljunggren, Hans. *Himmelska lador och jordiska tempel: Missionshus och församlingar anslutna till Svenska missionsförbundet i skärgårdskommunerna från Södertörn till Roslagen*. Stockholm: SMF i Stockholms distrikt, 1985.
Luhrmann, Tanya. *When God talks Back: Understanding the American Evangelical Relationships With God*. New York: Vintage Books, 2012.
Martikainen, Tuomas. *Immigrant Religions in Local Society: Historical and Contemporary Perspectives in the City of Turku*. Åbo: Åbo Akademy UP, 2004.
Nordin, Magdalena. *Religiositet bland migranter: Sverige-chilenares förhållande till religion och samfund*. Lund Studies in Sociology of Religion. Lund: Lund University, 2004. https://lup.lub.lu.se/search/publication/21918
Nordin, Magdalena. "Vad vi vet och inte vet om kristna migranter i Sverige" ["What We Know and Do Not Know About Christian Migrants in Sweden"]. In Anders Aschim, Olav Hovdelien and Helje Kringlebotn Sødal (eds), *Kristne migranter i Norden* [*Christian Migrants in the Nordic Countries*], 21–38. Oslo: Cappelen Damm, 2016.
Nordin, Magdalena. *Migration, religion och integration* [*Migration, Religion and Integration*]. Kunskapsöversikt, 2023:2, Delegationen för migrationsstudier, SOU Ju 2013:17. Delmi, 2023.
Nordin, Magdalena and Henrik Johnsén (eds). *Tradition och integration. Syrisk-ortodoxa kyrkan i Sverige* [*Tradition and Integration. The Syriac Orthodox Church in Sweden*]. Myndigheten för stöd till trossamfund (SST), 2023.
Nordin, Magdalena and Jonas Otterbeck. *Migration and Religion*. IMISCOE Short Readers. London: Springer, 2023.
Numrich, Paul D. and Elfriede Wedam. *Religion and Community in the New Urban America*. Oxford: Oxford University Press, 2015.
Pettersson, Per, and Annette Leis-Peters. "Religion i Sverige: kontinuitet och förändring." In Mia Lövheim and Magdalena Nordin (eds), *Sociologiska perspektiv på i Sverige*. Malmö: Gleerups förlag, 2022.
Pingströrelsens årsbok. *Pingströrelsens årsbok 1980*. Stockholm: Förlaget Filadelfia, 1980.
Pingströrelsens årsbok. *Pingströrelsens årsbok 1981*. Stockholm: Förlaget Filadelfia, 1981.
Pingströrelsens årsbok. *Pingströrelsens årsbok 2020*. Bromma: Pingst – fria församlingar i samverkan, 2020.
Statistisk årsbok. *Statistisk årsbok 1982/83: Årgång 69*. Stockholm: Statistiska centralbyrån, 1982.
Stepick, Alex, Terry Ray and Sarah J. Mahler (eds). *Churches and Charity in the Immigrant Church. Religion, Immigration, and Civic Engagement in Miami*. New Brunswick, NJ: Rutgers University Press, 2009.
Stevenson, Deborah, Kevin Dunn, Adam Possamai and Awis Piracha. "Religious Belief across 'Post-secular' Sydney: The Multiple Trends in (De)secularisation." *Australian Geographer* 41(3) (2010), pp. 323–350. https://doi.org/10.1080/00049182.2010.498039
Svenska Alliansmissionens årsbok. *Svenska Alliansmissionens årsbok*. Hässleholm: Alliansmissionens förlag, 1980.
Thurfjell, David and Erika Willander. "Muslims by Ascription: On Post-Lutheran Secularity and Muslim Immigrants." *Numen* 68(4) (2021), pp. 307–335. https://doi.org/10.1163/15685276-12341626
Willander, Erika. "What Counts as Religion in Sociology? The Problem of Religiosity in Sociological Methodology." PhD thesis, Uppsala University, 2014.

Chapter 3

Ecclesiology with Unintended Consequences: Pingströrelsen and the Integration of International Pentecostal Churches in Stockholm 1980–2020

Torbjörn Aronson

Introduction

The purpose of this chapter is to fill a gap of knowledge dealing with the on-going transformations of the religious landscape in urban Sweden: the rise of international Pentecostal churches. From the perspective of church history it is a relevant and important question to ask how the growth of international Pentecostal local churches has influenced the native Classical Pentecostal movement in Sweden, Pingströrelsen, in the Stockholm region and what has been the result. The tensions and challenges that arise when an older native religious community experiences a large influx of new co-believers in their local and national context are not unique to Pingströrelsen in Sweden. Older communities of Jews, Catholics and Muslims in Sweden and Pentecostals in Britain have experienced similar situations.[1] The results of the investigation presented in this chapter can be used in comparative analyses of the responses of older religious communities to the immigration of large groups of co-believers.

The major Classical Pentecostal denomination in Sweden from the 1920s has been Pingströrelsen (Pentecostal Movement), or Pingst – Fria Församlingar i Samverkan (Pentecost – Free Churches in Cooperation) which is the present formal name of the denomination. It became the largest free church in the country in the 1970s and is characterized by a radical congregationalist ecclesiology and a strong missionary focus. Pentecostal denominations in Latin America, Africa and Asia that were started by missionaries from Pingströrelsen currently total a membership of approximately 35–40 million people.[2] Now this overseas missionary movement is faced with a growing number of international churches at its doorsteps, and the question emerges how Pingströrelsen has interacted with the growing number of international Pentecostal churches in Stockholm during the four last decades and what role its particular ecclesiology has played in this.

Stockholm has experienced a demographic shift through immigration during the last decades of the twentieth century and the two first decades of the twenty-first century. The population of Stockholm Region has grown by more than 50 per cent during this time, from 1,528,200 in 1980 to 2,368,269 in 2020, with a considerable part of the population growth due to immigration.[3] This has made the global growth of Pentecostalism become visible in Stockholm Region. There has been a strong increase in the number of local churches with an international background in Stockholm and in some of the urban centres of the country.[4] In a global perspective, Pentecostalism has grown exponentially in the last half century, with strongholds of Pentecostalism in the Global South, while the English-speaking world plays a prominent role.[5] Although some immigration-related changes in the religious landscape in Sweden have caught the attention of secular media, immigrants with a Pentecostal affiliation have often been overlooked. Research on different religious communities is only just beginning and there are a few articles published on Pentecostal immigrants to this country.[6]

Migration to Sweden and its religious impact are of course not entirely new phenomena. Sweden experienced an influx of labour migrants from Finland and southern Europe in the 1960s. The influx of Finnish refugees and labourers led to a considerable increase of the already present Finnish-speaking minority during and after the Second World War. Some of these migrants were Pentecostals, and from the 1950s onwards Finnish-speaking worship groups and Finnish-speaking local churches were organized within Pingströrelsen.[7] The movement thus had an earlier experience of Pentecostal immigration before the latest influx of Pentecostal immigrants from all over the world. In addition, Pingströrelsen in Sweden also had congregations among two other officially recognized national minorities, that is the Sami population in the northern part of the country, and the Roma.[8] The first Sami-speaking Pentecostal congregation was already founded in 1925 in Ankarede, Jämtland.[9] One part of the Roma population where Pingströrelsen has made inroads are Travellers (in Swedish *resandefolket*). Travellers have closer historical links to ethnic Swedes than other Roma, often having common Swedish first names, despite speaking a dialect of the Romani language. Historically, they have seen heavy discrimination by the Swedish state and the Church of Sweden. In some parts of southern Sweden, especially the area around Jönköping, Travellers have joined local Pentecostal churches,[10] forming another experience with ethnic minorities in the movement, alongside Finnish and Sami Pentecostals.

In studying how the newer immigration movements have changed the main Pentecostal movement in Sweden, this chapter asks the following questions from the vantage point of church history:[11]

- What was the impact of the rise of international Pentecostalism in Stockholm on Pingströrelsen: did it affect growth, stagnation, or decline?

- What steps have been taken by Pingströrelsen to integrate, assimilate, or segregate the new international Pentecostal churches in Stockholm between 1980 and 2020?

- What role did the ecclesiology and ecclesial structures of Pingströrelsen play in the movement's response to the new international Pentecostal churches?
- In what ways have the earlier experiences with Finnish Pentecostal immigration and the integration of older national minorities contributed to the Pingströrelsen's integration, assimilation, or segregation of the new international churches?

After a brief discussion of methodology, the chapter will take these questions in turn. The first two questions will be answered together by delineating the development of the international churches in Stockholm and the Pentecostal movement's response to them. Next the chapter will turn to the third question in a historical survey of Pingströrelsen's ecclesiology of and its recent changes in ecclesial structures. Finally, the earlier attempts at integrating ethnic minority Pentecostals will be considered by way of comparison. The conclusion will deliver a short assessment of the response of Pingströrelsen to international Pentecostalism in Stockholm and point to areas in need of further research.

It is worth noting that "integration" is understood here as "a process of mutual adjustment and inclusion into a coordinated whole".[12] As such, "integration" sits between the two opposites of "assimilation" and "segregation", whereby the former is understood as the dissolution of a minority culture as it becomes absorbed into a majority culture, whereas the latter designates "the institutional separation of an ethnic, racial, religious, or other minority group from the dominant majority".[13] This means that the chapter has a special interest in studying processes of mutual adjustments between the native church and local international churches, rather than focus on instances of sustained segregation or absorption.

Theoretical and Methodological Considerations

The disciplinary locus of this study is church history, a scholarly discipline that seeks to combine historical methodology with theological analysis. As such, church history focuses on the interaction between theology and spirituality on the one hand and ideas, events and conditions in the social, political, economic, cultural, and ecclesiastical spheres on the other, all within a chronological perspective. By so doing, church history brings to light the influence of society and culture on theology and spirituality, and vice versa. In church history, *the church* is the primary object of study and research, and the interaction between church and society within a chronological framework is the central issue to be discussed. This means that if a major change occurs in a given ecclesial landscape over a particular period of time, church historians are interested in exploring its reasons and effects in both church and society. The immigration-related change in the Swedish Pentecostal landscape between 1980 and 2020 thus offers a typical case for a church historical exploration, in particular as it concerns transformations in both the Swedish Pentecostal movement and in Swedish society at large.

The material used for this chapter are denominational statistics and documents (including figures published on websites or contained in municipal and commercial registers) as well as field studies and interviews. Some of the underlying detailed research has already been published in 2021 in the project report "Pentecostal Migrants in Secular Sweden: Influences and Challenges".[14]

This study combines qualitative and quantitative methods, which is not unusual in church history. Concepts from ecclesiology and church history are used in the analysis. "Local church" refers in this chapter to a group of believers who regularly meet in a liturgical or congregational settings under local leadership and with an official registration as either an association or as a religious denomination. "Worship group" refers to a group of believers that are part of a local church but conduct additional, separate worship services. "International local church" thus means a local church using a language in worship other than Swedish and/or having a mother church in another country. "Pentecostal church" means a local church which is associated with one of the four major following historical groups in the Pentecostal tradition: classical Pentecostal churches, old independent Pentecostal-like churches of the majority world, Charismatic renewal movements within the historic churches and Neo-charismatic churches and networks. These categories are helpful in navigating the Pentecostal landscape but they are also loose and historically contingent. Because of their limitations, they are used here to indicate general patterns of development, which do, however, need to be complicated further by in-depth research.[15] Nonetheless, this rough typology can help understand why a local international Pentecostal church might not be interested in joining Pingströrelsen, which has a clear profile as a classical Pentecostal church with roots in the global and national Pentecostal revival of early twentieth century. Therefore, the typology is employed here to highlight historical, cultural and theological differences and how these impacted the integration of international churches into Pingströrelsen.[16]

The Impact of International Churches on the Pentecostal Landscape in Stockholm

It may seem trivial to ask whether Pentecostal immigration has contributed to the growth, stagnation or decline of Pentecostalism in Stockholm Region. Yet the seemingly self-evident answer of growth needs to be qualified when considering the different scenarios that have been observed among migrant Pentecostals in other European capitals. For example, in London, the religious fervor among of immigrant communities seems to have declined over time, with secularizing trends detected.[17] The staunchly secular character of Swedish society makes this such a development even more likely. Moreover, it is clear that Pingströrelsen in 2020 has a smaller national membership than in 1980, which set the growth observed in Stockholm in a different overall narrative of decline.

In 1980 there were six local Pentecostal churches in Stockholm Municipality and none of them had an international background. In the Stockholm Region the number of the local churches were 29. One of them was a new church plant and one was a Finnish-speaking church. Among these 29 local churches, 22 belonged to Pingströrelsen and six local churches were independent.[18] The total membership in 1980 was about 13,000, out of which 12,228 belonged to local churches in Pingströrelsen.[19]

In 2020, Pingströrelsen included a growing number of local churches and worship groups where the majority of the members were born in another country and where worship was conducted in a language other than Swedish. The number of local churches in the Stockholm Region belonging to Pingströrelsen had grown to 36 in four decades. These 36 local churches counted approximately 18,000 members, representing a growth of around 47 per cent between 1980 and 2020. Of these 36 local churches, 17 had an international background, with a worship language other than Swedish and/or a mother church in another country. Their membership totaled roughly 8100.[20] This means that the growth of Pingströrelsen in the Stockholm Region was fully explained by the integration of international local churches, in fact, the Swedish churches had seen a relative decline. This observation is strengthened by a look at the national development of Pingströrelsen, which saw a 9 per cent decrease in overall membership between 1980 and 2020 from 97,203 members to 88,222.[21] Thus, the integration of international churches has only buffered the decline of the national movement, and this integration was not always straightforward as the next section of the chapter will show. As Pingströrelsen in Stockholm Region went from a more or less ethnically homogeneous entity to one that consisted nearly half of international churches (in both local churches and overall membership), no structures and procedures had to be developed for the integration of these new churches.

Over the same period of time, Pentecostal churches in Stockholm overall have grown even more. In 2020 there were altogether 157 local Pentecostal churches in the Stockholm Region (including the Pingströrelsen churches) and 107 of these were international. Added to the 107 international local Pentecostal churches, there existed 15 worship groups within local Swedish Pentecostal churches, which used a language other than Swedish for worship. The number of members and affiliates in the 157 local churches can be estimated at around 35,000 people, although there is no official figure. Thus, while Pingströrelsen hosted roughly 69 per cent of the local Pentecostal churches in the Stockholm Region in 1980, this share had decreased to 23 per cent in 2020. In membership terms, the share of Pingströrelsen in Stockholm's Pentecostal population is probably around 50 per cent, down from around 90 per cent in 1980.[22]

It is clear from this short survey that Pentecostalism in Stockholm experienced a strong growth and diversification during the last four decades This general growth has benefited Pingströrelsen in Stockholm but has not reversed the national situation of membership decline. It is also clear that Pingströrelsen in Stockholm has only been able to integrate a minority of the international churches (17 out of 107) and about half of the international worship groups (8 out of 15). The largest local international Pentecostal church, Hillsong Sweden, belongs to both Pingströrelsen and the Australian international denomination

Hillsong Church.[23] No sources indicate any attempts of Pingströrelsen to apply an assimilationist or segregationist strategy in relation to the new international churches.

It is clear then, that Pingströrelsen has benefited to some extent from the growth of Pentecostalism in the Stockholm region, while also losing its dominant position in an increasingly fragmenting movement. It is not the focus of this chapter to discuss why many international Pentecostal churches did not find a home in Pingströrelsen. This would need further research into each church, considering factors like international connections to a mother church abroad, differences in spirituality or dogma between the aforementioned Pentecostal types, a particular competitive situation between or within migrant communities, or major cultural differences. Here we will instead proceed to analyse how the ecclesiology and institutional organization of Pingströrelsen impacted and was impacted by the integration of international churches into the movement.

The Role of Ecclesiology and Ecclesial Structures in the Integration of International Pentecostal Churches

The ecclesiology of Pingströrelsen was formed in the early decades of the movement's history with its prime architects being T. B. Barratt (1862–1940) and Lewi Pethrus (1884–1974). Lewi Pethrus became the leader of the new movement in the 1920s and dominated its ecclesiology until well into the 1960s.[24] There are several studies detailing the ecclesiology of Pingströrelsen in this period and Lewi Pethrus's influence.[25] In fact, his legacy was so resilient that it was not until the 1990s that the movement began to change with regard to it. It continued to influence the movement during the following decades. From the 1990s different challenges occurred and a development which led to new attitudes and policies concerning ecumenical relations, denominational structures, church planting and transdenominational and transnational networks.

Ecclesiology can be divided into two subcategories: "ecclesiology proper", which deals with the theological concept of the church, and the practical side of ecclesiology which deals with questions about ministry, structure and sacraments of the church.[26] We will begin with the "ecclesiology proper" of Lewi Pethrus and then move to the more practical issues. In the last part of the discussion we turn to the question of the long-lasting effects of Pethrus's ecclesiology and how the movement began to change in the 1990s.

Lewi Pethrus never used the Swedish word for "church" (kyrka) in the sermons published in his *Collected Writings* but used the Swedish equivalent of "congregation" or "assembly" (*församling*).[27] Pethrus argued that his use of the terms "congregation" or "assembly" was a more or less literal translation of the New Testament Greek word "ekklesia", which meant "those that are called out" or "those that are called together in a public assembly".[28] This not only allowed Pethrus to emphasize the separation between the believers in Jesus Christ and "the world" but also the restorationist character of his ecclesiology. The apostolic church of the New

Testament was the ideal church and thus the church he aimed to restore in these last days. Accordingly, this restored church was made out of individuals that by faith had become new creations in Christ according to 2 Cor. 5:17.[29]

Pethrus spelled out his restorationist ecclesiology in great detail in a 1919 pamphlet with the title *De kristnas enhet* (The Unity of Christian People). In six points Pethrus outlined an ecclesiology that affirmed a belief in the apostolicity, unity and holiness of "God's assembly" but also in its present decay and division. The decay and division could be remedied by a return to the Scriptures and by allowing "the Spirit freedom" to move in the "assembly".[30] The resulting "God's assembly" included both the local churches of the movement as well as a universal assembly of all true believers at all times, living and dead. There was no discussion about the relationship between the historic churches and "God's assembly".[31] Instead, the pamphlet offered an immediate synthesis between what Pethrus saw as the marks of the church and their practical application in the structure of "God's assembly". Pethrus began his argument by quoting a number of prominent Baptist leaders on the question of denominational structures and concluded that the present division of all Christians had one of its roots in the structures superimposed on the local congregations and that these structures were not motivated from Scripture.[32] The denominational structures also led to divisions among Christians because of the different creeds and confessions they espoused. Creeds and confessions thus were hindrances to the restoring work of the Spirit of God in his work of continuously revealing the meaning of Scripture. New outpourings of the Spirit always led to greater freedom through new "revelation". Denominational structures and confessions could never foresee or contain this liberating work of the Spirit and the result was always splits and divisions.[33]

The immediate historical background for Pethrus's congregationalist ecclesiology was his conflict with Svenska Baptistsamfundet (Swedish Baptist Denomination) and a similar conflict that the Norwegian Pentecostal leader T. B. Barratt experienced with the Methodist Episcopal Church in Norway. These experiences were reinforced by the writings of the Methodist missionary bishop of Africa, William Taylor (1821–1902).[34]

Lewi Pethrus repeated his tenets about the nature of the church twenty years later in a series of books called *På bibelns mark I-III* (*On Biblical Ground I-III*). The power and new life of the Spirit was seen in opposition to the structures and hierarchical organizations of denominations.[35] He also continued to affirm his belief in the present-day existence of the fivefold ministries in Eph. 4:11, including apostles and prophets.[36]

The practical ecclesiology of Lewi Pethrus had a number of distinctive features. Following the fundamental tenets of his ecclesiology, Lewi Pethrus fought for the formal independence of each local church and resisted the development of a common missionary board for the Pentecostal movement.[37] His criticism and practical prevention of denominational structures as well as a common confession of faith for all the churches to sign prevailed, and these things were never accepted or adopted by the increasing number of local Pentecostal churches in Sweden in the 1920s and the 1930s.

The early growth of this movement of local independent Pentecostal churches around Lewi Pethrus and the Filadelfia church was impressive. There were 129 local Pentecostal churches in Sweden in 1920 and 563 in 1940. This rise was often attributed to the movement's radical congregationalism, and while this did indeed make it easier for congregations from other denominations to associate with Pingströrelsen, it did not lead to greater Christian unity. The other Swedish free churches (i.e. those outside the Lutheran state church) instead perceived Pingströrelsen not only as a new and important actor, but more or less as a denomination like themselves. Though Lewi Pethrus continued to defend his practical ecclesiology in books, sermons and debates, the ensuing struggles over leadership, organization of missions, and church-internal politics marked Pethrus personal leadership as the decisive unifying trait of the movement rather than the independence of local churches.[38] From the 1950s and onwards practically no local churches from other denominations joined Pingströrelsen, and it has been suggested that the now growing homogeneity of the movement was a result of its lack of formal structures. Participating in the movement largely came down to signalling solidarity and rallying around common causes.[39]

What is clear from the discussion above is that the practical ecclesiology of Lewi Pethrus and Pingströrelsen was built on the assumption of a homogeneous population. There is no discussion about the relationship between congregationalism and ethnic or cultural diversity or about the role congregationalism could play in the integration of groups of Pentecostals with other ethnic backgrounds. When this ecclesiology was developed and put in practice, there was no intention that it should play an integrative role in that type of situation.

During the 1950s and 1960s, Pingströrelsen's practical ecclesiology was influenced by the pursuit of "one church in one city", which was a strategy to make best use of the movement's resources through centralization in urban areas. This brought with it a negative attitude to new church plants in larger towns if there already existed a local church that belonged to Pingströrelsen.[40] This was another feature of the practical ecclesiology that lacked awareness of situations that would arise if larger groups of Pentecostals with other ethnic or cultural backgrounds might like to join the movement.

The strategy of "one church in one city" culminated during the 1970s, leading to public debates and conflicts as new ideas were introduced promoting church plants as a strategy of evangelism in the new suburbs, which at the time grew strongly in Stockholm. In the 1973 yearbook of Pingströrelsen, two editorial articles were published with opposing views concerning church plants as a growth strategy.[41] One of the writers was Kjell Sjöberg (1933–1997), a former missionary to Pakistan who had returned to Sweden. In 1974, he founded a new autonomous local church in Järfälla, a suburb north of Stockholm, without asking permission from the older local Pentecostal churches in Stockholm city centre. The result was that the new church plant in Järfälla was boycotted by the other Stockholm churches of Pingströrelsen during the 1970s.[42] The conflicts subsided during the 1980s, but the overall strategy of the movement was the same. In 1985, the editorial of the yearbook of Pingströrelsen once again emphasized the established position under the heading "The strength of unity". Its author decried the growing interest in new church plants in suburban areas as a strategy of evangelism. He saw this type of strategy as a strategy that would lead to fragmentation.[43]

The regular steps to become a recognized and accepted local church in Pingströrelsen during these decades, consisted in first forming a worship group situated in a local community under the umbrella of an older mother church. When the worship group had grown enough to be able to carry the financial burden of regular congregational life, a process could be initiated that, if things worked out well, might result in a new autonomous local church. The new church was then founded and formally separated from the mother church and recognized by the other nearby Pentecostal churches. This process involved the support and consensus of the mother church and other geographically close local Pentecostal churches.[44]

By 1980, Pingströrelsen was still characterized by its congregationalist ecclesiology. Yet, a number of joint ventures and initiatives had been developed, built on some form of congregational support: a publishing house, mission in Africa, Latin America and Asia, local and international radio, a newspaper, a bank, and more. In an analysis of the organization and decision procedures, one pastor of the movement concluded that the motto seemed to be: "no to denomination – yes to its functions".[45] At the same time, Pingströrelsen was a homogeneous and uniform movement, where the local churches mostly held to a similar spirituality. One of the original *raison d'être* of the radical congregationalism, that a movement consisting of autonomous local churches would facilitate the inclusion of newly founded churches and pentecostalized churches from other denominations as well as new spiritual practices, had obviously faded into obscurity.

But, as will be discussed in the next part of the chapter, the ecclesial structures of the movement gained *a new and unintended life* through the growth of Finnish-speaking worship groups and local churches within the movement. This development began in the 1950s and culminated in the 1980s. While the earlier process of forming a worship group was organized on a territorial basis, worship groups now developed on an ethnic or cultural basis. This was something that never had been discussed or intended when the original system was put in place during the 1920s and the 1930s.

During the 1990s, the ecclesial structures of Pingströrelsen were challenged and a fierce debate erupted when a new local church, Stockholm Karisma Center, was founded in the capital in 1996. The debate that followed in *Dagen*, the newspaper of the movement, did not pertain directly to the congregationalist ecclesiology of the movement but to the still dominating ecclesial strategy of "one church in one city". The founders of Stockholm Karisma Center did not motivate their new church plant with reference to particular geographical or territorial factors, but to the need for new church plants in order to reach new segments of the population of Stockholm.[46] They emphasized the intrinsic value of new church plants, irrespective of the interests of older local churches of the movement. They were influenced by the research on church growth conducted at Fuller Theological Seminary, Pasadena, CA, which pointed to new church plants as a growth strategy. Their critics accused them of disrupting the movement and being disloyal because they had acted without having obtained the approval of the other local Pentecostal churches in Stockholm. In the conclusion of the debate, one of the commentators pointed to the need for formal denominational structures, where decisions and discussions of this kind could take place in an open and transparent process.[47] During the following year, in 1997, three old and relatively small Baptist denominations merged into a new denomination, which in 2002 got its new name, Evangeliska Frikyrkan (Evangelical Free Church).[48] These developments probably played a role when Pingströrelsen finally changed course concerning the question of denominational structures.[49] In the late 1990s another major legal change occurred when a new law that separated the Church of Sweden from the state was enacted. This new law came into effect in 2000. Parallel to this legislation, a new law about religious communities was enacted in 1998. The impact of these external legal developments should not be underestimated when seeking to understand why Pingströrelsen took steps in order to become a formal and legally recognized denomination.[50]

In 2001 a national association, Pingst – fria församlingar i samverkan, was founded and a formal application was filed with the Chamber of Deputies to register the new entity a legally recognized religious denomination. The national association was founded in order to enhance the coordination of the common enterprises of the movement. The application was accepted and from 2004, local churches that were part of the movement could join the national association and thereby the legally recognized denomination. One of the results of this process of becoming a denomination was that the movement established formal decision-making structures for electing a national leader and a national board and for admitting new local churches to the movement. In 2012 the church adopted a statement of faith and a formal process for adopting prospective new member churches. Another result was a stronger coordination of the common enterprises of the movement, as the national association became the platform for these.[51] Three additional structural innovations were introduced between 2001 and 2020: the possibility to admit congregations belonging to another denomination and/or a transnational church organization, a program for church planting, and a network for pastors, Pingst Pastor.

Iglesia del Pueblo in Sollentuna became the first local international church in Pingströrelsen in 1997, apart from the Finnish-speaking churches (see below). Given that this happened before the adoption of the new membership processes, this was a fairly irregular development because the church had not grown out of a Spanish-speaking worship group within a local Pingströrelsen church and there already was an older local Pentecostal church in the neighbourhood. What was the background for this change of practice in admitting Iglesia del Pueblo into the movement? One reason probably was the above-mentioned founding of Stockholm Karisma Center in 1995 and the public debate about the "one church in one city" policy that followed. Stockholm Karisma Center had stood its ground and won, as the debate did not lead to any kind of boycott or excommunication. It had become evident that the old strategy was being abandoned and that it could no longer be enforced. Thus, the old native Pentecostal church in Sollentuna, Filadelfiaförsamlingen, did not try stop the Latino church from being a member. The fact that it was an already existing and functioning Pentecostal church made it more than suitable for admission into the movement. The original *raison d'être* of the radical congregationalism of Pingströrelsen was now revived and allowed to triumph, meaning that a lack of denominational structures would facilitate the admission of churches from outside the movement. In 2001, Jerusalem Evangelical Church in Älvsjö, Stockholm, a local church formed predominantly by Ethiopian immigrants, was admitted into Pingströrelsen as the second international church in addition to the existing Finnish-speaking churches and Iglesia del Pueblo.[52]

Pingstkyrkan Gud är kärlek in Gothenburg (or Igreja Pentecostal Deus e Amor) and Hillsong Church Stockholm were the first local churches belonging to transnational church organizations that were admitted to Pingst FFS. Pingstkyrkan Gud är kärlek had begun a missionary work among Latinos in 2005 and was admitted as a member of Pingst FFS in 2009. Passion Church in Stockholm, founded in 2006, had joined the Hillsong Church in 2009, a transnational denomination which had been founded as a local Assemblies of God Church in Sydney in 1983 and had planted churches in major European cities in the 1990s. After changing its name to Hillsong Church Stockholm, the congregation joined Pingströrelsen in 2011.[53]

In 2001 an ecumenical church planting consultation was arranged, hosted by Evangeliska Frikyrkan. The consultation gradually developed into an ecumenical church planting network where most of the older free churches in the country became members. In 2016, Pingströrelsen became an active member of the network and upgraded its commitment to church planting. Since Pingströrelsen had already gradually changed its common policy concerning new church plants, the formal membership process now facilitated the recognition and support of new church plants in areas where older local churches exist.[54]

In 2012 a new formal network for pastors were started by Pingströrelsen, Pingst Pastor. This is a network for the pastors and travelling ministers of the movement, but it also introduced a novel inclusivity. Pastors from other denomination or from independent local churches may apply for membership here if they have some kind of a professed interest in joining the movement later on. This means that the pastoral network provides a bridge for pastors, and their churches, which presently do not belong to movement. It creates space for pastors, their churches and the movement to get to know one another, before any formal decisions concerning membership in the national association and the legal denomination are requested.[55] This has become a road into the movement for new international churches, for example in the case of the Arabiska församlingen i Centrumkyrkan (The Arabic Church in the Center church) in Sundbyberg, which is an international Arabic-speaking worship group within Centrumkyrkan, an independent local Pentecostal church. Sundbyberg is a municipality roughly 10 kilometres north of Stockholm city centre. The municipality has 52,000 inhabitants and about 30 per cent were born in another country.[56] Arabiska församlingen has a quite wide pastoral and legal autonomy, having registered as an association while also being represented on the board of Centrumkyrkan and having established a relationship to Pingströrelsen, independently of the Swedish mother church through Pingst Pastor.[57]

In short, Pingströrelsen has become a more diversified movement at the same time as its organizational and legal structures were strengthened and modified while the original congregationalism of the movement is still the operating ecclesiological principle. This means that the integration of new local international Pentecostal churches that has taken place in Stockholm 1980–2020 has in fact been facilitated through a rediscovery of the congregationalist ecclesiology of Pingströrelsen in the form of changes to its ecclesial structure that removed some of its tendencies toward uniformity.

Pingströrelsen's Experience of Finnish-Speaking Pentecostals and the Integration of Early Immigrant Groups

There has always been a Finnish-speaking population in Tornedalen in the very north of Sweden, close to the border to Finland.[58] The local churches belonging to Pingströrelsen here use *meänkieli* or Finnish as their language of worship.[59] The Finnish-speaking population in the southern parts of Sweden is the result of the labor migration after the Second World War. During the study period of 1980 to 2020, there have been no segregationist tendencies toward these churches in Pingströrelsen, neither were there any discussions that display an assimilationist strategy. In the magnum opus of the movement's historical writings, *Pingströrelsen, Del 1-2* (approximately 1000 pages in total), Bertil Bengtsson provides a short but survey of the movement's work among immigrant groups during the post-1945 era. In his survey, Bengtsson describes a number of diaconal initiatives to serve immigrants communities in Sweden from the late 1940s until the first years of the twenty-first century. He also relates the growth of immigrant worship groups within local Pentecostal churches and how some of them formed into autonomous local churches. Bengtsson's survey discusses the Finnish-speaking worship groups and local churches as well as the integration of Roma Pentecostals. As a result, Bengtsson clearly shows the link between Pingströrelsen's diaconal initiatives and the growth of immigrant worship groups within local churches. He concludes that Pingströrelsen in Sweden has had an integrationist approach during the post-1945 era. This approach was strengthened through diaconal initiatives and cooperation with local authorities, especially the municipalities, and sometimes encouraged by the positive media coverage of local initiatives to help refugees.[60]

This integrationist approach becomes clearly visible when we look at Finnish-speaking Pentecostals congregational life within Pingströrelsen. Already in 1938, Pentecostal refugees from Karelen, began to form small worship groups for Finnish-speaking people in Stockholm. This developed into a more structured community in 1947, which in 1951 got vital support from the head pastor of Filadelfia church in Stockholm, Lewi Pethrus. A Finnish-speaking worship group was formerly created within in the Filadelfia church, with public and regular worship services and a congregational life of their own from 1951. In 1954 an Estonian worship group within Filadelfia church followed, where Estonian-speaking refugees organized a congregational life and outreach.[61] After the resignation of Lewi Pethrus as head pastor of Filadelfia church in Stockholm in 1958, Willis Säwe (1907–1978) was called as his successor. Säwe shared Pethrus's concern for the Finnish and Estonian Pentecostals living in Sweden. Willis Säwe's support of their worship groups and their separate congregational life within Filadelfia church was crucial for the formation of similar worship groups in local Pentecostal churches in other parts of Sweden.[62]

The first autonomous Finnish-speaking local church was founded in Borås 1962, followed by Södertälje in 1972, Virsbo in 1981, Gothenburg in 1982, Upplands-Väsby in 1986, Söderfors in 1987 and Skene in 1988, and finally in Stockholm in 2018. In 1986 there were about 3,500 Finnish-speaking members in Finnish-speaking churches and worship groups in Pingströrelsen. There were around 50 worship groups, added to the above-mentioned local churches. The largest worship group at the time was Finska Filadelfia, with its own building in Stockholm and ca. 900 members.[63] In 2018, 67 years after its founding, it was decided that Finska Filadelfia should become an autonomous local church.[64]

The autonomous Finnish-speaking local churches have evolved out of worship groups within Swedish-speaking Pentecostal churches and were constituted as autonomous after some kind of consensus or joint agreement with a Swedish-speaking local mother church.[65] In 2010 a new network of Finnish-speaking worship groups and local churches in *Pingströrelsen* was established. According to their home page, there are still over 40 Finnish-speaking worship groups and local churches.[66]

The Finnish-speaking worship groups and local churches created a precedent that paved the way for worship groups and local autonomous churches among other minorities and immigrants from other countries. During the late 1960s and 1970s groups of Roma from Poland and other parts of Eastern Europe immigrated to Sweden. Gradually the number of Roma Pentecostals began to grow and during the 1980s, a revival occurred, which could be housed through the same type of ecclesial structures as the Finnish-speaking Pentecostals. One part of the Roma population had historical and linguistic connections to Finland and the Finnish language and was integrated in the Finnish-speaking worship groups and churches. In Stockholm and in Malmö, separate Roma worship groups were started.[67] David Thurfjell has emphasized that the ecclesiology of Pingströrelsen was a prerequisite for the integration of Roma.[68] The Roma population in Sweden has continued to grow during the first decades of the twenty-first century as a result of the large-scale immigration.[69] In 2016, Epic Church in Vällingby, became the first autonomous Roma local church to be admitted as a full member of Pingströrelsen.[70]

An immigration parallel to the Roma from Eastern Europe came from Latin America in the 1970s. Some of the immigrants found their way to local Pentecostal churches and were more or less treated in a similar way as the Finnish and the Roma. In the 1980s several Spanish-speaking worship groups were started in the larger Pentecostal churches in Stockholm (in Filadelfia Church and in Södermalms fria församling) and in Malmö (Elimförsamlingen). This was a result both of the immigration of Chilean Pentecostals and a revival among secular Latinos in Sweden. Many of these had their background in the Chilean exodus after the military coup in 1973.[71] For different reasons, these Spanish-speaking worship groups in Stockholm and Malmö never developed into new autonomous churches and full members of Pingströrelsen. Södermalms fria församling was more or less excommunicated from the Pentecostal movement because of a conflict related to its close cooperation with Livets Ord (Word of Life Church) in Uppsala, a new Neo-charismatic church 80 kilometres north of Stockholm.[72] Eventually two new churches were started by former members of the Spanish-speaking worship group in Södermalms fria församling, but none of them joined the Pentecostal movement.[73] In Malmö the worship group began to decline after its pastor moved to California to pastor Spanish-speaking churches in the US and to continue theological studies.[74] Both of these cases underscores the precariousness of international worship groups and international churches. The new local churches that eventually were founded by former members of Södermalms fria församling are still operating today, pointing to the congregational stability achieved by having to take full responsibility for church life.

The Spanish-speaking worship group in Filadelfia church began in the late 1980s, led by Eduardo Hurtado. Hurtado came to Sweden in 1975 as a political refugee from Chile together with his family. Being a secular political activist, he did not have any particular earlier experience of Pentecostalism before coming to Sweden. In Sweden, Hurtado came in contact with the Maranatha movement in Stockholm, a revival movement that had split from Pingströrelsen in the early 1960s. Later on, Hurtado became a member of Filadelfia church, while beginning a prayer group in his home. As the group grew, Hurtado was publicly handed the responsibility of leading its Spanish-speaking worship group. During the 1990s, the Spanish-speaking worship group cooperated with Finska Filadelfia and shared a common worship building in Stockholm city centre. In the middle of the decade, the Spanish-speaking worship group cut loose from Filadelfia church. Instead the group moved to Solna, and joined its local Pentecostal church. This local church had become autonomous and a full member of Pingströrelsen in 1946, in a process which also saw the involvement of Filadelfia church in the city centre. In 2008, the Spanish-speaking worship group moved to Sollentuna and decided to become an autonomous local church, Iglesia Para Todos, while also being accepted as a member church of Evangeliska Frikyrkan. The choice of Evangeliska Frikyrkan instead of Pingströrelsen, must be seen as a result of their long-term experience of Pingströrelsen in the Stockholm region.[75] The well-known reluctance and negative attitude to new churches in places where an older local church existed, was probably a background factor impacting this choice. In both Solna and Sollentuna, older Pentecostal churches existed and in Sollentuna there was already another Latino church admitted to the movement in 1997.[76]

To conclude, the Finnish-speaking worship groups and churches paved the way for greater ethnic and cultural diversity within Pingströrelsen. This benefited

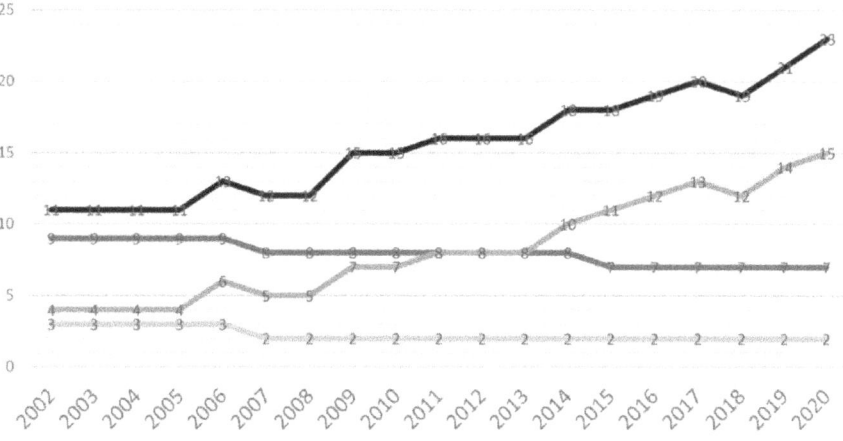

Figure 3.1. International churches in Pingströrelsen, 2002–2020.

Source: The list of churches belonging to Pingströrelsen is found the annual yearbook of the denomination, *Pingströrelsens årsbok 2002-2020* (Stockholm: Pingst fria församlingar i samverkan, 2002–2020)

both Roma and Spanish-speaking Pentecostals, and there are examples of constructive interaction between the different immigrant groups. The congregational space created for the Finnish-speaking Pentecostals was not a result of a change in ecclesiology, but rather a consequence of the prevailing ecclesiology. The strategy of "one church in one city" dominated the practical ecclesiological debate and several conflicts in the Pentecostal movement 1960s to the 1980s. This did not result in obstacles for the development of autonomous Finnish-speaking churches, and there was surprisingly not any explicit reference to this development in the ensuing debates. The reason for this is unclear and need further research. It may be that the historical connections between Sweden and Finland and the differences in languages influenced the situation. The arrival of Spanish-speaking worship groups became a more obvious challenge and the treatment of these did not lead to a satisfying long-term solution for Pingströrelsen.. Here, internal conflicts of the movement probably played a role, and probably also the continued policy of "one church in one city". The figure below shows the dominance of Finnish-speaking churches in relation to the total number of international local churches in Pingströrelsen until 2009. From 2009 and onwards other types of international local churches have continued to grow while the Finnish-speaking have slightly decreased.

Conclusions

The ecclesiology of Pingströrelsen was developed during the early decades of the twentieth century. It was a radical congregationalism emphasizing the possibilities of Christian unity and effective evangelism on the local level. This ecclesiology presumed a homogeneous population and did not foresee a situation characterized by ethnic and cultural diversity. Although this being the case, Pingströrelsen's early inroads among the old national minorities like the Sami population displayed an openness to adapt to such a situation. In a similar way, the immigration of Finnish and Estonian Pentecostals after the Second World War, showed a readiness to provide integrative space to accommodate these groups within the movement. They were allowed to create their own worship groups under the umbrella of a mother church and later the Finnish Pentecostals were allowed to start their own autonomous churches, while at the same time being a part of the movement. Obviously these earlier experience of Finnish Pentecostal immigration and the integration of older national minorities may have contributed to the integration of new international churches that have taken place in the twenty-first century in Pingströrelsen. There are examples of a constructive interaction between Finnish-speaking churches and worship groups and the accommodation of new groups of Pentecostal immigrants. But more research needs to be done to fully explore the connections between the older and newer Pentecostal immigrant groups, and what has been the result of those.

The practical ecclesiology of Pingströrelsen during the 1960s to the 1980s basically dissuaded the founding of new churches in cities were local churches belonging to the movement already existed. But the restrictive practical ecclesiology was not applied at all to the Finnish-speaking churches. When the immigration of Roma and Latin American Pentecostals increased during the 1970s and 1980, they were accommodated in basically the same way. But no autonomous Roma or Latino churches were founded or admitted to the movement before 1997, which was probably a consequence of the restrictive practical ecclesiology of "one church in one city". As has been shown, due to the fragile discussions about opening up new churches, Pingströrelsen made it difficult to enter as a new international church, and there seems to have been no dedicated outreach toward such churches. The socio-demographic changes and other international communities were not anticipated as long as the "one church in one city" policy was pursued. Different factors contributed to the abandonment of the restrictive strategy. From 2001 and onwards, Pingströrelsen developed a legal denominational structure and created structures for electing a national leadership, for transparent processes for prospective member churches, networks for pastors and acceptance of transnational and interdenominational networks of local churches. The mentioned changes have facilitated the integration of a growing number of international churches. At the same time, the present situation in Stockholm is that a majority of the local international Pentecostal churches are not part of Pingströrelsen.

The overall assessment of the integrative measures of Pingströrelsen is that these have been strengthened over time and that they presently have a potential to accommodate a larger number of the different groups and local churches of Pentecostal immigrants in the Stockholm region. A major question for further research is then why the number of international churches integrated into the movement has been limited in comparison with the overall figure of local international Pentecostal churches in the Stockholm Region.

Torbjörn Aronson is professor-at-large at Southeastern University (Lakeland), professor of church history at Scandinavian School of Theology (Uppsala) and associate professor in the same discipline at Uppsala University. He holds both a PhD in political science (University of Lund) and ThD in church history (Uppsala University). He has taught and conducted research at several universities during more than three decades. His main fields of research in political science are conservatism and nationalism, and in church history they are Lutheran ecclesiology, Pentecostalism, and the relationship between religion and migration.

Acknowledgement

This work was supported by the Swedish Research Council (no. VR 2018-01438).

Notes

1. See, for example, Malcolm J. C. Calley, *God's People: West Indian Pentecostal Sects in England*. (Oxford: Oxford University Press, 1965); Johan Gärde, *Från invandrarkyrka till mångkulturellt samfund. En kyrkosociologisk analys av katolska kyrkan i Sverige från 1970-tal till 1990-tal* (Uppsala: Teologiska institutionen, 1999), pp. 90–131; Rickard Lagervall and Leif Stenbeck, *Muslimska församlingar och föreningar i Malmö och Lund – en ögonblicksbild: En rapport från Centrum för Mellanösternstudier* (Lund: Lunds universitet, 2016), pp. 25–30; Per Hammarström, *Nationens styvbarn: Judisk samhällsintegration i några Norrlandsstäder 1870-1940* (Stockholm: Carlsson Bokförlag, 2007).
2. K. Lundström, K. Ahlstrand, J-Å. Alvarsson and G. Janzon (eds), *Svensk mission och kyrkorna som växte fram* (Skellefteå: Artos Norma, 2021), pp. 152, 232, 290, 422, 452, 584.
3. Data from www.usk.stockholm.se/arsbok/b049.htm, www.scb.se/hitta-statistik/statistik-efter-amne/befolkning/befolkningens-sammansattning/befolkningsstatistik/pong/tabell-och-diagram/kvartals--och-halvarsstatistik--kommun-lan-och-riket/kvartal-1-2020/, www.sll.se/globalassets/4.-regional-utveckling/alla-projekt-inom-regional-utveckling/demografidagen2019/lansprognosrapporten-2019.pdf
4. Torbjörn Aronson, *Ett nytt karismatiskt landskap i Sverige* (Uppsala: Areopagos, 2016); Torbjörn Aronson, "Tillväxten av pentekostala församlingar i Sverige 1974–2019", in Jan-Åke Alvarsson (ed.), *Pentekostalism i Sverige på 2020-talet* (Skellefteå: Artos Norma, 2021).
5. Allan Heaton Anderson, *An Introduction to Pentecostalism: Global Charismatic Christianity* (Cambridge: Cambridge University Press, 2014).
6. See e.g. Anne Kubai, "Singing the Lord's Song in a Strange Land: Challenges and New Frontiers for African Churches in Sweden", in Kwabena Asamoah-Gyadu, Andrea

Fröchtling and Andreas Kunz-Lübcke (eds), *Babel is Everywhere! Migration, Religion and Diaspora in Global Perspectives* (Berlin: Peter Lang, 2013), pp. 251–266; Jan-Åke Alvarsson, "Afrikanska pentekostaler i Sverige: Kyrkans roll i skapandet av en ny identitet", in Anders Aschim, Olav Hovdelien and Helje Kringlebotn Sødal (eds), *Kristne migranter i Norden* (Portal forlag, 2016), pp. 21–38.

7   Anoo Niskanen, *Religiös identitet hos första, andra och tredje generationens Sverigefinländare* (Gävle: Avdelningen för Humaniora, Examensarbete 30 hp, Religionsvetenskap, 2017), pp. 37–42, 61–85. Local Finnish Pentecostal churches existed in Borås and Södertälje in 1980: see *Pingströrelsens årsbok 1980* (Stockholm: Förlaget Filadelfia, 1980), pp. 61–62.

8   Concerning the Sami population, see Carl-Erik Sahlberg, *Frikyrka och väckelse i Jämtlands län 1850-1940* (Östersund, 1982), p. 205; *Dagen*, 21 July 2021.

9   *Midnattsropet* 5 (1974); *Dagen*, 30 June 2011; Claes Waern (ed.), *Pingströrelsen. Del 1: Händelser och utveckling under 1990-talet* (Örebro: Libris, 2007), p. 369.

10 "Hatten av för Målle 80 år", *Dagen* 23.9 (2009); "500 år av förtryck och diskriminering", *Miljömagasinet*, 23 October 2015.

11 For an introduction to Church history as a scholarly discipline, see Anders Jarlert (ed.), *Kyrkohistoria: Perspektiv från ett forskningsämne* (Stockholm: Kungliga Vitterhets Historie och Antikvitets Akademien, Konferenser 70, 2009).

12 See www.dictionary.com/browse/integration?s=t.

13 See www.dictionary.com/browse/assimilation, www.dictionary.com/browse/segregation.

14 Katarina Westerlund (ed.), *Internationell pentekostalism i Storstockholm: Tre församlingar i ett förändrat religiöst landskap* (Uppsala: CRS Working Papers, 2021).

15 Allan Heaton Anderson, *To the Ends of the Earth: Pentecostalism and the Transformation of World Christianity* (Oxford: Oxford University Press, 2013), pp. 4–10.

16 Ibid., pp. 4–10.

17 David Goodhew and Anthony-Paul Cooper (ed.), *The Desecularisation of the City: London's Churches, 1980 to the Present* (London: Routledge, 2018), pp. 50–52, 89–90.

18 *Pingströrelsens årsbok 1980*, pp. 60–65. There were five independent churches founded in the 1960s and early 1970s; see Torbjörn Aronson, *Maranata! Väckelse och samhällsförändring 1960tal till 1990tal* (Uppsala: EFS Budbäraren, 2021), pp. 186–188, 199–200, 332–334. There was one independent church plant in *Botkyrka*, which had been founded as a result of charismatic renewal; see Torbjörn Aronson, *Guds eld över Sverige: Svensk väckelsehistoria efter 1945* (Uppsala: Livets Ords Förlag, 2005), pp. 186–187.

19 *Pingströrelsens årsbok 1980*, p. 59.

20 *Pingströrelsens årsbok 2020* (Bromma: Pingst – Fria Församlingar i Samverkan, 2020), p. 46; Torbjörn Aronson, "Migration and Global Pentecostalism in the Greater Stockholm Area: A Mapping of the Growth of Local Migrant Churches in Stockholm", *Pentecostudies* 20(1) (2021), https://doi.org/10.1558/pent.41045. Fourteen international local churches are listed in *Pingströrelsens årsbok 2020*, p. 46. Three local churches are not listed in the yearbook for *Pingströrelsen 2020*, because they were admitted at the national council of denomination in 2020 and therefore listed as member churches in the yearbook of 2021: *Pingströrelsens årsbok 2021*, p. 48. The number of members of Hillsong Sweden (6052) includes members of three smaller campuses of the church in other cities.

21 *Pingströrelsens årsbok 1980*, p. 59, *Pingströrelsens årsbok 2020*, p. 44.

22 Aronson, "Migration and Global Pentecostalism in the Greater Stockholm Area".

23 *Pingströrelsens årsbok 2020*, p. 46.

24 Joel Halldorf, "En församling i varje stad: Ideal för lokal församlingsverksamhet i 1900-talets svenska pingströrelse", in Ulrik Josefsson and Magnus Wahlström (eds), *Församlingsplantering i Pingst: Rapport från ett forskningsprojekt på IPS 2015* (Alvik: Institutet för Pentekostala Studier, 2015), pp. 39–52.
25 Torbjörn Aronson, "Spirit and Church in the Ecclesiology of Lewi Pethrus", *PentecoStudies* 11(2) (2012), pp. 192–211; Tommy Davidsson, *Lewi Pethrus' Ecclesiological Thought 1911-1974: A Transdenominational Pentecostal Ecclesiology* (Leiden: Brill, 2015).
26 Veli-Matti Kärkkäinen, *An Introduction to Ecclesiology. Ecumenical. Historical and Global Perspectives* (Downers Grove, IL: IVP Academic, 2002), p. 14.
27 Lewi Pethrus, *Samlade skrifter, Band 3* (Stockholm: Förlaget Filadelfia, 1958), p. 116 is a very good example.
28 Lewi Pethrus, *Samlade skrifter, Band 6* (Stockholm: Förlaget Filadelfia, 1958), p. 92.
29 Ibid., p. 92.
30 Lewi Pethrus, *Samlade skrifter, Band 4* (Stockholm: Förlaget Filadelfia, 1958), p. 131. See also Ulrik Josefsson, *Liv och övernog: Den tidiga pingströrelsens spiritualitet*. (Skellefteå: Artos & Norma, 2005), p. 99.
31 Pethrus, *Samlade skrifter, Band 4*, pp. 148–158.
32 Ibid., pp. 132–138.
33 Ibid., pp. 139–179.
34 David Bundy, *Visions of Apostolic Mission: Scandinavian Pentecostal Mission to 1935* (Uppsala: Uppsala University, 2009).
35 Lewi Pethrus, *Samlade skrifter, Band 8* (Stockholm: Förlaget Filadelfia, 1958), pp. 143–168.
36 Ibid., pp. 88–101.
37 Pethrus, *Samlade skrifter, Band 6*, pp. 159–184.
38 Aronson, "The Spirit and the Church in the Ecclesiology of Lewi Pethrus".
39 Ulrik Josefsson and Magnus Wahlström, "Pingst i rörelse och samfund. En analys av Pingst – fria församlingar i samverkan", in Jan-Åke Alvarsson (ed.), *Pentekostalism i Sverige på 2020-talet* (Skellefteå: Artos Norma, 2021).
40 Halldorf, "En församling i varje stad", pp. 46–52.
41 *Pingströrelsens årsbok 1973* (Bromma: Förlaget Filadelfia, 1973), pp. 10–13.
42 Halldorf, "En församling i varje stad", pp. 52–53.
43 *Pingströrelsens årsbok 1985* (Stockholm: Förlaget Filadelfia, 1985), pp. 5–6.
44 Halldorf, "En församling i varje stad", pp. 44–46.
45 Carlsson, *Organizations and Decision Procedures within the Swedish Pentecostal Movement*, p. 79.
46 Halldorf, "En församling i varje stad", pp. 53–57.
47 See www.skr.org/medlemskyrkor/evangeliska-frikyrkan/
48 See www.riksdagen.se/sv/dokument-lagar/dokument/svensk-forfattningssamling/lag-19981593-om-trossamfund_sfs-1998-1593
49 Magnus Wahlström, "1990-talet – Omprövning av tidigare principer, 332–340", in Claes Waern et al. (eds), *Pingströrelsen, Del 1: Händelser och utveckling under 1990-talet* (Örebro: Libris, 2007).
50 Concerning the new laws about church–state relations and religious communities, see Cecilia Wejryd, "Från enhetssamhälle till mångreligiöst samhälle", in Martin Berntson et al. (eds), *Kyrka i Sverige: Introduktion till svensk kyrkohistoria* (Skellefteå: Artos & Norma Bokförlag, 2012), pp. 346–353. Concerning its impact on Pingströrelsen, see Tommy Davidsson, "Den svenska Pingströrelsens församlingssyn. Samfundsfri församling, riksförening, trossamfund", in Ulrik Josefsson and Magnus Wahlström, *Pingströrelsens*

ecklesiologi i förändring: Studier av Pingst som församling, rörelse och samfund (Alvik: Forskningsrapporter från Institutet för Pentekostala Studier 11, 2023), pp. 50–54.
51 Josefsson and Wahlström, "Pingst i rörelse och samfund".
52 Pingströrelsens årsbok 1998 (Stockholm: Förlaget Filadelfia, 1998), p. 54; Pingströrelsens årsbok 2002 (Stockholm: Pingst – Fira Församlingar i Samverkan), p. 47; Waern et al., Pingströrelsen, pp. 395–396.
53 Pingströrelsens årsbok 2011 (Stockholm: Pingst – Fira Församlingar i Samverkan, 2011), p. 43.
54 Världen idag, 26 August 2011; Hemmets Vän, 9 February 2017; Dagen, 4 April 2018; Josefsson and Wahlström, "Pingst i rörelse och samfund".
55 Daniel Alm (ed.), "Pingst Pastor: Självförståelse, organisation och aktiviteter", 2013, retrieved from http://docplayer.se/106433489-Pingst-pastor-sjalvforstaelse-organisation-och-aktiviteter-daniel-alm-december-faststallt-av-pingst-pastors-regionledare.html
56 Torbjörn Aronson, "Sundbybergs kommun", in Westerlund, Internationell pentekostalism i Storstockholm.
57 Émir Mahieddin, "Iglesia Nueva Creacion", in Westerlund, Internationell pentekostalism i Storstockholm.
58 See www.minoritet.se/jord-och-bergsbruk-lockade-till-invandring.
59 See www.helluntaiseurakunnat.fi/seurakunnat?areaCode=3&cpage=1&order=name &orderBy=DESC; Waern, Pingströrelsen, pp. 371, 389, 412.
60 Bertil Bengtsson, "Tyska krigsbarn och flyktingar från Mellanöstern. Svensk invandrarpolitik gav församlingarna nya uppgifter", in Claes Waern et al. (eds), Pingströrelsen, Del 2: Verksamheter och särdrag under 1900-talet (Örebro: Libris, 2007), pp. 218–229; Dagen, 15 January 2009.
61 Estniska Pingstförsamlingen i Stockholm 50 år (Stockholm: opublicerad jubileumskrift, 2004); Pingströrelsens årsbok 1980, p. 51; Bengtsson, "Tyska krigsflyktingar och flyktingar från Mellanöstern", pp. 222–223.
62 Pingströrelsens årsbok 1979 (Bromma: Förlaget Filadelfia, 1979), p. 42.
63 Pingströrelsens årsbok 1986 (Stockholm: Förlaget Filadelfia, 1986), p. 9; Pingströrelsens årsbok 1984 (Stockholm: Förlaget Filadelfia, 1984), p. 24.
64 See https://finskafiladelfia.se.
65 Pingströrelsens årsbok 1980, pp. 61–62; Waern, Pingströrelsen, Del 1. pp. 362, 370, 393, 399, 400, 404, 406; Finska Filadelfia 60 vuotta: Historiikki (Stockholm: Finska Filadelfia, 2011).
66 See www.finskapingst.se/seurakunnatjaryhmat.html
67 Bengtsson, "Tyska krigsflyktingar och flyktingar från Mellanöstern", 2007, p. 226.
68 David Thurfjell, Faith and Revivalism in a Nordic Romani Community: Pentecostalism amongst the Kaale Roma of Sweden and Finland (London: I. B. Tauris, 2013).
69 "Undervisning i och på de nationella minoritetsspråken – kartläggning av situationen 2001", Dnr 2000:3438 (Stockholm: Skolverket, 2002), pp. 37–56.
70 See www.pingst.se/content/uploads/2016/03/Medlemsarenden-Pingst-Radslag-2016. pdf; www.facebook.com/groups/544313818985748/
71 Magdalena Nordin, Religiositet bland migranter: Sverige-chilenares förhållande till religion och samfund (Lund: Lund University, 2004).
72 Owe Carlsson, Vilket himla liv! (Älmhult: Kom.at, 2009), pp. 329–336.
73 Torbjörn Aronson, "Största latinamerikanska församlingen i Stockholm planterar nya församlingar på flera platser i Sverige", Världen idag, 2 November 2016; Världen idag, 27 September 2018.
74 Carlsson, Vilket himla liv!, p. 343; https://generacionchurch.com/leadership

75 *Midnattsropet* 21–22 (1975); https://kyrkanforalla.org/quienes-somos/#historia, www.pingstkyrkansolna.nu/neve-home; Waern, *Pingströrelsen, Del 1*, p. 305; Émir Mahieddin, "Latin American Pentecostals in Sweden: Belief and Mistrust in Stockholm's Urban Space", in O. Larsson, M. Kindström Dahlin and A. Winell (eds), *Migration, Religion and Existential Well-being* (London: Routledge, 2020).

76 *Pingströrelsens årsbok 1998*, p. 54; Waern, *Pingströrelsen, Del 1*, p. 395.

Bibliography

Alvarsson, Jan-Åke. "Afrikanska pentekostaler i Sverige: Kyrkans roll i skapandet av en ny identitet." In Anders Aschim, Olav Hovdelien and Helje Kringlebotn Sødal (eds), *Kristne migranter i Norden*. Portal forlag, 2016.

Alm, Daniel (ed.). "Pingst Pastor: Självförståelse, organisation och aktiviteter." 2013. http://docplayer.se/106433489-Pingst-pastor-sjalvforstaelse-organisation-och-aktiviteter-daniel-alm-december-faststallt-av-pingst-pastors-regionledare.html.

Anderson, Allan Heaton. *To the Ends of the Earth: Pentecostalism and the Transformation of World Christianity*. Oxford: Oxford University Press, 2013.

Anderson, Allan Heaton. *An Introduction to Pentecostalism: Global Charismatic Christianity*. Cambridge: Cambridge University Press, 2014.

Aronson, Torbjörn. *Guds eld över Sverige: Svensk väckelsehistoria efter 1945*. Uppsala: Livets Ords Förlag, 2005.

Aronson, Torbjörn. "Spirit and Church in the Ecclesiology of Lewi Pethrus." *PentecoStudies* 11(2) (2012). https://doi.org/10.1558/ptcs.v11i2.192

Aronson, Torbjörn. *Ett nytt karismatiskt landskap i Sverige*. Uppsala: Areopagos, 2016.

Aronson, Torbjörn. "Största latinamerikanska församlingen i Stockholm planterar nya församlingar på flera platser i Sverige." *Världen idag* 2(11) (2016).

Aronson, Torbjörn. "Iglesia Icthus firar 12-årsjubileum." *Världen idag* 16(11) (2016).

Aronson, Torbjörn. "Ivar Svensson banade väg för spansktalande pingstkristendom i Stockholm." *Världen idag* 7(12) (2016).

Aronson, Torbjörn. "Tillväxten av pentekostala församlingar i Sverige 1974–2019." In Jan-Åke Alvarsson (ed.), *Pentekostalism i Sverige på 2020-talet*. Skellefteå: Artos Norma, 2021.

Aronson, Torbjörn. "Migration and Global Pentecostalism in the Greater Stockholm Area: A Mapping of the Growth of Local Migrant Churches in Stockholm." *Pentecostudies* 20(1) (2021). https://doi.org/10.1558/pent.41045

Aronson, Torbjörn. *Maranata! Väckelse och samhällsförändring 1960tal till 1990tal*. Uppsala: EFS Budbäraren, 2021.

Aronson, Torbjörn. "Sundbybergs kommun." In Katarina Westerlund (ed.), *Internationell pentekostalism i Storstockholm: Tre församlingar i ett förändrat religiöst landskap*. Uppsala: CRS Working Papers, 2021.

Bengtsson, Bertil. "Tyska krigsbarn och flyktingar från Mellanöstern: Svensk invandrarpolitik gav församlingarna nya uppgifter." In Claes Waern (ed.), *Pingströrelsen, Del 2: Verksamheter och särdrag under 1900-talet*. Örebro: Libris, 2007.

Bundy, David. *Visions of Apostolic Mission: Scandinavian Pentecostal Mission to 1935*. Uppsala: Uppsala University, 2009.

Calley, Malcolm J. C. *God's People: West Indian Pentecostal Sects in England*. Oxford: Oxford University Press, 1965.

Carlsson, Bertil. *Organizations and Decision Procedures within the Swedish Pentecostal Movement*. Alvik: Skrifter utgivna av Insamlingsstiftelsen för pingstforskning, 2008.

Carlsson, Owe. *Vilket himla liv! En pingstpastors bekännelser*. Älmhult: Kom.at förlaget, 2009.

Davidsson, Tommy. *Lewi Pethrus' Ecclesiological Thought 1911-1974: A Transdenominational Pentecostal Ecclesiology*. Leiden: Brill, 2015.

Davidsson, Tommy. "Den svenska Pingströrelsens församlingssyn: Samfundsfri församling, riksförening, trossamfund." In Ulrik Josefsson and Magnus Wahlström, *Pingströrelsens ecklesiologi i förändring. Studier av Pingst som församling, rörelse och samfund*, 50–54. Alvik: Forskningsrapporter från Institutet för Pentekostala Studier 11, 2023.

Estniska Pingstförsamlingen i Stockholm 50 år. Stockholm: opublicerad jubileumskrift, 2004.

Finska Filadelfia 60 vuotta: Historiikki. Stockholm: Finska Filadelfia, 2011.

Goodhew, David and Anthony-Paul Cooper (eds). *The Desecularisation of the City: London's Churches, 1980 to the Present*. London: Routledge, 2018.

Gustafsson, Berndt. *Svensk kyrkogeografi*. Lund: Gleerups, 1971.

Gärde, Johan. *Från invandrarkyrka till mångkulturellt samfund: En kyrkosociologisk analys av katolska kyrkan i Sverige från 1970-tal till 1990-tal*. Uppsala: Teologiska institutionen, 1999.

Halldorf, Joel. "En församling i varje stad. Ideal för lokal församlingsverksamhet i 1900-talets svenska pingströrelse." In Ulrik Josefsson and Magnus Wahlström (eds), *Församlingsplantering i Pingst: Rapport från ett forskningsprojekt på IPS 2015*. Alvik: Institutet för Pentekostala Studier, 2015.

Hammarström, Per. *Nationens styvbarn: Judisk samhällsintegration i några Norrlandsstäder 1870–1940*. Stockholm: Carlsson Bokförlag, 2007.

Hempton, David. *Methodism: Empire of the Spirit*. New Haven, CT: Yale University Press, 2005.

Jarlert, Anders (ed.). *Kyrkohistoria: Perspektiv från ett forskningsämne*. Stockholm: Kungliga Vitterhets Historie och Antikvitets Akademien, Konferenser 70, 2009.

Josefsson, Ulrik. *Liv och övernog: Den tidiga pingströrelsens spiritualitet*. Skellefteå: Artos & Norma, 2005.

Josefsson, Ulrik, and Magnus Wahlström. "Pingst i rörelse och samfund: En analys av Pingst – fria församlingar i samverkan." In Jan-Åke Alvarsson (ed.), *Pentekostalism i Sverige på 2020-talet*. Skellefteå: Artos Norma, 2021.

Kubai, Anne. "Singing the Lord's Song in a Strange Land: Challenges and New Frontiers for African Churches in Sweden." In Kwabena Asamoah-Gyadu, Andrea Fröchtling and Andreas Kunz-Lübcke (eds), *Babel Is Everywhere! Migration, Religion and Diaspora in Global Perspectives*. Berlin: Peter Lang, 2013.

Kärkkäinen, Veli-Matti. *An Introduction to Ecclesiology: Ecumenical. Historical and Global Perspectives*. Downers Grove, IL: IVP Academic, 2002.

Lagervall, Rickard, and Leif Stenbeck. *Muslimska församlingar och föreningar i Malmö och Lund – en ögonblicksbild: En rapport från Centrum för Mellanösternstudier*. Lund: Lunds universitet, 2016.

Lundström, Klas, Kajsa Ahlstrand, Jan-Åke Alvarsson and Göran Janzon (eds). *Svensk mission och kyrkorna som växte fram*. Skellefteå: Artos Norma, 2021.

Mahieddin, Émir. "Iglesia Nueva Creacion." In Katarina Westerlund (ed.), *Internationell pentekostalism i Storstockholm: Tre församlingar i ett förändrat religiöst landskap*. Uppsala: CRS Working Papers, 2021.

Mahieddin, Émir. "Latin American Pentecostals in Sweden: Belief and Mistrust in Stockholm's Urban Space." In O. Larsson, M. Kindström Dahlin and A. Winell (eds), *Migration, Religion and Existential Well-being*, 168–183. London: Routledge, 2020.

Niskanen, Anoo. *Religiös identitet hos första, andra och tredje generationens Sverigefinländare.* Gävle: Avdelningen för Humaniora, Examensarbete 30 hp, Religionsvetenskap, 2017.

Nordin, Magdalena. *Religiositet bland migranter: Sverige-chilenares förhållande till religion och samfund.* Lund: Lund University, 2004.

Pethrus, Lewi. *Samlade skrifter, Band 3-8.* Stockholm: Förlaget Filadelfia, 1958.

Pingströrelsens årsbok 1979-1986. Stockholm: Förlaget Filadelfia, 1980.

Pingströrelsens årsbok 1998. Stockholm: Förlaget Filadelfia, 1998.

Pingströrelsens årsbok 2002-2020. Stockholm: Pingst – Fria Församlingar i Samverkan, 2002–2020.

Sahlberg, Carl-Eric. *Frikyrka och väckelse i Jämtlands län 1850-1940.* Östersund, 1982.

Struble, Rhode. *Den samfundsfria församlingen och de karismatiska gåvorna och tjänsterna: Den svenska pingströrelsens församlingssyn 1907-1947,* 2nd edition. Alvik: Skrifter utgivna av v Insamlingsstiftelsen för pingstforskning, 2009.

Suhonen, Unto-Einar. *Finland i Borås: Ett stycke Borås nutidshistoria under fyra decennier 1944-1984.* Borås: Invandrarförlag, 1985.

Thurfjell, David. *Faith and Revivalism in a Nordic Romani Community: Pentecostalism amongst the Kaale Roma of Sweden and Finland.* London: I. B. Tauris, 2013.

Waern, Claes (ed.). *Pingströrelsen. Del 1: Händelser och utveckling under 1990-talet.* Örebro: Libris, 2007.

Wahlström, Magnus. "1990-talet – Omprövning av tidigare principer, 332–340." In Claes Waern (ed.), *Pingströrelsen, Del 1: Händelser och utveckling under 1990-talet.* Örebro: Libris, 2007.

Wejryd, Cecilia. "Från enhetssamhälle till mångreligiöst samhälle." In Martin Berntson et al. (eds), *Kyrka i Sverige: Introduktion till svensk kyrkohistoria,* 346–353. Skellefteå: Artos & Norma Bokförlag, 2012.

Westerlund, Katarina (ed.). *Internationell pentekostalism i Storstockholm: Tre församlingar i ett förändrat religiöst landskap.* Uppsala: CRS Working Papers, 2021.

Chapter 4

"Living Theology": Everyday Life, Challenges and Resources among International Pentecostals in Stockholm

Katarina Westerlund

Introduction

It's difficult being an international.

(Man, age 42, Kenya)[1]

You know, when you mention Jesus, people look at you like you're crazy.

(Woman, age 36, Tanzania)

These quotes are from interviews with a man and a woman belonging to an international Pentecostal church in Stockholm, Sweden. Both of them have migrated to Sweden from the African continent and find the situation in Sweden challenging. Being an international and a Pentecostal could be seen as a double challenge, that gives rise to feelings of otherness or alienation in encountering Swedish society. The picture is thus not that straightforward, as will be shown. Both an international identity and a Pentecostal life could be resources in everyday encounters with a new "homeland". The Swedish context is crucial in shaping and understanding these experiences.

In Sweden, more than half of the population belongs to the former state church, the Lutheran Church of Sweden.[2] This heritage shapes Christian religious normality in Sweden, where religion is supposed to be private, primarily defined by a set of cognitive beliefs, and preferably to be found inside religious organizations, and at home.[3] Other spheres are to be ruled by secular logic.

However, the commitment and formal affiliation to institutionalized and organized religion, especially to Christian churches, are in decline in Sweden.[4] Studies of the population in Sweden show a gradual decline in the number of people that report a belief in God or regularly engage in some sort of religious activity. This pattern changes when looking at migrants. Behind a general decline in religious beliefs and practices, there is a growing group where religious activity is well and thriving.[5] This points towards a seemingly contradictory trend: on the one hand, there is rising secularization in the population; and on the other hand, increasing religious and ethnic plurality. Furthermore, these trends are expressed differently, and sometimes in contradicting ways, at the macro, meso and micro levels of society.[6]

In this chapter, I will explore challenges and resources among international Pentecostals living in the capital of Sweden. The analysis will highlight the meaning of religious belonging and spiritual practices in contemporary Sweden. The chapter thus contributes to the larger picture of the role of religion in migrants' lives and to the results of the research project on "Pentecostal Migration in Secular Sweden: Influences and Challenges".[7] It will explore in particular the personal experiences of living as a Pentecostal Christian in the secular and institutionalized Swedish society and culture will be explored. The chapter also makes a theoretical contribution by using a strong practice perspective that is explored theologically.

Practical Theology, Theoretical and Methodical Considerations

The scholarly perspective in the text is practical theology, reflecting the ongoing empirical turn in the theological field in general and in practical theology especially.[8] This empirical turn, also described as a turn to practice, is visible not only in practical theology.[9] Ways of elaborating and labelling this turn are lived theology, ordinary theology, and empirical theology.[10] Within religious studies and the sociology of religion, we see a similar trend in the rise of an interest in lived religion.[11]

A basic argument for adopting an empirical and lived approach to religion is the common neglect of ordinary people's religious life. Starting from the assumption that religion is inseparable from life in general, this lived approach favours everyday life over formal religion as organizations, elites, religious texts, or doctrine.[12] However, this does not mean a one-sided focus on what happens inside designated religious spaces but also takes seriously religious organizations and the wider cultural context.[13] All practices, including religious practices, are always situated in both macro and micro contexts, which shape and are shaped by the practices.[14]

In the initial analysis, I will draw on the later work of sociologist of religion Nancy Ammerman on lived religion.[15] Her understanding of lived religion builds on empirical findings grounded in theories of social practice. This means first that religion is distinguished by its social actions. This foregrounds what people are doing in their everyday lives. Secondly, the use of practice theory provides analytical tools for understanding actions both "inside" and "outside" religious institutions, by identifying different dimensions of social experiences. Consequently, and thirdly, Ammerman's approach to lived religion is useful for situating everyday practices in a cultural and legal context. A practice-based study of religion thus links what people are doing with the larger structural possibilities and limits in society. Thus, from a practice approach the shared patterns of action that engage persons are in focus.

Scholars within the field of lived religion have suggested different and overlapping dimensions of practice such as materiality, embodiment, spatiality, rituals, emotions, and narratives.[16] The perspective of lived religion has proved useful in studying charismatic Christianity in an urban setting, exploring embodiment, narratives, ritualization, performance, and materiality.[17] Furthermore, scholars have highlighted the practice dimension of Pentecostalism by studying its spirituality.[18]

However, the strength of a lived religion perspective using practice theory is faced with the problem of how or if to distinguish between religious or non-religious practices. From an emic perspective, such a difference is presumably not productive. But from an etic or theoretical perspective, it is hard to avoid the question of what should or could be labelled a *religious* practice. Ammerman suggests the use of a spiritual dimension that invokes a direct or indirect connection to something that is "other than" everyday life, as a way to distinguish religious practice.[19] This means that religious practices are patterns of social practices recognized by the participants as including spiritual experiences, or what could be called "more-than ordinary realities". The perception of a spiritual dimension is thus foundational for the study of lived religious practices.[20] I hypothesize that in a study of Pentecostal Christianity this dimension will permeate every aspect of life.[21] Thus, the entire lives and practices of the Pentecostal Christians studied will be of interest. The lens structuring the material will be the question of what stands out as a challenge or a resource for the international Pentecostal Christians in the urban setting of Stockholm.

In the scope of the research project "Pentecostal Migration in Secular Sweden", ethnographic fieldwork was conducted in one African, one Arabic, and one Latin American Pentecostal church in the Stockholm region.[22] The interviews and participant observations considered in this chapter are limited to the City Church International (CCI) and the Arabic Church, Stockholm. CCI could be labelled African with a majority of members originating from countries like Ghana, Kenya, Ethiopia, Tanzania, Sierra Leone, but not excluding other parts of the world, like India and Korea. In this church the main language used in the services, in personal interactions, and on the church's homepage was English. In the Arabic church, members mainly originated from Egypt, Syria, Lebanon, and Iraq, and used Arabic and Swedish in the services and personal gatherings.[23]

The label international Pentecostal Christians refers to persons born outside Sweden that use a primary language other than Swedish. Furthermore, they belong to churches, as those mentioned above, that are connected to some historic branch of Pentecostal Christianity. Furthermore, international marks a connection to an international church, church assembly, or an international network.

The interviews with church members, consisting of stories about their practices and experiences, are used as the main material but are complemented by participant observations from worship services, Sunday school, and more informal gatherings such as church coffee.[24] Interviews were also conducted with the pastors in the churches, exploring the rationale, activities in the church, and experiences of the pastors. Furthermore, written texts describing the churches and their activities and mission, both internal and external, complement the source material.

The analysis of challenges and resources in the lives of these African and Arabian Pentecostals is formed in an abductive process, in dialogue with theoretical tools to reach an enhanced understanding or explanation.[25]

Nancy Ammerman posits seven dimensions shaped by the intersection of practice theories and lived religion research: embodiment, materiality, emotion, aesthetics, moral judgment, and narrative structuring, together with a spiritual dimension that distinguishes religious practices from other practices. Not all seven dimensions are used in this analysis. Foundational for lived religion, as well as in this analysis, is spirituality. Religious practices are thus constituted by the spiritual dimension, including experiences of extraordinary realities.

Spirituality is an expansive and elusive concept, and its meaning and content have shifted throughout history and are culturally sensitive. It could comprise rituals in organized settings, traditionally studied by practical theologians as liturgy, or individual experiences of union, inner peace, awe, connectedness with people, nature, or a greater reality.[26] An extraordinary reality could be experienced and referred to in numerous ways and related to several different practices.[27]

An important dimension of lived religion, used in the analysis, is embodiment. Bodies are constitutive of the way we experience the world.[28] Agency involves bodily senses, one sees, tastes, smells, touches, moves, and hears. This does not mean to ignore spirit or mind, but to emphasize that experiences cannot be separated from the body.[29] In addition, the dimensions that have been productive while searching for challenges and resources for the international Pentecostals in the analysis are materiality, emotions, moral judgment, and narrative structuring.

The material dimension directs attention to the places where a practice take place and to the concrete objects it involves. Studying emotions in religious practice means not only acknowledging and naming different emotions but also recognizing that they are part of social patterns. Situations that evoke feelings come from past experiences, our relationships, and our surroundings.

Morality, in turn, directs our attention to norms and to expectations about how to behave, and to understand what kind of person and society is good. Actions could be constrained, reinforced, or consolidated by morality. Furthermore, the moral dimension of (religious) practices could enforce or preclude boundaries between people.

Lastly, the narratives in religious practice include the way people communicate with each other. There are religious practices of storytelling but stories could also be acted out. By the way one acts there is a story of "who I am", located in a collective story about "who we are". In this way, our identities and personal stories are present in our actions together with a claim and trust in identification and membership in a community.[30]

The narrative dimension of lived religion could also express theology in a more narrow meaning, as doctrine or perceptions of God, human beings, and the world.[31] The title of this chapter – "Living Theology" – makes this point. I will thus also draw on theoretical and methodological resources from Systematic Theology together with Theological Action Research (TAR). Material from a Christian context could be potentially theological, understood as faith seeking understanding. This means that practices and people in these settings are "bearers" of theology.[32] TAR has developed a scheme where theology is understood in four voices. Two of these voices in TAR named, "espoused" and "operant" theology, are useful in highlighting theological perceptions and thus theological resources in the material. Espoused theology is theology embedded in a group's articulation of its beliefs, and operant theology is embedded in the actual practice. Both of these voices, are what could be called theology from below, or lived theology.[33] The lived religion, practices, in the material will thus be phrased in a systematic theological language, which will qualify and elaborate specific theological resources.

The results of the thematic analysis of lived religion and "living theology" in the material gave rise to the following three sections. In a fourth and final analytic section, I will interpret or elucidate some theological perspectives, thereby framing the resources theologically, as "living theology". The chapter thereby contributes to the study of Pentecostalism by thoroughly applying lived religion, and showing the meaning and significance of practices, as part of a larger cultural context.[34] Thus, "living religious practices will be shaped by the readiness of migrants to negotiate with outsiders and cope with limitations in their context".[35] Practices, as lived religion, furthermore become a way to explore theology. Thus, in this perspective, theology is primarily practice.

Living as International Pentecostal Christian – the Challenge of Swedish Secular Homogeneous Culture

The woman in the introductory quote captures an important and painful experience among these Pentecostals. Being a Pentecostal, a person of faith, is met with suspicion and even condemnation. "You know, when you mention Jesus, people look at you like you're crazy" (woman, age 36, Tanzania). The challenge of living as a Pentecostal Christian in Sweden can be framed in these five themes: *intolerance*, *discrimination*, *closed society*, *holding back* and *questioning faith*.

This first theme of the challenge of being a Pentecostal Christian means dealing with *intolerance* of one's embodied faith. There are examples in the material of prejudice due to the faith Pentecostal migrants express. In a Christian majority culture, this could be hard to understand. But this has more to do with a specific intolerance, as one woman explains, recounting what others have said about her: "I've met Christians, but you're like the serious Christian, they say. ... like weird, like you are weird, you know" (woman, age 40, Kenya).

Embodying a Pentecostal Christianity could thus be met with strong moral judgment that evokes a negative emotional response. Lived religion in this shape and tone are not entirely accepted in Swedish society. As one woman explains: "You want to begin a conversation, and the person blocks you immediately. Or the look they give you" (woman, age 34, Tanzania). Intolerance towards this kind of religious expression outside church or in public has also been noted historically in Sweden.[36]

There are also stories in the material of *discrimination*. A person with a "different body" that looks African or Arab is recognized as the "other" or different then the Swedish norm. There are examples of "blatant" hot prejudice, where informants are called names or taken for being a prostitute. This kind of discrimination is tied to embodiment, based on biological differences, and tells a story of bodies that do not fit, that look different. Confronted with the majority culture, the embodied difference conveys overt discrimination and examples of xenophobia; fear, aversion or negative stereotyping.

But there are also "subtle" cool and distant prejudice in the material. Internationals living in Sweden find it difficult to make new friends outside the church and get in contact with other people. Sweden is experienced as *a closed society*. On man explains: "It is difficult to get to know people, to get close. Also, if you invite them to your home, they are hard to get to know" (man, age 42, Ghana). This kind of experience could leave one with a feeling of otherness or alienation. There are places where they are not allowed to go which carry negative emotions such as loneliness and even shame. This kind of prejudice conveys a perceived threat to the majority's traditional values, which reinforces the cultural difference between the minority and the majority.[37]

The intolerance against Pentecostal Christianity and experiences of discrimination also means that the informants are *holding back* and are not able to express their faith. The informants' stories show how difficult or impossible it is to express or talk about faith in their daily lives outside the church. This holding back is experienced in several public areas. In school or higher education, at work, or meeting people in the street, they are not able express their faith and thereby experience limitations to their identities as Christians. One man who has lived in several different countries gives an example: "In China, it's much easier for me to go to the street, the train, the bus, and talk to people about my faith" (man, age 42, Ghana). In Sweden, by contrast, he often encounters silence or being shunned when he talks about his faith. Another informant recalls a situation at her work as a nurse. During a regular paediatric check-up, the child's mother was in deep distress because of problems in her family:

> And then, I do not know what grasped me, I have never done this before. Maybe it was because I knew that I would soon leave this workplace. I asked her, do you believe in God? And she nodded, crying. ... And I then asked her, would you like me to pray for your situation? And she said yes, and we began to pray.
> (Woman, age 36, Tanzania)

The language of exceptionality is interesting here. The informant notes that she has never done anything like this before and that it was a profound healing moment for the woman in distress. Yet at the same time, she also notes that she had broken a taboo.

There is a conception, among the informants, that people in Sweden do not practise nor talk about their religion. As a result, Pentecostal migrants refrain from expressing faith in public spaces. "Well, I do know that there is some sort of stigma against believers and being Christian" (woman, age 36, Kenya). Not being able to practise their Christianity in public is accompanied by feelings of grief, loss, and resentment. The negative moral judgments and emotions experienced by the informants result in refraining from expressions of faith in public spaces.

These regular encounters with rejection and judgment can eventually lead these International Pentecostal Christians to *question their faith*. Encountering such a different mindset every day can lead to confusion and doubt, affecting the previous self-evidence of faith. When one is not able to live one's faith, to speak and perform according to one's inner core, it influences the person as a whole. The previous narrative identity is silenced. As one woman phrases it: "And you become more like a thinker Christian" (woman, age 36, Kenya). She explains that she has started to doubt and that she does not know how to behave and talk in situations outside the church. Such difficulties in publicly living one's faith can thus bring about negative emotions such as loneliness, confusion and sadness.

Being both Pentecostal and international thus reinforce the challenges they encounter in Swedish secular homogeneous culture. Thus, ethnicity and religion are independent concepts, they intersect and interact in complex ways. The religious identity of migrants thus may have a racial meaning extended to a religious identity or affiliation.[38]

Church as Extended Family – a Multidimensional Resource

Given the multifaceted and complex challenges international Pentecostals in Stockholm face, religion is often framed as a recourse in our interviews with them. Generally speaking, the Pentecostal church functions as an embodied extended family, comprising emotional and material dimensions. Thus, church is much more than Sunday service. The main themes emerging in our interviews in this regard are *spiritual and emotional belonging, practical support and knowledge*, as well as *education*.[39]

Both the African and the Arabic churches offer several different groups, activities, and meetings. Beyond worship services, prayer groups, Sunday school, church coffee, and Bible studies, there are women's ministries, youth groups, healing groups, soup kitchens or coffee houses for the homeless, choir and music groups, study groups, business education, as well as online broadcasts and recordings.[40] In the African church, there is a system of home groups or cell groups, consisting of 3–5 persons who meet every week in someone's home. These many different groups and activities provide a varied and important context that serves as the organizational and material basis for this extended family. Some of the activities are spiritual at their core, like Bible studies or prayer groups, also including religious or theological narratives.

The first profound and important aspect of this extended family is *spiritual and emotional belonging*.[41] The church's importance in this respect is highlighted throughout the material. In their churches international Pentecostals find a new family, consisting of brothers and sisters in faith. Here they feel accepted, supported, and safe. One woman describes it like this:

> We are one group with Jesus – like siblings. When I come here, I see my sisters and brothers. I am so happy that I found this church – we are all connected in the name of Jesus. We have different nationalities, Syriac, Iranian, Swedish, and Egyptian, and have become one body – we are like organs, organs with different functions.
> (Woman, age 54, Syria)

In this narrative, the church becomes a kind of family that in its different activities unites people of different gender, ages, and from various parts of the world. This narrative dimension, the story of family, creates both an individual and collective identity and belonging as individuals locate themselves in relation to a larger whole. Their church family meets for explicitly religious activities, such as worship and prayer, but also for social and educational purposes.

Moreover, given that Swedish is a foreign language for many of these international Pentecostals, the organization of their churches around a shared language and regional identity contributes to the creation of this extended family. Being able to meet, worship, and share experiences in a familiar language reinforces spiritual and emotional belonging, be it in English or Arabic.

A second theme emerging from this sense of church as an extended family is *practical support and knowledge*. Encountering Swedish laws, administrative authorities, rules, and norms could be tough for migrants coming from an African or Arab country. In church, they support one another in dealing with Swedish authorities and institutions. This includes learning how to apply for jobs, help with finding accommodation, contacting the immigration authorities, or finding one's way through the health care system. Understanding Swedish institutions, customs and norms is especially important for those with children, and here the church becomes an important venue of support and knowledge exchange as one of our interlocutors noted: "Because all of us go through the same thing, things with our kids, all of us worry when they go to school and come back home with funny things" (woman, age 41, Tanzania).

In home groups and at different meetings in the church, international Pentecostals discuss practical matters related to social institutions but also how to understand and deal with questions of gender equality, children's autonomy, and discrimination. Gender roles, in particular, form an area of debate as different cultural ideas encounter the Swedish ideal of gender equality. One Arab woman clearly felt the need to stand up for the gender values she inherited: "It's our role to take care of the home, cook, and take care of the children. I don't think that I am different or less valued than a man in the eyes of God" (woman, age 48, Syria). But a younger woman, with parents from Syria, explains that this is a generational matter. "I am raised in Sweden, so, for me, it's normal that both the man and the woman work, and chair the responsibility for homework" (woman, age 23, Egypt). Other female informants even noted how Swedish gender equality had given them freedom because they were able to divorce their husbands and live an independent life: "It's an amazing country, Sweden, how to live after the divorce" (woman, age 60, Singapore).

The churches also provide shelter, clothes, and food for newly arrived migrants, and provide food and a weekly place to meet for homeless people in Stockholm. In this way, the churches embody practical and material support with delivering the knowledge needed to navigate Swedish society.

The third way the church function as an extended family is by organizing *education*. Both the African and Arabic churches provide different learning opportunities and educational support. They offer Swedish language courses and thereby also support the national program for learning Swedish. There are also business courses, for example in how to start one's own company. More expectedly, they also arrange Bible studies and other opportunities for learning in the Christian faith, at times in collaboration with international networks and Bible schools. This enables some members to go abroad for Bible schools or longer ministerial training.[42]

Altogether then, the churches provide a *spiritual and emotional belonging*, which is expressed by the wide-spread notion of a "family of believers". The spiritual dimension is foundational for this narrative of a "family abroad", but arguably the emotional and material support these churches deliver is just as crucial. I will return to the spiritual dimension of the extended family in the section below on living theology, but from a lived religion perspective, it is important to foreground the practical and material dimension of mutual support, knowledge exchange, and educational opportunities that make these churches a place of belonging and safety for international Pentecostals.

Purpose and Mission – as Resources for Meaning and Identity

The Pentecostal faith and the church could also be viewed as a resource that gives one's life a purpose and a mission. Two themes can be distinguished here by elaborating on purpose and mission: *meaning* and *identity*.[43]

The first theme concerns the *meaning* provided by God's calling, giving purpose to the life and work of international Pentecostals both inside and outside the church. Many see themselves as called by God to come to Sweden in order to evangelize this secular nation. As noted previously, this notion is especially prevalent among African Pentecostals.[44] One of our male interlocutors states it like this:

> I have come to Sweden, as a part of a plan for my life. The Lord has a great plan for me here in Sweden. ... Sweden needs us now and that's why God is bringing us. ... So, I believe there will be a revival for sure.
>
> (Man, age 43, Ghana)

For some, this also means staying in Sweden until God reveals a new mission to go somewhere else as part of a larger global plan: "God is doing something and he's taking us somewhere. He is using all these churches who are awake to build an army" (man, age 48, Ghana). The notion of God's calling thus gives a temporary character to life in Stockholm with all its joys and challenges. The mobility of international Pentecostals is anchored in this sense of a divine plan as they come to Sweden, on circuitous routes, move back and forth between various countries, and are often ready to move on.

One other aspect of Pentecostal purpose and mission is the *identity* it provides.[45] There is a sense that all of life should be integrated in one fundamental sense of self, fortified by everyday practices that embodies praying and reading the Bible at home, following preachers on the internet and on podcasts, listening to Christian music, and participating in church services. One of our female interlocutors explained this overarching sense of identity in the following words: "You know, every other area in your life is affected. So that is how I identify myself as a child of God. It makes all the difference in the world" (woman, age 60, Singapore,). These practices have an important material dimension as they primarily take place at home and in church rather than in public places.

In this way, embodied faith practice becomes the foundation of one's identity. "It's the core of a person, it's the making of a person", one African woman tells us (woman, age 40, Kenya). The firm basis and courage this Pentecostal identity provides can help resist prejudice and other forms of discrimination or alienation in Sweden. As another of our African interlocutors states: "Nothing can be taken away from me because the real me is inside" (woman, age 36, Tanzania). This kind of identity transcends difficulties and holds out hope in times of challenge, and it provides security and orientation when encountering new and different social norm and customs. When this faith identity is ridiculed or marginalized by Swedish society, an important resource in the lives of international Pentecostals is challenged.

A narrative structuring, then, is constitutive of Pentecostal meaning and identity. The precariousness and fluidity of the migratory situation gains meaning through the biographical narrative of God's calling upon one's life, which integrates all past and future movements. Moreover, this biographical narrative is a totalizing one, subsuming all of one's life in the identity of a Christian, as fortified by daily spiritual practices at home and at church. This identity is an important resource of hope, trust in the future, safety, and courage.

Living Theology as a Resource

In the analysis above, different challenges and resources were elucidated along with several dimensions of lived religion. I have highlighted the importance of embodiment, emotions, moral judgment, materiality, and narrativity in the lives of international Pentecostals in Stockholm. In this final section, I will explore these aspects further and synthesize them in a concept of "living theology", as a kind of practised or practical theology. By naming it "living theology" I hope to reinforce the meaning of theology as a living force in the lives of the Pentecostals, and that theology is in process of being shaped and reshaped.

Pentecostalism and its spirituality have been described as experiential and culturally constructed.[46] Its oral and performative dimensions thus tend to be in focus like in lived religion. The lived religion explored in the material can thus be viewed as theology. Without a theological interpretation some of the meaning and power of the lived religion in this context are lost. Lived religion, in its oral and experiential dimensions, embodies the ongoing construction, reshaping, and re-presentation of theology.[47] The themes and aspects above will thus be rescripted and elaborated in a theological language.

"Living theology" could be viewed as an articulation of the spiritual dimension of the lives of the international Pentecostals studied. However, I want to go beyond restating the spiritual beliefs of my informants and instead offer a theological reflection upon them that shows how Pentecostal spirituality is linked to specific traditional Christian beliefs and concepts. This serves to highlight the dogmatic basis and importance of this living theology among international Pentecostals. I will focus here mainly on the resources of the extended family and of the purpose and mission claimed by international Pentecostals.

In the material collected during research, the extended family forms a strong, embodied, and narrated vision that is explicitly described as *the body of Christ*. The body of Christ is a theologically informed concept with biblical references.[48] Moreover, this concept draws on the image of the human body, where all the different parts are interconnected and all indispensable to the full life and flourishing of the body. This image or metaphor of the body of Christ not only gives the members their place and worth, but also makes them see themselves united in and as the body of Christ. This unity in Christ also inscribes a divine presence into the community. It is not merely up to individual members of the church to shape and uphold this body, from in a theological perspective, it is first and foremost the work of God. Furthermore, in the celebration of the Eucharist, the image of the body of Christ is used as a lived and embodied reality that the communicant participants both shape and take part in.

In both the Arabic and the African churches, the celebration of the Eucharist was accompanied by Jesus words of institution as cited in 1 Cor. 11.[49] As such the celebration of the Eucharist and its connection with incarnational theology thus reinforce the divine origin and meaning of the extended family as the body of Christ. This theological foundation of the extended family thus reinforces the spiritual and emotional support provided by the church and the sense of belonging it invokes, thus fostering trust in the church and motivating the members to live together as a community.

The body of Christ could also be seen as an embodiment of *God's family*, with all members equally being children of God. In this family, one is welcome and accepted as both an international and a Pentecostal, not only by other Christians but ultimately by God. As a child of God, one is given an identity that transcends human interaction and thus provides an important protection against prejudice and discrimination. As a child of God, in God's family, one is protected, valued, and safe. In such a safe place, there is room for growth as a person and in knowledge.

The body of Christ and God's family could be linked to another theological theme, namely the *Kingdom of God*. The purpose and mission that is expressed among the international Pentecostals point towards an eschatological future, a hope for a better world in this life, and in afterlife. The informants' stories and ways of organizing church are characterized by a hope for a better future for both the individual member and the church. This is what has been described as a "passion for the Kingdom".[50] God's good future for the wider society is pictured in the mission and purpose, but humanity is simultaneously in need of salvation, which provides a missionary motivation. This could also be phrased as an eschatological orientation towards mission and justice that brings empowerment, especially for the marginalized.[51]

Due to its eschatological orientation, Pentecostal Christianity is sometimes described as a Jesus-is-coming movement. Such a belief in the imminence of Christ's return can also be found in the churches studied.[52] The members are urged to contribute and making visible the Kingdom of God to all people. In this way, the mission and purpose embodied among the informants are harbouring a theological vision of the Kingdom of God. One's own life thus could be an expression of, and a contribution to, God's plan for humankind and creation. Furthermore, God is viewed as an active agent, with a plan and purpose for everyone, providing meaning and purpose in everyday experiences and encounters, as well as for the future. This could be described as radical openness to God, and the continuing activity of the Spirit in every-day life.

The metaphor the Kingdom of God, evoked in the New Testament, is thus useful in uniting the family of God and the mission found in the material. The Kingdom of God comes as God's new creation and as a manifestation of the church, but could at the same time also be viewed as something that was prepared for the church.[53]

A starting point in the analysis of lived religion in this chapter was the foundational importance of the spiritual dimension. Furthermore, I presumed that Pentecostal Christians would place all of life in this context and that, therefore, the lives of international Pentecostals are best understood from a spiritual or religious dimension. Against the backdrop of the theological themes and concepts visited in this section, this could be described in terms of a comprehensive view of life. The extended family as the body of Christ, as God's family, and as the Kingdom of God reveals lives that are spiritually permeated by God. This is also visible in a reversed and negative meaning by the challenges the informants experience when they can't express or live according to this embodied all-encompassing spirituality. Life is one, a reality in and with God. The material world is "charged" with the spiritual, with the presence of the Spirit.[54] The force and scope of this way of spiritual living are at odds with secular Swedish culture, where religion is primarily institutional or interstitial.[55]

Conclusions

The lived religion and living theology explored in this chapter are shaped by the Swedish context.[56] The exploration of lived religion shows the importance of religion as embodied in specific material practices and places, combined with expression of both positive and negative emotions, moral judgments and narrative structuring. As such international Pentecostal religion is not compatible with the secular logic of Sweden and its specific institutional and interstitial religious context. Overtly expressing one's religiosity in public spaces will stand apart from the Swedish cultural context. International Pentecostals are met with suspicion and discrimination in public spaces, giving rise to negative emotions, the occlusion of one's faith and questioning of one's identity and safety.

Lived religion as living theology in the Swedish context reveals theological resources for the churches and their members as the body of Christ, God's family and the Kingdom of God. Living theology in this form provides a spiritual identity and support in everyday life. The cultural institutionalization of religion thus supports the studied churches' religious activities, as long as they remain inside the organization or take place in the members' private homes. Living religious practices at home and in church create safe, multi-functional social spaces, where practices are sustained and also adapted.[57]

In the Swedish cultural context, international Pentecostals often feel challenged, tied up and muted, leading them to question and hide away their religious identity. One of our informants summed up this challenge as follows: "It's a narrow path. You have to come back to your faith, your origin, remind yourself of what God has done. Stick to your identity" (woman, age 40, Kenya).

It is debated whether these kinds of international churches contribute to the segregation or integration of migrants.[58] However, when moving the focus away from the churches and to society at large, it becomes clear that the Swedish secular logic restricts the lives of internationals or migrants, lives that are religious at their core.

International Pentecostalism as seen from the lens of lived religion and living theology, thus clarifies the profound meaning of these groups' practices for thriving. At the same, this practice perspective elucidates challenges for Swedish society on both the individual and organizational level, and it challenges the notion of a cultural homogeneity or normality. In this way a practice-based study provides knowledge about societies as well as of the importance of religion for understanding change.

Katarina Westerlund is professor in practical theology at the Department of Theology, Uppsala University, and project leader for the research project *Pentecostal Migration in Secular Sweden*. Her research interests include studies of worldview in contemporary society, with a focus on youth, family, and existential health, and practice, learning, and lived religion. Among recent publications we find "And the Word Was Made Flesh? - Exploring Young People's Situated Learning in Leadership and Spirituality in a Secular Context" in *Journal of Youth and Theology* (2021) and "Turning to Practice in Academic Theology and Religious Studies: Research Circles as an Example" in *Studia Theologica* (2021).

Acknowledgement

This work was supported by the Swedish Research Council (no. VR 2018-01438).

Notes

1. This man called himself "international", meaning that he had moved between several countries. The term international will be clarified and discussed throughout the chapter, and is discussed in the introductory chapter.
2. The Lutheran Church of Sweden has been governed by the state until the year 2000.
3. Erika Willander, *The Religious Landscape of Sweden: Affinity, Affiliation and Diversity in the 21st Century* (Stockholm: Swedish Agency for Support to Faith Communities, SST, 2019).
4. During the last three decades, the number of churchgoers has more than halved.
5. Willander, *The Religious Landscape of Sweden*.
6. Inger Furseth (ed.), *Religious Complexity in the Public Sphere Comparing Nordic Countries* (New York: Springer, 2018), p. 17. See also Chapter 2, this volume, which analyses the changes in numbers of churches in relation to international Pentecostalism.
7. Philip Connor, *Patterns of Immigrant Religion in the United States, Canada, and Western Europe* (New York: New York University Press, 2014), pp. 70–75.
8. Birgit Weyel, Wilhelm Gräb, Emmanuel Lartey and Cas Wepener (eds), *International Handbook of Practical Theology* (Berlin: De Gruyter, 2022).
9. Malin Löfstedt and Katarina Westerlund, "Turning to Practice in Academic Theology and Religious Studies: Research Circles as an Example", *Studia Theologica – Nordic Journal of Theology* 75(1) (2021), pp. 79–98.
10. See Charles Marsh et al. (eds), *Lived Theology: New Perspectives on Method, Style, and Pedagogy* (New York: Oxford University Press, 2017); Leslie J. Francis and Jeff Astely, *Exploring Ordinary Theology, Everyday Christian Believing and the Church* (New York: Oxford University Press, 2017); *Journal of Empirical Theology* (https://brill.com/view/journals/jet/jet-overview.xml); *Empirical Studies in Theology* (https://brill.com/view/serial/EST).
11. Meredith B. McGuire, *Lived Religion: Faith and Practice in Everyday Life* (New York: Oxford University Press, 2008); Nancy T. Ammerman, "Lived Religion as an Emerging Field: An Assessment of its Contours and Frontiers", *Nordic Journal of Religion and Society* 29(2) (2016), pp. 83–99; Nancy T. Ammerman et al., *Everyday Religion: Observing Modern Religious Lives* (New York: Oxford University Press, 2007); Nancy T. Ammerman, *Sacred Stories, Spiritual Tribes: Finding Religion in Everyday Life* (New York: Oxford University Press, 2013); Nancy T. Ammerman, "Rethinking Religion: Toward a Practice Approach", *American Journal of Sociology* 126(1) (2020).
12. Samuel Schielke and Liza Debevev (eds), *Ordinary Lives and Grand Schemes: An Anthropology of Everyday Religion* (New York: Berghahn Books, 2012).
13. Ammerman, "Rethinking Religion".
14. Nancy T. Ammerman, *Studying Lived Religion: Contexts and Practices* (New York: New York University Press, 2021), p. 63.
15. Ammerman, "Rethinking Religion".
16. See McGuire, *Lived Religion*; Ammerman, *Sacred Stories, Spiritual Tribes*; Julia Kuhlin and Yonatan N. Gez (guest eds), *PentecoStudies* 20(2) (2021).
17. Jessica Moberg, *Piety, Intimacy, and Mobility: A Case Study of Charismatic Christianity in Present-day Stockholm* (Stockholm: Södertörn Doctoral Dissertations 74, 2013).

18 James K. A. Smith, *Thinking in Tongues: Pentecostal Contributions to Christian Philosophy* (Grand Rapids, MI: William B. Eerdmans Publishing Co., 2010); Julia Kuhlin, *Lived Pentecostalism in India: Middle Class Women and Their Everyday Religion* (Uppsala: Studia Missionalia Svecana CXXV, 2022).
19 Ammerman, "Rethinking Religion".
20 Ammerman, *Studying Lived Religion*, p. 51.
21 Smith, *Thinking in Tongues*, p. xiv; Connor, *Patterns of Immigrant Religion*.
22 See Katarina Westerlund (ed.), *Internationell Pentecostalism i Storstockholm: Tre församlingar i ett förändrat religiöst landskap*, CRS rapporter no. 1 (Uppsala: Uppsala universitet, 2021), www.crs.uu.se/digitalAssets/981/c_981614-l_3-k_internationell-pentekostalism-i-storstockholm--21-12-01-.pdf.
23 Services in the Arabic church are simultaneously interpreted into Swedish. Interviews in the Arabic church were done in Swedish and English. The pastor in the Arabic church and his family all speak Swedish. Members interviewed had various fluency in Swedish. The interviews in the African church were done mainly in English, with a few conducted in Swedish.
24 Fourteen interviews from the African church and one focus group interview with women from the Arabic church are used in the analysis. Participatory observations from five services, Sunday school, and church coffee, in the African church, and four participant observations from services and church coffee in the Arabic church are included. The interviews were recorded and transcribed at full length. The participant observations were documented in a filed diary.
25 Stefan Timmermans and Iddo Tavory, "Theory Construction in Qualitative Research: From Grounded Theory to Abductive Analysis", *Sociological Theory* 30(3) (2012), pp. 167–186.
26 Philip Sheldrake, *Spirituality: A Brief History* (New York: John Wiley and Sons, 2013).
27 Ammerman, *Studying Lived Religion*, p. 7.
28 Ammerman, "Rethinking Religion".
29 Ammerman, *Studying Lived Religion*, p. 76.
30 Ibid.
31 Mark J. Cartledge, "Pentecostal Experience: An Example of Practical Theological Rescriping", *Journal of the European Pentecostal Theological Association* 28(1) (2008), pp. 21–33.
32 Helen Cameron, Deborah Bhatti, Catherine Duce, James Sweeney and Clara Watkins (eds), *Talking about God in Practice: Theological Action Research and Practical Theology* (London: SCS Press, 2010).
33 Ibid.
34 Anne Kubai, "Accommodation and Tension: African Christian Communities and their Swedish Hosts", in Helena Vilaça, Enzo Pace, Inger Furseth and Per Pettersson (eds), *The Changing Soul of Europe: Religion and Migrations in Northern and Southern Europe* (Farnham: Ashgate, 2014).
35 Kim Knott, "Living Religious Practices", in J. Saunders, E. Fiddian-Qasmiyeh and S. Snyder (eds), *Intersections of Religion and Migration: Religion and Global Migrations* (New York: Palgrave Macmillan, 2016), p. 86.
36 Jan-Åke Alvarsson (ed.), *Pentekostalism i Sverige på 2020-talet*, Studia pentecostalia upsaliensia vol. 5 (Skellefteå: Artos & Norma Bokförlag, 2021), pp. 55–56.
37 Kubai, "Accommodation and Tension", p. 156.
38 Khyati Y. Joshi, "Racialization of Religion and Global Migration", in J. Saunders, E. Fiddian-Qasmiyeh and S. Snyder (eds), *Intersections of Religion and Migration: Religion and Global Migrations* (New York: Palgrave Macmillan, 2016).

39. Knott, "Living Religious Practices", p. 85. According to Knott living religious practices enable migrants to i.e., travel, settle with God, and clearing obstacles and providing material assistance.
40. For instance, in CCI there is a Focus Business School, which is an international entrepreneur school with education in Scandinavia, Asia, and Eastern Europe (see http://focusbusinessschool.org).
41. Kubai, "Accommodation and Tension", p. 157.
42. CCI has long-standing connections with the British Pentecostal church Kensington Temple, and the ecumenical network New Wine. The Arabic church has regular contact with the Evangelical Alliance of Arabic Speakers in Europe.
43. See Knott, "Living Religious Practices", p. 85. Living religious practices contribute to the formation of persons, and of their religious and ethnic identities.
44. Jan-Åke Alvarsson, "Afrikanska pentekostaler i Sverige", in Aschim Anders, Olva Holverlien and Helje Kringleotn Sødal (eds), *Kristne migranter i Norden*, Kyrkjefag Profil no. 28 (Oslo: Portal forlag, 2016), pp. 181–182.
45. Stian S. Eriksen, "The Diversification of Norwegian Pentecostalism: Changing Cultures, Identities, and Theologies through Migration", *Journal of Pentecostal and Charismatic Christianity* 43(1) (2023).
46. Allan Heaton Anderson, *An Introduction to Pentecostalism* (Cambridge: Cambridge University Press, 2014), p. 192.
47. Cartledge, "Pentecostal Experience", pp. 21–33.
48. Frank S. Thielman, *Theology of the New Testament* (New York: Zondervan, 2005).
49. The words used in the liturgy of the Eucharist are found in the synoptic Gospels Mt. 26:26-28, Mk. 14:22-24, and Lk. 22:17-20. These words were recapitulated by Paul in his writings to the Corinthians about the order of worship. Accordingly, in both in the African and the Arabian church 1 Cor. 11:11-32 were used for celebrating the Eucharist.
50. Anderson, *An Introduction to Pentecostalism*, pp. 195–196.
51. Smith, *Thinking in Tongues*, p. 12.
52. See https://cks.se/var-tro.
53. Cyril Hovorun, *Meta-Ecclesiology: Chronicles on Church Awareness* (London: Palgrave Macmillan, 2015), pp. 4–6.
54. Smith, *Thinking in Tongues*, p. 12.
55. Institutional religion is supposed to happen in specific places, and not others, and has its organization, activities, and rules, and interstitial in this context means that religious authorities and organizations are weak, and religious practices, are individualized, fluid, and diffuse. For further explanations and decription of the Swedish society and cultiure, see the introductory chapter. Ammerman, *Studying Lived Religion*, pp. 30–40.
56. Peter Kivisto, *Migrant Faiths in North America and Western Europe* (Cambridge: Polity Press, 2014).
57. Ammerman, *Studying Lived Religion*, p. 41.
58. See Kubai, "Accommodation and Tension", pp. 170–171.

Bibliography

Ammerman, Nancy T. "Lived Religion as an Emerging Field: An Assessment of its Contours and Frontiers." *Nordic Journal of Religion and Society* 29(2) 2016, pp. 83–99. https://doi.org/10.18261/issn.1890-7008-2016-02-01

Ammerman, Nancy T. "Rethinking Religion: Toward a Practice Approach." *American Journal of Sociology* 126(1) 2020. https://doi.org/10.1086/709779

Ammerman, Nancy T. *Sacred Stories, Spiritual Tribes: Finding Religion in Everyday Life.* New York: Oxford University Press, 2013.

Ammerman, Nancy T. *Studying Lived Religion: Contexts and Practices.* New York: New York University Press, 2021.

Ammerman, Nancy T. et al. *Everyday Religion: Observing Modern Religious Live.* Oxford: Oxford University Press, 2007.

Alvarsson, Jan-Åke. "Afrikanska pentekostaler i Sverige." In Aschim Anders, Olva Holverlien and Helje Kringleotn Sødal (eds), *Kristne migranter i Norden.* Kyrkjefag Profil no. 28. Oslo: Portal forlag, 2016.

Alvarsson, Jan-Åke (ed.). *Pentekostalism i Sverige på 2020-talet.* Studia Pentecostalia Upsaliensia vol 5. Skellefteå: Artos & Norma Bokförlag, 2021.

Anderson, Allan Heaton. *An Introduction to Pentecostalism.* Cambridge: Cambridge University Press, 2014.

Cameron, Helen, Deborah Bhatti, Catherine Duce, James Sweeney and Clara Watkins (eds). *Talking about God in Practice. Theological Action Research and Practical Theology.* London: SCS Press, 2010.

Cartledge, Mark J. "Pentecostal Experience: An Example of Practical Theological Rescriping." *Journal of the European Pentecostal Theological Association* 28(1) (2008). https://doi.org/10.1179/jep.2008.28.1.003

Connor, Philip. *Patterns of Immigrant Religion in the United States, Canada, and Western Europe.* New York: New York University Press, 2014.

Eriksen, Stian S. "The Diversification of Norwegian Pentecostalism: Changing Cultures, Identities, and Theologies through Migration." *Journal of Pentecostal and Charismatic Christianity* 43(1) 2023. https://doi.org/10.1080/27691616.2023.2188897

Francis, Leslie J. and Jeff Astely. *Exploring Ordinary Theology: Everyday Christian Believing and the Church.* Farnham: Ashgate, 2013.

Furseth, Inger (ed.). *Religious Complexity in the Public Sphere Comparing Nordic Countries.* New York: Springer, 2018.

Hovorun, Cyril. *Meta-Ecclesiology. Chronicles on Church Awareness.* London: Palgrave Macmillan, 2015.

Kivisto, Peter. *Migrant Faiths in North America and Western Europe.* Cambridge: Polity Press, 2014.

Knott, Kim. "Living Religious Practices." In J. Saunders, E. Fiddian-Qasmiyeh and S. Snyder (eds), *Intersections of Religion and Migration: Religion and Global Migrations.* New York: Palgrave Macmillan, 2016.

Kubai, Anne. "Accommodation and Tension: African Christian Communities and their Swedish Hosts." In Helena Vilaça, Enzo Pace, Inger Furseth and Per Pettersson (eds), *The Changing Soul of Europe: Religion and Migrations in Northern and Southern Europe.* Farnham: Ashgate, 2014.

Kuhlin, Julia. *Lived Pentecostalism in India: Middle Class Women and Their Everyday Religion.* Uppsala: Studia Missionalia Svecana CXXV, 2022.

Kuhlin, Julia & Yonatan N. Gez (eds). "Special Issue: Pentecostalism and Lived Religion." *PentecoStudies* 20(2) 2021. https://doi.org/10.1558/pent.43392

Lundgren, Linnea. *A Risk or Resource? A Study of the Swedish State's Shifting Perception and Handling of Minority Religious Communities between 1952-2019.* Stockholm: Ersta Sköndal Bräcke University Collage, 2021.

Löfstedt, Malin, and Katarina Westerlund. "Turning to Practice in Academic Theology and Religious Studies. Research Circles as an Example". *Studia Theologica – Nordic Journal of Theology* 75(1) 2021. https://doi.org/10.1080/0039338X.2021.1917158

Marsh, Charles, Peter Slade and Sarah Azaransky (eds). *Lived Theology: New Perspectives on Method, Style, and Pedagogy*. New York: Oxford University Press, 2017.

McGuire, Meredith B. *Lived Religion: Faith and Practice in Everyday Life*. New York: Oxford University Press, 2008.

Moberg, Jessica. 2013. *Intimacy, and Mobility: A Case Study of Charismatic Christianity in Present-day Stockholm*. Stockholm: Södertörn Doctoral Dissertations 74, 2013.

Schielke, Samuel and Liza Debevev (eds). *Ordinary Lives and Grand Schemes: An Anthropology of Everyday Religion*. New York: Berghahn Books, 2012.

Sheldrake, Philip. *Spirituality: A Brief History*. New York: John Wiley and Sons, 2013.

Smith, James K. A. 2010. *Thinking in Tongues: Pentecostal Contributions to Christian Philosophy*. Grand Rapids, MI: William B. Eerdmans Publishing Co., 2010.

Thielman, Frank S., *Theology of the New Testament*. New York: Zondervan, 2005.

Timmermans, Stefan and Iddo Tavory. "Theory Construction in Qualitative Research: From Grounded Theory to Abductive Analysis." *Sociological Theory* 30(3) 2012. https://doi.org/10.1177/0735275112457914

Westerlund, Katarina (ed.). *Internationell Pentecostalism i Storstockholm: Tre församlingar i ett förändrat religiöst landskap*. CRS rapporter no. 1. Uppsala: Uppsala universitet, 2021. www.uu.se/download/18.300bef8f18f0f87bbe9ab06/1714063783038/c_981614-l_3-k_internationell-pentekostalism-i-storstockholm--21-12-01-.pdf

Weyel, Birgit, Wilhelm Gräb, Emmanuel Lartey and Cas Wepener (eds). *International Handbook of Practical Theology*. Berlin: De Gruyter, 2022.

Willander, Erika. *The Religious Landscape of Sweden: Affinity, Affiliation and Diversity in the 21st Century*. Stockholm: Swedish Agency for Support to Faith Communities (SST), 2019.

Chapter 5

Suburbia and the Subway: Pentecostalism and Migration in Stockholm

Émir Mahieddin

> God's intention is for the city to be a place of refuge, a place of communion and a place of personal liberation.[1]

Introduction

This chapter intends to give an account of the different ways in which the figures of the "immigrant" and the "refugee", as well as the question of migration at large, are conceived in the Pentecostal congregations I visited between 2018 and 2020 in Stockholm and its outskirts. I propose to reflect further on the effects of urbanity on Pentecostalism, and reciprocally on the interpretations that Pentecostals make of the city. In so doing, this chapter aims to contribute to one of the research questions raised by our collective project, which was concerned with highlighting the fluidity of the contemporary logics of religious belonging in a late modern cosmopolitan landscape such as the contemporary urban Swedish society?

Urbanity is the object of a significant imaginary[2] investment on the part of Pentecostals, as the opening quotation from John Dawson – one of the founders of the charismatic missionary movement *Youth with a Mission* – emphasizes.[3] This chapter will discuss the category of "suburbia" (*förorten*), commonly imagined as a place peopled by "immigrants", and the way it is used by some congregations as a space to deploy an ethical practice of hospitality, aiming at strengthening their Christian moral subjectivity in the encounter with otherness. This chapter will also address some of the political translations of the theological interpretations of the relationship to the "immigrants", or to religious otherness that some of the latter may represent in the urban Pentecostal setting.

This chapter is based on 20 months of fieldwork in Spanish- and Arabic-speaking Pentecostal groups in Stockholm, the majority of which were considered as "migrant", consisting of daily visits to congregations, informal conversations and formal interviews with pastors and worshippers, both men and women. This did not prevent me from meeting on a regular basis with Swedes whose families had no migrant background. The so-called "migrant churches" (*migrantförsamlingar* or *migrantkyrkor*) and the "other churches", therefore considered as "national" by contrast (may it be explicitly or implicitly) are porous environments whose actors intermingle.[4] It is because of this porosity, and given the fact that not all the members of the "migrant churches" were migrants per se (many were born in Sweden and/or had Swedish citizenship for decades), that we favored the use of the notion of "international Pentecostalism". It is in this world of contact and encounter where Pentecostal congregations are formed that a religious imaginary is shaped, in which urban territory and national and/or ethnic-racial origins are invested with spiritual and prophetic meaning. How are these Pentecostal imaginaries of the city and of migration fashioned? To what kinds of social practices are these imaginaries articulated? What are their potential political translations?

After reviewing a series of social practices that I observed in the course of my fieldwork, that relate to a Pentecostal conception of the city, I propose to focus on the broader social context in which these practices are embedded and make sense, particularly in the wake of what has come to be known as the "refugee crisis". Finally, at a time when Pentecostalism in Sweden is increasingly taking shape as a clearly urban anthropological phenomenon,[5] like religion in general in large European cities,[6] I will try to propose some research avenues on the way in which the urban setting, as a matrix of religious networks, is articulated in the shaping of Pentecostal imaginaries and beliefs.

Suburbia: Moving to Counter-places as Spiritual Warfare

17 September 2017. This day, a small charismatic Vineyard congregation of a few hundred people is realizing the "vision" shared by Anders one January evening, at a meeting earlier that year. Seized by emotion and, he recounts, his eyes flooded with tears, he had then shared his disappointment and shame that his co-religionists were focusing on unimportant issues in the warmth of their venue, while in the street, migrants and asylum seekers were sleeping in the bitter cold of the Stockholm winter. On this Sunday in September, Anders, a young pastor in his forties, took the stage to recall the "vision" that led the congregation to move from its premises in downtown Stockholm to the northern outskirts of the capital. The church is celebrating this missionary move and the inauguration of their new venue, which is a rental from the municipality. He insists on the fact that the role of the Church is to be played in the most vulnerable areas of society, "where the social bond is broken". The Church must act, according to him, as a restorative force (*en helande kraft*) for society, to work in priority for the poor and the excluded.

In the weeks and months that followed, the congregation would become involved on several fronts with the small suburban town. Some volunteered to pick up waste in the public space, others volunteered in a local youth association to work with the most disadvantaged populations, and others got engaged in an ecumenical project called *Vinternatt* (lit. "winter nights"). From November to March, on the coldest nights of the Swedish winter, the project, in cooperation with two other Pentecostal congregations in the city, offered a shelter to Romanian people begging and living in the streets, the majority of whom were

Muslims in that case. The congregation's leaders had several meetings with local political representatives to make it clear that they were able to offer their services and volunteer support in any area that was deemed necessary.

This commitment to the community on the part of this congregation coincided with the recent merger with a Spanish-speaking congregation, primarily attended by Latin Americans who had come to Sweden a few years before, which operated as an autonomous group with its own pastors: two couples, Anibal and Deisy, originally from Uruguay and who arrived in Sweden in 2014, and Nicolas and Johanna, respectively from Argentina and Chile, who had been in Stockholm since the late 1990s for the first one and early 2000s for the second. One night at a church vigil, Nicolas told me that the vision that called them to move the church facilities to the northern outskirts of Stockholm was also inspired by what their Latin American group had done in the southern suburbs of the city, where several of their congregants resided. Many of them had economic and administrative difficulties, some of them being in an irregular situation. Nicolas' and Johanna's support to newcomers to Sweden inspired many of the congregants to see this as the role that true Christians should play in the society in times of crisis. The installation of the new premises in the northern outskirts of the city would complement the presence of the Spanish-speaking group in the southern outskirts, and would thus make it possible to spiritually encircle Stockholm from both cardinal points.

Many young charismatics and Pentecostals live in the romantic ideal of the Christian as a spiritual "soldier for Jesus", fighting for social justice at the shadow of housing projects, serving in the most stigmatized areas of the city. In so doing, by moving down the ladder of socio-economic topography and away from the city centers, these Pentecostal activists, "missionaries in the concrete"[7] (*betongmissionärer*) as there are missionaries in the jungles, spiritually elevate themselves by reaching out to the peripheries. In this way, they reverse the hierarchies of the city: the spaces that are the lowest on the socio-economic scale become the highest in the spiritual order.[8]

One hypothesis that would require being backed up by a more systematic quantitative approach to be corroborated is that this move also corresponds to sociological dynamics of gentrification in the segregated geography of Stockholm, the economic middle-classes being pushed away from the inner city where it becomes more expensive to afford housing. They are thus led to live in spaces characterized by a higher density of populations with a migrant background and low income9. This physical co-presence, which by no means inherently implies sociological mixing in daily face-to-face interactions10, might result in the development of a romanticized social concern of some middle-class individuals for their lower-class neighbours, which would in turn be translated in spiritual terms in the Pentecostal milieu. Indeed, on the day they officially inaugurated the congregation in Sollentuna, Jakob, a young Swedish man in his twenties with whom I had lunch, acknowledged that moving the congregation's venues there from Stockholm's center was both spiritually significant and convenient. As it happened, many congregants, many of which were educated white people from 20 to 50, already lived in the area.

These young Swedish Christians are not the only ones who live under the seductive power of marginalized urban peripheries, which often appear as areas invested with a certain charisma, producing fascination as a place of the Other, charged with a certain exoticism.[11] As the Swedish geographer Irene Molina notes, the peripheries of the city function as "counter-places" for the construction of "Swedishness", which makes them central places in the definition of the Swedish national character, and endows them with a certain charisma. They are the negative polarity against which normality is defined.[12] Here, suburbia becomes a symbolically charged place for Pentecostals, as a space to sharpen one's Christian qualities by performing an exercise of subjectivation: helping the Other, offering hospitality beyond difference. And these suburbs, as an "Orient from the inside", are *the* place of difference in Sweden.[13]

Rinkeby, for example, is a highly stigmatized area of the country, considered as paradigmatic of the failure to integrate immigrant populations as a result of the disastrous urban architecture of the Million Homes Program implemented in the 1960s-1970s in Sweden[14]. An Arabic-speaking evangelical group, mostly Egyptian and Syrian, has been established there since the 1980s and the pastor considers it an outpost on the missionary front, operating at the heart of what had become in his words a "Muslim territory" over the years. The heart of mission is thus, in his eyes, at the heart of the margins, in one of the city's neighborhoods with the worst reputation. At the moment of my fieldwork, most of the congregation's members no longer lived in Rinkeby, tired and sometimes worried by the increasingly "Islamized" atmosphere and the "moral pressure of the Islamists". They had often left after a trajectory of social ascension parallel to the decline of the district, and preferred to meet in a chapel several kilometers away from Rinkeby, of which the church finally only kept the name, except for some occasional apparitions to evangelize and a Christian crib held by some Swedish volunteers of the church, which was about to get closed. But keeping this name had a symbolic importance for the congregation, the pastor said: it reminds us of its "presence" in a place considered abandoned by the authorities and nibbled away by the "obscurantist forces of radical Islam".

The strategies of territorial anchorage deployed by the Spanish- and Arabic-speaking churches described here derive from a well-documented logic of "spiritual mapping", which participates in a dynamic of (re)semantization of the urban territory by Pentecostals and Charismatics, well underlined by the works of the sociologist Yannick Fer,[15] the Church historian Harvey Cox[16] before him, or the ethnologist Nadège Mézié.[17] It is particularly within the framework of what has been identified as "third-wave Pentecostalism", under the aegis of theologian Peter Wagner of the Fuller Theological Seminary of Pasadena, that cities have become the object of particular attention.[18] It is a question of working for the liberation of cities by confronting the "territorial spirits" that occupy them and that need to be identified. Each city is said to have a tutelary spirit or demon that determines its personality.[19] The urban territory can thus be seen as a spiritual entity in itself, which holds the fate of its inhabitants in its hands. Beyond converting individuals, Pentecostals thus also intend to convert territories.[20]

To give just one example, on a much larger scale than that of the city of Stockholm, the Arab-Muslim world is thus found in the famous "10/40 window", considered a priority evangelization zone.[21] Certain areas can thus be identified as being places of good or evil, and the Churches can choose to establish themselves there in order to combat Evil in places where its action is identified, notably through the prevalence of certain social problems (economic exclusion, alcoholism, drug trafficking, prostitution, etc.). They thus promote a spiritual reading of the urban frame, which gives rise to very particular urban prayer practices, both at a collective and individual scale.

To mention a prominent example of these practices, in November 2020, the Stockholm Arab Pentecostal church organized a day of prayer and fasting. After gathering at their venue in Rissne, dozens of worshippers dispersed in teams to 30 different sites to pray for the city of Stockholm, joined by people from all over the country. On the Facebook account of the church pastor, one could thus read:

> A week ago, the Lord moved our hearts to stand up for our nation as an army of God ready to fight the spiritual battle through fasting. In our prayer we proclaim the precious blood of Jesus on different sites in Sweden. By His authority we pray for the failure of the Enemy's plans for this country.[22]

In addition to a team stationed in front of the Swedish Parliament in the city center, there were prayer groups in front of subway stations or suburban shopping malls (Akalla, Rinkeby, Tensta, etc.), but also a team that shared the eucharist in front of an Islamic center in Järfalla. This is a common practice in Pentecostal settings around the world. Kristin Krause shows, for example, that African Pentecostals pray weekly in front of the Berlin Museum where the Pergamon Altar, held to be the throne of the Devil, is located.[23]

Other variations of this practice of spiritual mapping can be found in many places and at different scales: Merzek Botros, a well-known Egyptian-Swedish televangelist and pastor of an Arab Pentecostal church in Stockholm, sees the city of Malmö as the "gateways to Sweden", dominated by Islam because of its high proportion of immigrants from the Middle East, and where a stronger missionary presence is needed: "These are the gates to Europe", he says. In 2019, he rushed to create an evangelization program in Arabic to reach Muslim migrants who recently had arrived from the Middle East, but also Arab Christians from the historical churches.

This practice of spiritual prayer for the territories also has individual variations, as techniques of spiritual warfare circulating at a global scale. For example, I met a young Swedish Pentecostal woman whose parents were from the Middle East who told me that she woke up every morning at dawn to pray and celebrate an individual eucharist for Stockholm and for Sweden, so that the blood of Jesus would bless the territory she was standing on. She said that she started doing this after attending an international evangelical summer camp in Egypt, where she met people from Indonesia, a country where the vast majority of the population is Muslim.[24] Every morning, at the call of the muezzin, they would stand up and pray in the name of Christ, in order to oppose to prayers invoking the prophet of

Islam, Muhammad, who is considered a usurper, the creator of a fake religion that has distorted the message of the gospel.

However, the relationship of Pentecostals to Islam should not be caricatured, especially in the case of Arabic-speaking Pentecostals, who refer to Islam much more often than other Pentecostals in Sweden, for reasons of obvious symbolic proximity, since most of the converts in these churches come from Muslim-majority countries if they are not former Muslims themselves. While Islam is considered a deception, it is common for Arabic-speaking Evangelicals and Pentecostals alike to distinguish Islam from Muslims, as explained by one of the Arab world's leading televangelists, *Akh* Rasheed (Brother Rasheed), a well-known presenter on the Arab Evangelical Christian channel *Al Hayat,* who converted from Islam himself, and to whom many of my interlocutors referred as an authority on these issues. During an extract of one of his most famous TV-shows, *Souâl Jâria* (lit. "Daring questions"), he stated:

> There is a difference between Islam and Muslims. Islam is defined by the texts and the sunna. It is also defined by its symbols, those who lived it concretely, like the prophet Muhammad and his companions: the "founders of Islam" [the preacher marks the quotation marks with a movement of the hands] ... Islam as a religion should not be confused with Muslims as individuals, who have been raised in this doctrine and belong to it by tradition ... Daesh represents Islam, not the Muslims. That is the difference. The representative of Islam is the one who respects the teachings of its texts, not the one who ignores them or does not practice them, who does not know much about them or does not give them any importance.[25]

A difference is thus established between an "essential Islam", that of the texts only practised by the fundamentalists, and a "real Islam", that of the majority of Muslims, most of whom would live in ignorance, sometimes deliberate, of the essence of the religion that they would merely practice by "tradition". There is therefore no contradiction in the eyes of these actors between "fighting Islam" and "loving Muslims" by hosting them and helping them in the refugee camps when they arrive in Sweden, an activity in which the Church of Merzek Botros has worked for years, voluntarily, by lending a hand to the municipality through translation, language courses, distribution of clothing or food aid.

Whether working in the suburbs, in refugee camps or at the borders with Muslim otherness, it is the idea of a movement towards the peripheries (peripheries of the cities, peripheries of the nation, peripheries of Christianity) that appears to be recurrent in the practices of the city that I was able to observe during my fieldwork in Stockholm, re-conducting a Christian grammar that consists of putting one's faith to the test in marginal places, or places thus constituted as margins.

The Political Translations of a Spiritual Practice

The theme of the elective affinity between mission and social margins emerges as an important axis of analysis of the Pentecostal churches' activities in the city. Mission is aimed at the margins as well as being carried out by the "marginalized", "immigrants" being seen as missionary forces sent by God to (re)christianize a highly secularized Sweden or Europe.[26] Mission can reinforce or constitute socio-cultural margins as such, turning certain spaces into missionary hotspots.[27] The missionary activities of Pentecostals described here can thus be seen as a symbolic construction of a frontier – in the sense of a pioneering front. Anthropologist Mathijs Pelkmans writes that *frontiers* evoke the idea of wildness, of a potential yet to be realized, of an "elsewhere" that needs to be pacified and regulated. They become horizons towards which to project the imagination, invested with ambivalent feelings (fear and desire, anxiety and hope) and which lead the actors through action: they are thus both margins and projects.[28] It is a question of regenerating – and thus constituting – a symbolic center for Christianity by working at the boundaries of its group and/or at the border of its territory. Margins, boundaries and borders thus have a spiritual value, both for the work on oneself of the believers, who put their faith to the test by going into contact with the national and/or religious Other, but also as places to revitalize Christianity at a collective scale.

This attraction to the margins and peripheries, which is linked to a form of evangelical xenophilia, inevitably has political implications. Many Pentecostals, whether or not their families have a migrant background, have become advocates of hospitality at the borders of the Swedish nation. In this urban environment, which has also become one of confessional pluralism, new religious projects have emerged, often ecumenical, which place hospitality towards the foreigner at the heart of their practice, often in poor and segregated neighborhoods: churches become temporary shelters for Romanian migrants who came to Sweden to collect money through begging, language cafes are organized to promote the integration of Syrian refugees, and families welcome Afghans or Iranians to accompany them in their asylum applications – I met a Pentecostal couple who hosted more than 30 Afghan refugees at once in their house. But what used to be a regular exercise of Christian hospitality has, in recent years, become a vehicle for the criticism of public policies regarding the reception of foreigners, thus fitting part of a trend towards a "politicization of hospitality" noted elsewhere in Europe.[29]

In a context where the influence of the extreme right is growing, where national hosting policies are more restrictive and while migrants are dying in the Mediterranean in the indifference of European governments, opening the doors of one's home, when governments fail to open those of the nation, is an eminently political gesture. Through their sense of hospitality, many believers have become activists. Several networks of Christian actors in support of refugees and migrants have been organized in Sweden in recent years, sometimes led by Pentecostal figures, such as Pastor Christian Mölk: Rätt till tro (lit. "The right to faith"), which defends the right to protection for refugees who have converted to Christianity, and Flyktingvänliga kristna (Christians in support of refugees).

These actors are publicly committed to the cause of migrants and refugees while displaying their religious conviction as a sign of selflessness, seeking to signify the absolute, even sacred, character of the duty of hospitality. For example,

Micael Grenholm, a young radical Pentecostal who calls himself a "charismactivist", was touring churches in Sweden with his book *Jesus Too Was a Refugee*.[30] Repeating a verse from the Gospel of Matthew (25:41–43), he reminded his hearers and readers that every Christian should be a host for the stranger: "Depart from me, accursed ones, into the eternal fire which has been prepared for the devil and his angels; for I was hungry, and you gave me nothing to eat; I was thirsty, and you gave me nothing to drink; I was a stranger, and you did not invite me in."

This positioning obviously does not meet with consensus in the spheres of the Pentecostal churches, which went through an intriguing political sequence during the Swedish electoral campaign of the summer 2018. In contrast to Grenholm, the preacher Lars Enarson published a prophecy announcing that God wanted the Swedish Democratic Party (SD) to rule the country. He was immediately challenged publicly by Joakim Lundqvist, pastor of the famous Livets Ord charismatic church in Sweden, who called on his followers from his pulpit to stay away from the temptation of the far-right. Following this episode, the charismatic preacher Runar Sögaard invited Jimmy Åkesson, leader of the SD party, to a "revival election evening": an astonishing mix of registers, at the crossroads between political meeting and religious revival, reminding that Pentecostal churches also house voters worried about immigration.[31]

Nader Helawi, who claims he was the first far-right candidate with a foreign background in Sweden, is part of the Stockholm Evangelical spheres in greater Stockholm, attending a small Arabic-speaking congregation affiliated with the Swedish Lutheran Church's internal revival movement, Evangeliska Fosterland Stiftelse.[32] Chaldean and socialist, he fled from Iraq as an adult in the early 2000s, and joined the ranks of the Sweden Democrats (Sverigedemokraterna) for the 2010 election campaign, where he was among the party's many local candidates in the municipality of Södertälje. He was also fiercely opposed to same-sex marriage and warned against the danger of an Islamization of Swedish society, linking sexual and reproductive mores (the number of children per woman and abortion) to the issue of the demographic balance that would be posed by the massive immigration of Muslims into the country.[33] Some of my interviews with Pentecostal Arabs confirmed that there are affinities with the ideas defended by the Swedish Democrats among the Arabic-speaking Pentecostals in Stockholm, including people who were activists in the Christian Democratic Party (Kristdemokraterna). That being said, the "Pentecostal vote" in Sweden, if it exists as such at all, should not be reduced to these two parties.

In the interviews I conducted during my fieldwork, I was able to meet voters from all sides, from the far-right to the far-left. Without a rigorous statistical survey, one can unfortunately only make approximations and conjectures about the political weight of the migration issue in the Pentecostal churches. On the one hand, there are many other economic and sociological factors that determine voting, and the correspondence between religious commitment and political options seems to have become looser in recent years in Sweden;[34] on the other hand, while there is no recent study of the Pentecostal vote in particular, there are surveys on the vote of those who attend church regularly in Sweden (at least once a month). Although Evangelicals and Pentecostals probably make up a significant part of this contingent, they do not represent all of it, but it can give a glimpse of the electoral distribution in this population of "practising" Christians. The survey showed that, despite an upward dynamic, the vote for the far-right party is significantly underrepresented for practising Christians (9% voted for SD, compared to 17% of all votes cast in Sweden in 2018; 14% against 20.5% in 2022). The leading party for regular church-goers remained the Social Democrats, gathering around 30 per cent of the votes of Christians who regularly attend worship. The Christian Democratic Party was losing ground, but nevertheless gathered 24 per cent of the votes among this same population (it would have been probably higher if the free churches alone were considered in the poll). The most clearly xenophobic political option thus remained a minority among Christians who regularly attend church.[35] For several years now, the Swedish political scientist Magnus Hagevi has been defending the idea that the free churches constitute an ideological bulwark against xenophobia, the protection of refugees, sometimes at the risk of illegality, being an old practice on their part in Sweden.[36] But the recent evolutions of the national political landscape, as made manifest in the 2022 electoral campaign, indicate that this might be less true nowadays. At least, it underlines that churches are following the national trend and are not so immune to being gained by xenophobic ideas. The proportion of practising Christian SD voters increased indeed, and in 2022, the party contracted a political alliance with a conservative government which included the Christian Democrats. However, this also points to the pervasiveness and fluidity of the political options of churches, which, at least electorally speaking, seem to follow more or less the general political trends in Sweden. Besides, one thing appears as certain, Evangelical and Pentecostal Christianity in Sweden, whatever the trends followed by the relative majority as elsewhere, is not monolithic but a politically heterogeneous block, pervaded by conflicts of interest and values. Pentecostals can serve diverging political projects, work against each other. Some of them, when engaged with ethno-nationalist ideologies, might even participate to creating difficulties for their own coreligionists with a foreign background.

There is no doubt anyway that the new religious pluralism of the contemporary Swedish cities and the accompanying processes of othering that goes along with the territorial marginalization of some populations with a foreign background are working in depth on the political imaginaries of urban Pentecostalism, in which the question of migration seems to have a central importance. The imaginary representations of suburbia (*förorten*) that we can come across in these milieus are particularly significant in this respect.

Alongside the suburbs, another space in the city deserves ethnographic attention: the subway, which is just as saturated with religious imaginaries as the urban peripheries.

The Subway: A Non-place and Matrix of Religious Networks

Each fieldwork has its own specificities. Because it was anchored on the outskirts of the city, the fieldwork I carried out in Stockholm was characterized by long hours spent in the capital's subway system, traveling from the northern to the southern outskirts to reach the congregations where I was conducting ethnographic observations. For a while, I took these journeys as a mere inconvenience of the urban fieldwork and as a sign of the physical distance that marked the sociological gap between the places where I worked and lived, the central places of the privileged classes, and the outskirts of the city where many "immigrants" lived and where the international Pentecostal churches were mainly located[37]. I then used to think of the subway as nothing more than the infrastructure that would make possible the existence of churches forged on networks of linguistic or national affinities on a city-wide scale – which is of course no small thing in itself.

Meeting Zakaria, aka Ziko, a Coptic man who, after spending years in Italy, immigrated to Sweden, changed my perspective on what the subway can be in a city. Ziko used the subway as a place of missionary opportunities. He regularly approached people he heard speaking Arabic or who had a cross tattooed on their wrist or on the top of their hand, indicating that they, like him, were Copts. He would not hesitate, within seconds, to invite them to follow him to church, and some would indeed follow. He also boasted to his friends that he knew all the Christian Egyptians in Stockholm. Ziko attended several Arabic-speaking Evangelical and Pentecostal churches a week, which also meant that he spent a lot of time in the subway, sometimes making trips lasting more than an hour and a half to reach a congregation.

This missionary dynamic in the subway goes far beyond the case of Ziko. To give just one example, a Uruguayan pastor, Anibal, who arrived in Stockholm in 2014, told me in an interview that he began attending his congregation after he happened to meet a Peruvian congregant in the subway. Hearing him speak Spanish, they began to talk, and the latter informed the former that his pastor was very helpful to Latin American migrants with their administrative procedures with the migration services. Anibal followed him and met pastor Nicolas, an Argentinean immigrant, with whom they shared a common vision of the Church. They became friends and, a few years later, became copastors of a Spanish-speaking group in the congregation mentioned at the beginning of this chapter, the Vineyard. In fact, I have often observed discussion groups between strangers forming around a common language on the subway, whether it was Arabic or Spanish. I also heard many stories of the kind during my interviews and casual conversations, including Pastor Merzek Botros, who told me that he met his wife to be, who had a decisive influence on his vocation as a pastor, during a subway ride when he arrived in Sweden.

Subway stations are also important places for evangelization. It is often at the exit of the station that evangelist teams from Spanish-speaking and

Figure 5.1. A worshipper at an Arab Pentecostal church in Stockholm hung informational materials on the church before getting off the subway after an evening of prayer. January 2020.

Source: Émir Mahieddin

Arabic-speaking churches are stationed. Some leave information material on the Gospel or on the Church, sometimes in several languages, on their seat – or close to it – in the train they ride to get home after prayer meetings (see Figure 1).

The meeting with Ziko, as well as the collection of these multiple stories of chance encounters in the subway, as hazardous as they were significant, led me to reconsider the role that this underground infrastructure might play in the structuring of the networks of churches in Stockholm, which did not correspond to the territorial logic of the parish that had long prevailed in the Swedish Church history.[38] On the one hand, at the level of representations, these accounts of chance encounters in the subway were salient because they underlined the "part of God" in the bifurcations that could durably mark the lives of my interlocutors, constituting moments of meaning in places commonly associated with meaninglessness, moments of bonding and connection in places known to produce a sense of isolation and anonymity.[39] This implies that, on the other hand, at the level of practices, the subway is invested as a place of possibilities and missionary opportunities. This dynamic goes beyond the case of Stockholm. In Paris, as in London or Amsterdam, one meets "missionaries on the rush" in the tube who, sometimes on their way to work, shout some words from the Gospel, calling the passengers to conversion and repentance, a few seconds before getting off at their station and disappearing into the crowd. The metro thus no longer appears as a non-place, a simple interstice or transport infrastructure, a "mobile parenthesis",[40] between supposedly "real" places, such as churches for example, merely allowing the passengers to get on and off. It is not a mere transitory structure that allows physical mobility. It is a place in itself, loaded with meaning, producing identity, relationship and memory,[41] which is also invested as a strategic place in the spiritual battle for the urban territories on the surface. If the subways intuitively appear as symbols of the solitude and anonymity that characterize contemporary urban sociality, they are in practice full places of "city-making", as possible spaces for the projection of representations and imaginaries, and even places of encounter and creation of social ties, which in the end appear more as a "porous parenthesis" permeable to the codes from other social spheres,[42] in this case the religious sphere of Pentecostalism and its prophetic interpretations.

It is in this sense that the anthropologist Michel Agier calls for a shift in the ethnographic gaze, to study not urban structures but, taking up the proposals of the Swedish anthropologist Ulf Hannerz,[43] urban forms of situational engagement,[44] insisting on the capacity of actors to reframe their experience of the moment, which reintroduces complexity into the analysis of individuals and groups in migratory situations. They are no longer seen as carrying a cultural stock that predetermines their behavior, but are considered as capable of adjusting their role according to the interaction situations. In the case that interests us here, we can see the Pentecostals' desire to transform "situations of passage" into "extraordinary situations", to use the typology proposed by Agier. While the former are mainly marked by the relationship of the individual to space alone – in the sense that they are marked by individualization and a spatio-temporal marking of the paths where the relationship of *ego* to society does not crystallize in any precise interpersonal relationship, immersed as he or she is in an excess of materialities,[45] the latter being characterized by their accidental and unforeseen character, which only take on a social meaning if they are subject to a minimum of interpretation.[46] Pentecostalism, with its insistence on the effectiveness of the Holy Spirit in intervening at the spur of the moment (*kairos*), suggesting that anything can happen at any time,[47] offers a privileged interpretative framework to enable actors to define the extraordinary situations that are so common in the urban setting, potentially turning them into a "ritual situation",[48] in which the individual-space relationship is supplemented by the symbolic mediations of a style of society-making. The journey in the subway becomes a possible performance, implying ethical and aesthetic aspects, which allows to exploit the potential of non-places to make them, by renewing the meaning of urban situations, places in their own right, matrices of socialities and renewal of urban networks. The lived city itself is then transformed.

Conclusion

David Martin described Pentecostalism as "a 'religious movement' accompanying and facilitating the movement of people".[49] Pentecostalism is indeed often described as a religion of mobility, with a great capacity for adaptation and plasticity that makes it a particularly exportable religious form,[50] based on the very value of movement, with the city appearing as the place par excellence where individual mobility can be fulfilled.[51] There are certainly many demographic, sociological and economic factors that make the city a privileged place for the development of Pentecostalism in Europe. Here, through the example of Stockholm, I have merely sought to underline, through ethnography, the elective affinities between the situations of cosmopolitan and pluralistic interactions to which urban settings and technostructures give rise and Pentecostal imaginaries of space and time. I have emphasized the tactics of Pentecostalism's implantation in non-places (subway) and counter-places (suburbs) as a strategy for conquering urban territories through their margins, referring to the antique theme of the affinity between mission and marginalized spaces. Paying attention to these intertwined imaginaries and practices of urbanity and Pentecostalism may help to shed light on the reasons for the relative growth of this type of Christianity in Sweden's major cities in recent years.

I have also looked at the possible political translations of this affinity, but have had to content myself with assumptions, given the lack of conclusive statistical data on the links between Pentecostalism and ideological options in Sweden. The only certainty lies in the deeply heterogenous character of Evangelical Christianity in political terms, Pentecostals of diverging opinions and interests might work against each other in the political arena: while brothers and sisters in the religious field, they become enemies on the political front. As Antonio Gramsci wrote when thinking through the relations between Catholicism and politics: "Every religion ... is in reality a multiplicity of distinct and often contradictory religions".[52] What is true of Catholicism is even truer of Pentecostalism. Since it is a fiercely decentralized movement which is deprived of a uniting institutional authority, it can interplay with radically different political ideologies.

Émir Mahieddin is a Franco-Algerian anthropologist, CNRS researcher and member of the Centre d'études en sciences sociales du religieux (CéSor) at the School of Advanced Studies in Social Sciences (EHESS) in Paris. He is the author of a monograph on Swedish Pentecostalism, *Faire le travail de Dieu. Une anthropologie morale du pentecôtisme en Suède* (2018, Karthala), and edited a special issue of the French journal *Multitudes*, offering a comparative gaze on the political engagements of Evangelicals in five continents (*Evangéliques: combien de division ?*, 2024). In 2022, he was awarded with the CNRS Bronze Medal.

Acknowledgement

This work was supported by the Swedish Research Council (no. VR 2018-01438).

Notes

1. John Dawson, *Conquérir nos villes pour Dieu* (Brutigny: Jeunesse en Mission, 1991), p. 25.
2. The notion of "imaginary" refers not to fantasy or the unreal but to a network of social practices, a form of incessant work of creating figures and images (including

mass-produced, industrially or digitally) that allow us to apprehend a phenomenon or a problem. See Arjun Appadurai, *Modernity at Large: Cultural Dimensions of Globalization* (Minneapolis, MN: University of Minnesota Press, 1996); and Cornelius Castoriadis, *L'institution imaginaire de la société* (Paris: Seuil, 1975).
3   For a detailed study of the movement, see Yannick Fer, *L'offensive évangélique: Voyage au cœur des réseaux militants de Jeunesse en Mission* (Geneva: Labor & Fidès, 2010).
4   Although they can be intuitively distinguished by the language they use in worship in Sweden, this linguistic criterion does not apply to other European countries where "migrants" may share the mother tongue of their host society. See Jeanne Rey, *Pentecôtisme et migration en Suisse* (Paris: Karthala, 2019).
5   Torbjörn Aronson, "Tillväxten av nya pentekostala församlingar i Sverige 1974–2020", in J.-Å. Alvarsson (ed.), *Pentekostalismen i Sverige på 2020-talet* (Skellefteå: Artos & Norma, 2021), p. 82.
6   David Goodhew and Anthony-Paul Cooper (eds), *The Desecularization of the City: London's Churches, 1980 to the Present* (London: Routledge, 2020).
7   "The concrete" (*betongen*) is a common metaphor to refer to suburbia.
8   Contrary to what is still a surprisingly widespread idea, not all Evangelicals and Pentecostals preach the gospel of prosperity, as a religious version of neoliberal conservatism. There are many currents preaching social justice, some even claiming to be anti-capitalist theologies of liberation. Mae Elise Cannon and Andrea Smith (eds), *Evangelical Theologies of Liberation and Justice* (Downers Grove, IL: InterVasity Press, 2019). See also David Simbsler, "'Trusting the Lord, Conquering the Land': Pentecostals, Landless Movement and Grassroots Politics from Dilma Roussef to Jair Bolsonaro", *Bulletin of Latin American Research* (2021), https://doi.org/10.1111/blar.13167.
9   On social and ethnic segregation in Stockholm, see Jonathan Rokem and Laura Vaughan, "Geographies of Ethnic Segregation in Stockholm: The Role of Mobility and Co-presence in Shaping the Diverse City", *Urban Studies* 56(12) (2018), pp. 2426–2446.
10 Ibid.
11 Per-Markku Ristilammi, *Rosengård och den svarta poesin: En studie av modern annorlundahet* (Stockholm: Symposion, 1994).
12 Irene Molina, "Koloniala kartografier av nation och förort", in P. De Los Reyes and L. Martinsson (eds), *Olikhetens Paradigm* (Lund: Studentlitteratur, 2005), pp. 99–121.
13 Émir Mahieddin, "Latin American Pentecostals in Sweden: Belief and Mistrust in Stockholm's Urban Space", in O. Larsson, M. Kindström Dahlin, A. Winell (eds), *Migration, Religion and Existential Well-being* (London: Routledge, 2020), pp. 168–183.
14 After a housing shortage due to urban exodus which was a major political concern for decades, the Swedish government launched a national housing policy known as *Miljonprogrammet* to build one million new homes between 1965 and 1974, mainly in the outer suburbs of large cities, which resulted in large scale modernistic inward-looking autonomous neighbourhoods. See T. Hall and S. Vidén, "The Million Homes Programme: A Review of the Great Swedish Planning Project", *Planning Perspectives* 20 (2005), pp. 301–328.
15 Yannick Fer, "Pentecôtisme et modernité urbaine: entre déterritorialisation des identités et réinvestissement symbolique de l'espace urbain", *Social Compass* 54(2) (2007), p. 204.
16 Harvey Cox, *Fire from Heaven: The Rise of Pentecostal Spirituality and the Reshaping of Religion in the Twenty-First Century* (Cambridge, MA: Da Capo Press, 1994).
17 Nadége Mézié, "Les évangéliques cartographient le monde: Le *spiritual mapping*", *Archives de sciences sociales des religions* (2008), pp. 63–85.

18 Cox, *Fire from Heaven*; Fer, *L'offensive évangélique*, pp. 62–69.
19 Fer, "Pentecôtisme et modernité urbaine", pp. 204–205.
20 Ibid., pp. 205
21 This is an area located between the 20th and 40th parallels that includes regions and countries where Christianity is not in the majority, such as North Africa, the Middle East, Central Asia, India and China.
22 Facebook post by Merzek Botros, 14 November 2020, www.facebook.com/pastor.merzek.botros/posts/10224156593839507 (accessed 31 October 2021).
23 Kristine Krause, "Orientations. Moral Geographies in Transnational Ghanaian Pentecostal Networks", in S. Coleman and R. Hackett (eds), *The Anthropology of Global Pentecostalism and Evangelicalism* (New York: New York University Press, 2015), pp. 75–92.
24 Indonesia is the largest Muslim country in the world. With 87% Muslims in the 2010 census, it is home to around 12.7% of the world's Muslims.
25 Frère Rachid, "Qui représente l'islam? French Version", www.youtube.com/watch?v=jmvVM6Mx0TA.
26 Sandra Fancello and André Mary (eds), *Chrétiens africains en Europe* (Paris: Karthala, 2010).
27 Émir Mahieddin and Katia Boissevain, "Thinking through Missionary Work", in N. Neveu, A. Turiano and K. Sanchez-Summerer (eds), *Missions & Preaching* (Leiden: Brill, 2022), pp. 382–409.
28 Mathijs Pelkmans, "Frontier Dynamics: Reflections on Evangelical and Tablighi Missions in Central Asia", *Comparative Studies in Society and History* 63(1) (2021), pp. 212–241.
29 Michel Agier, *L'étranger qui vient: Repenser l'hospitalité* (Paris: Seuil, 2018).
30 Michael Grenholm and Stefan Swärd, *Jesus var också flykting: invandring, främlingsfientlighet och kristen tro* (Stockholm: Libris, 2016).
31 Émir Mahieddin, "Le migrant et le militant religieux: Le renouveau du labyrinthe théologico-politique en Suède", *Bulletin de l'Observatoire international du religieux* 23 (2018).
32 Interview with N. Helawi conducted in January 2020 in Södertälje, Sweden. Helawi has since left the far-right party, arguing that he and his Iraqi colleagues elected on the same list were victims of racism there.
33 Émir Mahieddin and Fatiha Kaouès, "Médiateurs évangéliques entre 'Orient' et 'Occident'", *Journal des anthropologues* 166–167 (2021), pp. 87–109.
34 Magnus Hagevi, "Religionsröstning i Sverige 1988–2018", *SurveyJournalen* 5(1) (2018), pp. 2–14.
35 Sara Anderson, "Undersökning: så röstade de kyrkliga väljarna", *Världen idag*, 12 September 2018, www.varldenidag.se/nyheter/undersokning-sa-rostade-de-kyrkliga-valjarna/reprij!f1sdNf2PMaj8rqp80OOniQ.
36 Magnus Hagevi, "Xenophobic Opinion, a Populist Radical Party, and Individuals with Different Religious Contexts in Sweden", *Journal of Church and State* 60(3) (2017), pp. 449–471.
37 Torbjörn Aronson has shown that, in 2020, 40% of Stockholm's international Pentecostal congregations are in the southern suburbs, half of which have African roots and a third of which have Latin American origins. The west of Stockholm is also a concentration of international churches (26%), with the city centre lagging far behind (16%), partly because of unequal economic access to these relatively expensive areas of the Swedish capital. Cf. Torbjörn Aronson, "Internationell pentekostalism i

Stockholms kommun", in K. Westerlund (ed.), *Internationell pentekostalism i Stockholm: Tre församlingar i kontext*, CRS Rapporter no. 1 (Uppsala: Uppsala University, 2021), pp. 73-87. The northern suburbs are also more invested than the city centre by international Pentecostal churches, especially in the neighboring commune of Sollentuna. Cf. T. Aronson, "Internationell pentekostalism i Sollentuna", in Westerlund, *Internationell pentekostalism i Stockholm*, pp. 45-55.

38 It is commonly assumed that Pentecostalism is based less on territorial affiliations predetermined by birth or place of residence than on deterritorialized networks of affinities. Sébastien Fath, *Billy Graham, pape protestant?* (Paris: Albin Michel, 2002), pp. 154-155. See also Chapter 3, this volume.
39 Marc Augé, *Non-lieux: Introduction à une anthropologie de la surmodernité* (Paris: Seuil, 1992).
40 Jean-Charles Depaule and Phillipe Tastevin, "Deux ethnologues dans le métro", *Égypte/Monde arabe* 3 (2006), p. 28.
41 This is the threefold anthropological definition of a "place" according to the anthropologist Marc Augé (*Non-lieux*, p. 100). In a later work, Augé revisited his conception of places of public transportation and transit as non-places, criticizing his own past analysis, and affirming that the metro was indeed a "place". Marc Augé, *Le métro revisité* (Paris: Seuil, 2008).
42 Depaule and Tastevin, "Deux ethnologues dans le metro", pp. 28-29.
43 Ulf Hannerz, *Exploring the City: Inquiries Toward an Urban Anthropology* (New York: Columbia University Press, 1983); Ulf Hannerz, *Cultural Complexity: Studies in the Social Organization of Meaning* (New York: Columbia University Press, 1992).
44 Michel Agier, *Anthropologie de la ville* (Paris: Puf, 2015), pp. 93-94.
45 Ibid., p. 100.
46 Ibid., p. 98.
47 Simon Coleman, "'Right Now!': Historiopraxy and the Embodiment of Charismatic Temporalities", *Ethnos* 76(4) (2011), pp. 426-447.
48 Agier, *Anthropologie de la ville*, pp. 102-104.
49 David Martin, *Pentecostalism: The World Their Parish* (Oxford: Blackwell, 2002), p. 23.
50 C. Pons, "Ce qui circule, ce qui change, ce qui reste. Mobilité et plasticité dans les pentecôtismes au Cap-Vert et en Islande", *Migrations et société* 184(2) (2021), pp. 43-57.
51 Fer, "Pentecôtisme et modernité urbaine", p. 203.
52 Antonio Gramsci, *Selections from The Prison Notebooks* (London: Lawrence & Wishart, 1971), pp. 419-420.

Bibliography

Anderson, Sara. "Undersökning: så röstade de kyrkliga väljarna." *Världen idag*, 12 September 2018. www.varldenidag.se/nyheter/undersokning-sa-rostade-de-kyrkliga-valjarna/reprij!f1sdNf2PMaj8rqp80OOniQ/

Agier, Michel. *Anthropologie de la ville*. Paris: PUF, 2015.

Agier, Michel. *L'étranger qui vient: Repenser l'hospitalité*. Paris: Seuil, 2018.

Appadurai, Arjun. *Modernity at Large: Cultural Dimensions of Globalization*. Minneapolis, MN: University of Minnesota Press, 1996.

Aronson, Torbjörn. "Tillväxten av nya pentekostala församlingar i Sverige 1974-2020." In J-Å. Alvarsson (ed.), *Pentekostalismen i Sverige på 2020-talet*, 71-120. Skellefteå: Artos & Norma, 2021.

Aronson, Torbjörn. "Internationell pentekostalism i Stockholms kommun." In Katarina Westerlund (ed.), *Internationell pentekostalism i Stockholm: Tre församlingar i kontext*, 73–87. CRS Rapporter no. 1. Uppsala: Uppsala University, 2021.

Aronson, Torbjörn. "Internationell pentekostalism i Sollentuna." In K. Westerlund (ed.), *Internationell pentekostalism i Stockholm. Tre församlingar i kontext*, 45–55. CRS Rapporter no. 1. Uppsala: Uppsala University, 2021.

Augé, Marc. *Non-Lieux: Introduction à une anthropologie de la surmodernité*. Paris: Seuil, 1992.

Augé, Marc. *Le métro revisité*. Paris: Seuil, 2008.

Cannon, Mae Elise and Andrea Smith (eds). *Evangelical Theologies of Liberation and Justice*. Downers Grove, IL: InterVarsity Press, 2019.

Cornélius Castoriadis. *L'institution imaginaire de la société*. Paris: Seuil, 1975.

Coleman, Simon. "'Right Now!': Historiopraxy and the Embodiment of Charismatic Temporalities." *Ethnos* 76(4) (2011), pp. 426–447. https://doi.org/10.1080/00141844.2011.580354

Cox, Harvey. *Fire from Heaven: The Rise of Pentecostal Spirituality and the Reshaping of Religion in the Twenty-First Century*. Cambridge, MA: Da Capo Press, 1994.

Dawson, John. *Conquérir nos villes pour Dieu*. Burtigny: Jeunesse en Mission, 1991.

Depaule, Jean-Charles and Phillpe Tastevin. "Deux ethnologues dans le metro." *Egypte/Monde arabe* 3 (2006), pp. 23–34. https://doi.org/10.4000/ema.1073

Fancello, Sandra and André Mary (eds). *Chrétiens africains en Europe*. Paris: Karthala, 2010.

Fath, Sébastien. *Billy Graham, Pape protestant?* Paris: Albin Michel, 2002.

Fer, Yannick "Pentecôtisme et modernité urbaine: entre déterritorialisation des identités et réinvestissement symbolique de l'espace urbain." *Social Compass* 54(2) (2007): 201–210. https://doi.org/10.1177/0037768607077031

Fer, Yannick. *L'offensive évangélique: Voyage au cœur des réseaux militants de Jeunesse en Mission*. Genève: Labor & Fidès, 2010.

Gramsci, Antonio. *Selections from The Prison Notebooks*. London: Lawrence & Wishart, 1971.

Grenholm, Micael and Stefan Swärd. *Jesus var också flykting: invandring, främlingsfientlighet och kristen tro*. Stockholm: Libris, 2016.

Goodhew, David and Anthony-Paul Cooper (eds). *The Desecularization of the City: London's Churches, 1980 to the Present*. London: Routledge, 2020.

Hagevi, Magnus. "Xenophobic Opinion, a Populist Radical Party, and Individuals with Different Religious Contexts in Sweden." *Journal of Church and State* 60(3) (2017), pp. 449–471. https://doi.org/10.1093/jcs/csx056

Hagevi, Magnus. "Religionsröstning i Sverige 1988–2018." *SurveyJournalen* 5(1) (2018), pp. 2–14. https://doi.org/10.15626/sj.20180501

Hall, Thomas and Sonja Vidén. "The Million Homes Programme: A Review of the Great Swedish Planning Project", *Planning Perspectives* 20 (2005), pp. 301–328.

Hannerz, Ulf. *Exploring the City: Inquiries Toward an Urban Anthropology*. New York: Columbia University Press, 1983.

Hannerz, Ulf. *Cultural Complexity: Studies in the Social Organization of Meaning*. New York: Columbia University Press, 1992.

Krause, Kristine. "Orientations: Moral Geographies in Transnational Ghanaian Pentecostal Networks." In S. Coleman and R. Hackett (eds), *The Anthropology of Global Pentecostalism and Evangelicalism*, 75–92. New York: New York University Press, 2015.

Mahieddin, Émir. "Le migrant et le militant religieux: Le renouveau du labyrinthe théologico-politique en Suède." *Bulletin de l'Observatoire international du religieux* 23 (2018).

Mahieddin, Émir. "Latin American Pentecostals in Sweden: Belief and Mistrust in Stockholm's Urban Space." In O. Larsson, M. Kindström Dahlin and A. Winell (eds), *Migration, Religion and Existential Well-being*, 168–183. London: Routledge, 2020.

Mahieddin, Émir and Katia Boissevain. "Thinking through Missionary Work." In N. Neveu, K. Sanchez-Summerer and A. Turiano (eds), *Missions & Preaching*, 382–409. Leiden: Brill, 2022.

Mahieddin, Émir and Fatiha Kaouès. "Médiateurs évangéliques entre 'Orient' et 'Occident'." *Journal des anthropologues* 166–167 (2021), pp. 87–109.

Martin, David. *Pentecostalism: The World Their Parish*. Oxford: Blackwell, 2002.

Mézié, Nadége. "Les évangéliques cartographient le monde: Le *spiritual mapping*." *Archives de sciences sociales des religions* 142 (2008), pp. 63–85. https://doi.org/10.4000/assr.13973

Molina, Irene. "Koloniala kartografier av nation och förort." In P. De Los Reyes and L. Martinsson (eds), *Olikhetens Paradigm*, 99–121. Lund: Studentlitteratur, 2005.

Pelkmans, Mathijs. "Frontier Dynamics: Reflections on Evangelical and Tablighi Missions in Central Asia." *Comparative Studies in Society and History* 63(1) (2021), pp. 212–241. https://doi.org/10.1017/S0010417520000420

Pons, Christophe. "Ce qui circule, ce qui change, ce qui reste: Mobilité et plasticité dans les pentecôtismes au Cap-Vert et en Islande." *Migrations et société* 184(2) (2021), pp. 43–57. https://doi.org/10.3917/migra.184.0043

Rachid Frère. "Qui représente l'islam ? French Version." www.youtube.com/watch?v=jmvVM6Mx0TA.

Rey, Jeanne. *Pentecôtisme et migration en Suisse*. Paris: Karthala, 2019.

Rokem, Jonathan and Laura Vaughan, "Geographies of ethnic segregation in Stockholm: The Role of Mobility and Co-presence in Shaping the Diverse City." *Urban Studies* 56(12) (2018), pp. 2426–2446.

Ristilammi, Per-Markku. *Rosengård och den svarta poesin: En studie av modern annorlundahet*. Stockholm: Symposion, 1994.

Simbsler, David. "'Trusting the Lord, Conquering the Land': Pentecostals, Landless Movement and Grassroots Politics from Dilma Roussef to Jair Bolsonaro." *Bulletin of Latin American Research* 41(5) (2021), pp. 710–723. https://doi.org/10.1111/blar.13167

Chapter 6

Legal Regulation of Religious Minorities in Sweden: The Example of International Pentecostals

Victoria Enkvist

Introduction

This chapter is about some of the legal possibilities and challenges concerning human rights, that religious minorities, such as Pentecostal migrants, may face coming to Sweden. In the interviews conducted within the "Pentecostal Migrants in Secular Sweden: Influences and Challenges" research project (see Chapter 1, this volume), the parishioners expressed an ambivalence towards Swedish laws concerning religion. Interpretation of how the parishioners experience these rules and Swedish society emerges from the fieldwork that the other researchers in this project have conducted and written about in their chapters. Some of the references are directly from transcripts from the conducted interviews. The sources that emanate from the interviews that are used in this chapter are therefore secondary sources in some sense.

While parishioners expressed gratitude for some of the legal regulations in Sweden, for example, freedom of religion, scepticism was expressed about the "control" of the content of what can be said in sermons as this "control" can imply that institutions exercise power over what one believes in.[1] The perceived control emanates from the interview subjects' perception of the regulations of freedom of religion and freedom of expression and other legal rules, such for example the Education Act. The parishioners also expressed their feeling of moral and political pressure from Myndigheten för stöd till trossamfund (the Authority for State Aid to Religious Communities) (SST) regarding the promotion of Swedish values. This made some parishioners hesitant to register and apply for state funds and aid.[2] In these statements, it is possible to discern a duality that the aid can entail, which is partly about the actual impact that the rules on aid have on the internal organization, and content of the religious communities, but which also affects the actual actions of the individuals in relation to the state.[3]

To some extent, the feeling or concern expressed by the parishioners in the interviews is correct. Freedom of religion in Sweden means the right to think and believe what you want. However, the protection does not cover all ways of manifesting or otherwise expressing one's faith. Due to the importance of the legal rules concerning religion for religious minorities such as Pentecostals, and the different ways in which these rules were mentioned in the interviews, this chapter focuses on the most important legal rules concerning religion

The Legal Perspective and the Legal Method

Unlike the other disciplinary perspectives in this project, there are not several different methods in legal research. The starting point in legal research, in general, is based on what is usually referred to as the legal dogmatic method, which involves examining the various sources of law in Sweden that exist in order to arrive at what is the law in force. The accepted sources of law are legislation, preparatory works, case law and doctrine. In this chapter, I have used these sources but also other literature to provide a broader perspective and a context for the research results from the other researchers in the project.

The chapter mainly concerns a discussion about freedom of religion, according to the Instrument of Government (IoG) and the European Convention on Human Rights (ECHR). Other rights and principles such as freedom of expression and fundamental principles of legality, objectivity and neutrality are also discussed. Questions about religion and how religion is facilitated in various ways by the public authorities, including the rules on support for religious communities are central in this chapter.

The reason for choosing the above-mentioned systems is that IoG sets the constitutional frames for all legislation in Sweden and the ECHR is an international obligation and Swedish law since 1995. The ECHR has a unique role in the Swedish Constitution because it is protected in an 2:19 in the IoG.

Migration or Mobility?

A defining feature of society today is globalization and the mobility of people. As a result of migration, the composition of the Swedish population has changed. It has affected society in many ways, not least the religious landscape. In Sweden, population movements have, among other things, led to greater diversity in terms of people's religious affiliations and religious practices.[4] For a long time, Sweden was a country with a relatively homogeneous population both from a cultural and religious perspective.[5] As society has become more heterogeneous in terms of both national origin and religious affiliation, various challenges have arisen at different levels of society, not least concerning issues of equal treatment and rights and possibilities to manifest different religions.[6]

Many texts are written about various religious minority groups and their role and place in Swedish society, not least about Muslims. Considerably less is written about various Christian minority groups and congregations and their place in Swedish society, at least from a legal perspective. This text originates from the project Pentecostal Migrants in Secular Sweden: Influences and Challenges.[7]

The project deals with what we initially in the project description decided to call "migrant churches" in Sweden. One of the main reasons for our interest in the selected congregations was that a majority of the congregation members had their origins in other countries. People from different parts of the world sought out religious groups that seemed to originate from the same or nearby geographical areas as themselves, or at least chose them out of linguistic affinities.[8] The mobility or what we call fluidity itself, was another reason for our research interest. Thus, from the start of the project, the issue of the concept of "migrant churches" was discussed, as it was considered problematic for various reasons. One of the reasons for questioning the concept was the lack of added scientific value in the different research disciplines. And eventually, we chose another term, internationals.[9] The focus of this text is the legal conditions and the social context in which these groups operate

Within the legal framework in Sweden, encounters between different groups, religious and secular, have given rise to various conflicts where different values are measured against each other. The examples that have emerged in the last decade relate primarily to Islam. Muslims are categorized in various contexts as "the other" and increasingly as a threat to Swedish values, security and culture.[10] Historically, however, Christian minority groups have been labelled as "the other".[11] The question of integration, assimilation, acceptance and the relationship of the state also to Christian minority groups is central to the contemporary Swedish situation. Furthermore, there is an intermingling between religion and ethnicity that can be misleading in relation to the state and governmental bodies.

Definitions and Narrative – a Matter of Perception

One focus of the project was to examine the legal aspects of the individuals and congregations in question. In this context, it is important to consider how we choose to categorize people and how these categorizations have consequences for the legal status of individuals, which in turn affects the life of that individual, in terms of opportunities and access to society at large.

Dividing churches into different country/origin designations or calling them, "migrant churches" can have other consequences beyond the obvious and intended. In this context, it should be emphasized that migration is one way of describing movement across borders.[12] Another way of referring to the same phenomenon is mobility. The choice of concept directly determines how the person concerned will be treated by society. As Magdalena Kmak puts it:

> [W]hen we consider the cross-border movement problematic or unwanted we use the word migration. To be sure, mobility has become synonymous with freedom and choice, something central to our identity as researchers and academics for example, perhaps also a feature of what is being called a European Way of Life.[13]

The members of the different congregations who met with the project researchers are from different parts of the world. Many of them are members of transnational networks, which raises the question of whether their movement across borders can be described in terms of mobility or migration according to Kmak.

Using different forms of categorization is human and a way to relate the subject of categorization to the surrounding society. But categorizations have consequences, desired and sometimes undesired.[14] Referring to a Latin-American community, an African community and an Arab community of Pentecostals as migrant congregations can contribute to an image of the congregations that may not be appreciated by the members of the congregations themselves and is not necessarily entirely accurate either, some of the adherents being born and raised in Sweden. What is the unifying factor: the religion, the faith, the origin of the parishioners, or the language? About the latter, the question can also be asked, based on Kmak's research, whether it is a question of migration or mobility of religious groups. Moreover, is there only one root cause?

Regardless of whether the displacement as such is based on religion or not, some of the people who come to Sweden are religious and some may become religious along the way or after their arrival to Sweden. In other words, people's religiosity can both increase and decrease in the context of migration/fluidity, or it can change through conversion (for example from Islam to Christianity, or from one Christian tradition to another).[15] The reasons for this change in religiosity are manifold and occur at the state-individual, state-group, group-individual and individual-individual levels. That is, the influencing factors are many and varied and can have a variety of outcomes.[16] The legal status of individuals depends on a variety of factors, which makes it impossible to highlight any concrete issues of legal relevance because people, adherents to Pentecostalism, have crossed borders.

Religious Movements in Time, Space and Thought

The basis of this text is, as mentioned, three Pentecostal congregations, a Latin American community, an African community and an Arab community. Several of the members in these congregations either are aliens or have their origins in other parts of the world. Some of them settle in Sweden, while others continue to travel, and some return to their previous countries of residence. During their journey, the travellers will be affected by different legal systems. Some legal systems are universal, for example, the Universal Declaration of Human Rights. The UN Universal Declaration as such, affects all humans. Other legal systems are regional and national and their jurisdiction depends on different factors.

As mentioned above this text is about people coming to Sweden. The legal status of those who have migrated to Sweden depends on the cause of their migration. The legal system in Sweden is not always as transparent as one would like it to be and for aliens newly arrived in Sweden, the legal system can be perceived as an impenetrable web. Because of the general application of human rights, most of them apply to all people whether they are citizens or not. Only a few human rights systems differentiate between people depending on their citizenship.

In Sweden, for example, the chapter about human rights in the Instrument of Government (IoG) differentiates between citizens and aliens. Chapter 2 article 25 provides a constitutional basis for discriminating against certain aliens. In para 10 for example, it is stated that freedom of religion can be restricted through law in contrast to Swedish citizens for whom the prohibition on restricting religious freedom is stated in IoG 2:20–2:21. For Swedish citizens limitations in freedom of religion are prohibited, even in times of war. The legal possibilities for an individual to both hold and practise his or her religion may therefore vary depending on whether the individual in question is a Swedish citizen or not.

The Legal Frames of Freedom of Religion

The regulations concerning rights and freedoms in Sweden and the relationship between the various rights complexes and legislations concerning religion are to some extent difficult to grasp and require knowledge of both the legal system as a whole and of rights in a more in-depth manner. It can be difficult to understand and relate to the different possibilities and requirements that legislation places on individuals and groups, especially for people who have recently moved here. Challenges related to language, and understanding how the public system works are some of the challenges that new citizens or newly arrived individuals may face.

The two most important rules concerning religion in the second chapter of the IoG are the rules regulating freedom of religion, 2:1 p 6 and 2:2. Freedom of religion according to both the Constitution protects people´s right to hold and practise their religion without state interference. Both regulations are absolute, which means that they cannot be restricted. Due to their absolute nature, the protection and scope of the rights are interpreted restrictively. The latter protects citizens from having to state which, if any, religion they belong to.

The general development of human rights discourse and more specifically freedom of religion during the last decade is extensive, at least in theory, in the way politicians and the general public talk about it. It is getting more and more common for human rights arguments to be presented in courts although the actual impact of human rights still can be debated. For religious adherents' freedom of religion for obvious reasons is an important right. The focus of the text is how religion is regulated and protected according to the IoG and how this legislation may affect religious adherents and congregations. The contrast between the utopic view of rights and how rights are realized is important to shed light on. In recent decades, the issue of religious freedom has become increasingly important. Freedom of religion is described as a key to prosperity, emancipation and a foundation for a vital democracy. This has, among other things, prompted states to create clearer protection for this freedom, while old regulations have been retained and placed in new systems.[17]

It is clear, however, that all individuals, regardless of whether they have migrated or not are protected by the freedom of religion in both 2:1 p 6 and 2:2

in the IoG, and the European Convention in article 9, and that this right entails a right to practise one's religion and to assemble with others. Freedom of religion can be restricted in various ways, but the core of the right is to guarantee the right to believe what one wants. This part of the right is not subject to restriction, while the part that deals with the actual practice can be restricted in different ways but under certain conditions.

Certain manifestations of religion have been the subject of debate, both politically and legally. In Sweden, for example, the issue came up in the so-called the Green case. The question was whether the Swedish Pentecostal pastor Åke Green's sermon about homosexuals constituted hate speech and whether the fact that Green's speech was a form of religious expression meant that freedom of religion had to be taken into account.[18] In this case, regulations concerning hate speech and freedom of religion conflicted. According to the Constitution, the rules on freedom of expression are used in legal assessments because the expression i.e. religious manifestation in these cases meets the very nature of freedom of expression. This, in turn, means that the rules limiting freedom of expression apply.[19] That means that it is possible to restrict various forms of religious expression through the limitations on freedom of expression in the Constitution. The offence of incitement to hatred is one such constitutional restriction on freedom of expression and it was held to be applicable in the Green case. If these had been the only rules that the Supreme Court had to take into account in its judgment, Pentecostal Pastor Green would have been convicted of incitement to hatred. However, there was another system of rights to be taken into account in the proceedings, namely the ECHR. When the Supreme Court took into account Article 9 of the ECHR, the freedom of religion under the Convention was considered to cover the type of sermon that Mr. Green gave and he was acquitted.[20]

Taking the European Convention into account, the same issues fall within the framework of Article 9, which deals with freedom of religion. The practical significance of this may vary, but the symbolic significance is not negligible. The issue of Pastor Green's sermon came up and concerns were expressed about what could be expressed during a sermon due to the legal regulations regarding religion, and freedom of religion in Sweden. While there is gratitude for the freedom of religion, scepticism was expressed about the "control" of the content of what can be said in sermons as this "control" can mean a control of what one believes in.[21] To some extent, the feeling or concern expressed by the parishioners is correct. Freedom of religion in Sweden means the right to think and believe what you want. However, the protection does not cover all ways of manifesting or otherwise expressing one's faith.

Part of the freedom of religion is the right to practise one's religion by oneself or with others. Joining with others may involve gathering in different ways. There are many different ways in which religious groups organize themselves. The different ways can result in the legal status of the congregation itself varying. Gathering with other religious people in an orderly fashion is protected by freedom of religion regardless of the form of the gathering but depending on the type of gathering, the freedom of Assembly may also be relevant. The right as such is regulated in Chapter 2 article 1 para 4 in the IoG and Article 11 of the European Convention. This right is subject to different restrictions than freedom of religion and freedom of expression, which must be taken into account in different situations, such as in the legislative process but also when existing legislation is to be applied in such a way that it may restrict freedom of Assembly.

The above-mentioned rights are important for all people and citizens, but perhaps especially for minority groups. It is one of several tools to maintain some of what they have left behind. It is also an important part of the integration process to be able to be who you are and believe in what you want regardless of the surrounding society.

Secular Values Meet Religion

Sweden is a democratic state. Freedom of expression, religion, association and assembly have each played prominent roles in building our society. The challenges that Sweden, like many Western democracies, is facing today with criticism of the current democratic systems and security issues are undermining the relatively strong position of these rights.[22] The suspicion of non-Swedishness affects religious groups increase. Questions about what protection different minority groups should receive are raised in various contexts. The starting point seems to be to protect the society and the systems that are the basis for it. In these discussions and court cases, the question of the protection of the individual is often relegated to the background, especially those individuals belonging to minority groups whose views are not entirely compatible with the values considered "traditional" Swedish values.

What the concept of democracy means in concrete terms is a difficult question. What characterizes a democracy can be answered in different ways depending on which theories of democracy are used. This is important from a legal perspective, as the legislation surrounding various religious issues contains several links and references to the concept of democracy. Among other things, we can see the concept of democracy raised in the limiting rules for freedom of religion. A more indirect link to democracy can be found in the legislation concerning religious communities, where there is a provision on societal values. This has been concretized in legal cases such as the cases concerning Jehovah's Witnesses, where the legal issue was whether the congregation as such fulfilled the requirements for being a religious community because of its social values.[23] In a state investigation, SOU 2018:18 regarding changes in the Act on support to religious communities (1999:932)where, among other things, a proposal related to values was presented. In the inquiry, it is stated that Swedish society has changed since the act on support to religious communities came into force and that several shortcomings in the current system were the reason for the revision of the legislation. One of the gaps identified was the democracy requirement in the legislation and the lack of clarity in the legislation regarding that requirement. Another uncertainty identified was how to interpret the democracy criterion in light of the ECHR. A further shortcoming was the possibility of withdrawing support to the communities if the community in question did not fulfil the democratic requirement. The inquiry proposes a new objective for the State's support to religious communities and new criteria for receiving that support, including a clearer democracy criterion compatible with freedom of religion.[24]

In parallel with the requirements of democracy, it can be emphasized that the inquiry also finds that the support can strengthen fundamental democratic values and stimulate participation in democracy. However, this is not always the case. In some cases, religious communities have maintained values and structures that restrict individuals in terms of enjoying their freedoms and rights. The report concludes "The legitimacy of the support also presumes that public funding is not paid out to religious communities that conduct activities incompatible with our fundamental values." Against this background, the inquiry considers that a democracy criterion should be set. However, the report notes that this may violate the freedom of religion in the ECHR and must therefore be compatible with the limitation requirements of the Convention. What is not mentioned is the freedom of religion in the IoG, which cannot be limited. The question can also be asked whether these changes, like the current legislation in the area, already pose a challenge to the content of the religion and the religious congregation, since recognition by society requires some adaptation and change of the core of the religion.[25]

An important question in this context is what the protection of religion means. Does adequate protection mean that minorities are assimilated into the majority in different ways, or does it allow minorities to preserve their characteristics, and, if so, at what price? The relationship between the minority interest and the majority interest is interesting for several different reasons. When it comes to understanding and protecting majority interests and expression of these interests, tradition and culture often weigh heavily as arguments, while the opposite applies to minority expressions that can be traced to culture and tradition.[26]

Is there a clear link between democracy and religious freedom? It depends. The majority has always had interpretive precedence over what is considered religion and what is to be protected. Although the provisions on freedom of religion, in particular in Chapter 2, Section 1(6) of the Constitution, appear to be broad by design, the provision has a narrow scope of application. It can also be argued that the very fact that the protection of freedoms and rights sets limits on the governing power means that democracy and the protection of freedoms and rights are not compatible per se. In this context, it can be important to raise the question of if there is an inherent conflict between the liberal democratic system and the protection of religion especially among religious minorities in society.

Another key concept is the rule of law. There are several different definitions of what characterizes a rule of law. A checklist concerning the rule of law has been issued by The Venice Commission. In the rule of law checklist, it is stated that the rule of law is linked not only to human rights but also to democracy.[27] In the checklist, it is stated, "while democracy relates to the involvement of the people in the decision-making process in a society, human rights seek to protect individuals from arbitrary and excessive interferences with their freedoms and liberties and to secure human dignity".[28] The rule of law focuses on limiting and reviewing the exercise of public powers.

The supremacy of the law is emphasized in the checklist concerning the rule of law. Closely linked to the supremacy of law is compliance with law. Another important factor is legal certainty, which is the principle that is relevant to this chapter. Clarity in legislation and regulations is fundamental to ensure compliance with the rules in question and to minimize the possibility of arbitrariness in their application.[29] One problem that exists in most regulations and rules concerning religion is the wide scope for interpretation. When concepts such as religion and democracy are used in rules, it is difficult for those to whom the rules are addressed to comply with them.

> The legislation must also be formulated with sufficient precision and clarity to enable legal subjects to regulate their conduct in conformity with it. Instability and inconsistency of legislation or executive action may affect a person's ability to plan his or her actions. However, stability is not an end in itself: law must also be capable of adaptation to changing circumstances. The law can be changed, but with public debate and notice, and without adversely affecting legitimate expectations.[30]

Another component of a functioning rule of law is access to justice, which the Raoul Wallenberg Institute describe as follows:

> Access to justice means that individuals have fair and equal access to the legal system and legal remedies; e.g. access to legal information, representation, and a fair trial. Procedures and practices for fair, efficient, humane, and accountable justice determine the chances of us enjoying our human rights. This is why justice systems constitute a cornerstone in a society based on human rights and the rule of law.[31]

So why is this important in this context? One of the challenges for aliens and the authorities they come into contact with is communication. Sometimes difficulties occur in the communication on what is required in the meeting with the public sector, both in terms of obligations and rights. To be able to regulate one's way of life according to existing rules, it is necessary not only to understand the language of the rules but also to understand the rules and their purpose. A current example of this is a new political proposal for an interpretation fee for people who do not speak Swedish when seeking medical care. Interpreting has so far been free of charge in Sweden, and the proposal has been widely criticized by the public sector employees affected, as the care for care patients risks deteriorating due to a lack of communication. The rules themselves, not least the rights rules, are there to protect individuals against the government in particular. This places great demands on accessibility and trust.

State Neutrality and Support to Faith Communities

In the interviews, the parishioners expressed an ambivalence towards Swedish laws concerning religion. On the one hand, some of the parishioners expressed gratitude for freedom of religion, and on the other hand, they felt moral and political pressures that could come from SST regarding the promotion of Swedish values. This led some people to hesitate to register and apply for state funds and aid.[32] Applying for recognition as a religious community can be done for various reasons.

Religion and freedom of religion in Sweden have undergone several changes during history. Sweden was for a long period a society with a state church. Swedish citizens were obliged to be members of a religious community. The Parliament passed a decision in the year 1998 concerning changed conditions between the state and the church. The relation between the state and the Swedish church is now regulated in a special act, Lag (1998:1591) om Svenska kyrkan (Act about Church of Sweden). The decision can be seen as the last step in a long road to reaching an agreement on the issue of the church's relationship with the state. During the same time, the Act (1998:1593) on religious communities was introduced. Due to the different legislations, one can say, that the Swedish church still has a special position, at least from a judicial perspective. The Acts concerning religion and faith communities and the relation between the state and the faith communities are few, but they have a great impact on the opportunities for the religious group's possibilities to be heard in the public discourse and to influence society.

Apart from the individual protection offered by the legal system, the question of how the government relates to religious groups is important for religious minorities. This affects individuals who are members of the various communities. It is also relevant to the wider issue of integration and the sense of belonging to the majority society. Besides the constitutional protection of religion regulations concerning religion can be found in Legislation on Religious Communities and the legislation on Support to Religious Communities. The latter contains some interesting rules; For example, it is stated that the aid is intended to help create the conditions for religious communities to conduct active and long-term religious activities in the form of worship, spiritual care, teaching and care. The prerequisites for government grants are as follows: State aid may only be given to a religious community that contributes to the maintenance and strength of fundamental values on which society is based, and is stable and has its vitality. Some prerequisites are more interesting than others, such as the word religious. What defines a religion and what is worship in the eyes of the law? The last sentence in article 3 is also interesting because state aid can only be given to a religious community that contributes to maintaining and strengthening the fundamental values on which society is based upon. This wording is open to a broad interpretation and may mean that less well-known religions with forms of expression unknown to Swedish society may not be accepted due to misconceptions and prejudices. Being recognized as a religious community is a prerequisite for receiving state aid. Such support provides a form of confirmation from the public sector, but can also mean that the state influences the group as a whole, as it requires a certain adaptation to expectations for the creation of a group's internal and external forms.[33]

Another way to go is not to see the religious parameter as governing, but instead focus on other parts and values of the group and see it as a political association. Financial assistance may then be sought via support to civil society organizations. Recently a new legislation has been proposed concerning public aid to civil organizations.[34] The proposed legislative changes are similar to the rules proposed for state aid for religious communities. Various consultative bodies regarding this proposed legislation have raised the same concerns.[35]

One interesting underlying question is on what grounds the parishes have made their choice to undergo an application process or not and what consequences this has had for the parish itself. As previously stated, the support is not only financial but has other consequences, not least a stamp of approval that can be important for the view of the community from the surrounding society. This reasoning is also relevant for political associations. A third and quite different way of being religious in a group is to be completely outside the public system in the sense that there is no registration of any kind. In this case, there is no possibility of seeking financial support for the group in question. This option can also be problematic from a societal perspective, as there is no possibility of insight into the group's inner life and organization.

Therefore, the regulations surrounding religious and political groups and their ability to receive grants and support from the public sector have two purposes, so to speak. One is slightly more explicit, the support of minority groups and minority religions. A second, more implicit purpose is to create a relationship with the public sector that provides an opportunity for transparency and influence from the state. The design of the system, i.e. the requirements that may force the religious group seeking support to organize itself in such a way that affects the content of the religion may lead to different religious groups refraining from seeking support. Legislation is a way for the state to influence religious groups in the desired direction. There is nothing unique or strange about the state making demands on how and what they should provide funding for, but it may affect the possibilities of controlling the content and activities of the religious congregation. It may be possible to claim that religious freedom is affected.

The principle of objectivity is an important principle in the Swedish judicial system, see 1:9 IoG. All faith communities are covered by the same legislation apart from the Church of Sweden. The reason why there is special legislation concerning the Church of Sweden is that for a long time, it was closely linked to the state and when the division between state and church took place this required special legislation. A large number of investigations in which the question of how religion should be regulated was thoroughly discussed preceded the division. In these inquiries, the question of state neutrality and support for religious communities was thoroughly examined. These issues have not been discussed legally to any great extent since then but deserve further analysis, not least in light of current social developments.

So, what does the Act on faith communities have to do with religious freedom? The formal connection is that the first section of the law refers to the rules on religious freedom in the IoG and the ECHR. The purpose of the Act was to create as good conditions as possible for equal treatment of different faith communities. When the Act on faith communities came into force, the Religious Freedom Act of 1951 was repealed. Some articles from the Religious Freedom Act were transferred to the new Act. For example, the concept of religious community has the same meaning as it did in the fourth article of the Religious Freedom Act.

Another important question that has been discussed thoroughly in the preparatory works is the issue of state neutrality. The neutrality question is important in this context because most of the legislations regarding religious freedom were introduced during a time when Sweden was not neutral from a religious point of view partly due to the state-church system.

The discussion about neutrality in the preparatory works for the state-church relationship is extensive and very interesting. In the preparatory works, a neutral state is defined as a state that does not interfere with people's religion and conscience. Furthermore, the state should be passive to all types of religious views, as well as to all forms of expression of non-religious views.

Table 6.1. The state can have any of four different attitudes to religion: an active or passive positive attitude, or an active or passive negative attitude.

Positive	Active
	Passive
Negative	Active
	Passive

Source: SOU 1972:[36]

In addition to this form of neutrality, which is referred to as passive neutrality, the preparatory works also contain concepts like positive and negative neutrality, which means that the state takes a positive or negative attitude towards different groups.

A non-denominational society can be based on four different approaches to religious groups and communities. An active positive attitude from society promotes the activities of religious and other life-view groups. In the final report "Society and Religious Communities" it was stated that society should adopt an actively positive attitude, as it is society's most important task to ensure that the individual needs of citizens in all sectors of society are covered.36

> In addition to satisfying the needs of the citizens, it was considered important for the vitality of Swedish democracy that all different ideologies and faiths have good opportunities to assert themselves. These views on life, as well as much of the activities conducted within non-profit organizations based on various views on life, are valuable sources of inspiration also for the general debate.[37]

Within the framework of the passive positive method, there is the possibility that the state allows free competition between different groups. The actively negative attitude means that the state does not support religious activities in any form and also seeks to hinder religious activities. The passive negative attitude is based on the fact that society does not support any religious activity but it also requires that the state does not create any obstacles to religious activity.[38]

Concerning the issue of equal support for different groups, the inquiry found that it must be required both from a religious freedom point of view and a democratic point of view that religious minorities should have the same right to their beliefs as the majority.[39]

It can be problematic for the state to take a different attitude to different groups or for that matter to take an equal attitude to different groups because it is the task of the state to convey democratic values to the citizens. Chapter 1 article 9 in the IoG, states that Courts, administrative authorities, and others performing public administration tasks shall take into account the equality of all before the law and observe objectivity and impartiality in their activities.

The state's ethical values, which are the basis for various forms of legislation, are not always compatible with the values of religious groups. The state investigation, Society and Religious Communities called into question the concept of neutrality, as it was considered that total neutrality in matters of religion and conscience is not possible or desirable as our democratic system is based on certain fundamental values.[40]

The state's positive attitude towards different religious orientations can be defined as states directly or indirectly creating favourable conditions for the activities of the various groups. It has been considered important to strive to achieve equal treatment of different faiths and conscience. It was stated in the preparatory works that state support and state control are valued differently by different groups. What is perceived positively by one group may be perceived negatively by another group. The ambition for state neutrality was therefore considered difficult to achieve, which is why one conclusion in the report was that the state should strive for the benefits offered to religious communities to be perceived as equally valuable. However, it was found that it is impossible to create an objective standard for estimating such a value.[41] In a chapter on Religion and Human Rights Slotte presents different researchers' criticism against neutrality: "thus, according to the critics, what has been considered and portrayed as neutrality comes across as instead as partially-selective blindness".[42]

In a State inquiry, SOU 2018:18, suggestions were made concerning inter alia concepts like religion. The investigation is complex and covers several areas. One of the most important questions from a human rights perspective that is discussed in the investigation is the question of freedom of religion. For some reason, the investigation focuses mostly on freedom of religion according to Article 9 in the ECHR. Given that the constitution is of higher value this can be questioned. Prerequisites that must be met when limiting Article 9 is that the limitation has to be necessary for a democratic society, the purpose must be legitimate and the means must be proportional. There are several different definitions of democracy, why it is difficult to understand the lack of discussion of democracy in the investigation. This is important because it is related to the role and weight of human rights. In the investigation, it is stated that conditions in the legislation must be done with caution.[43] If for example, the conditions interfere with the right to expression the limitations must be formulated in accordance with the IoG.

If the support to faith communities aims to safeguard freedom of religion and the democratic values in Sweden the requirements concerning the limiting criteria can be perceived as a bit problematic. In a referral by Uppsala University, it was expressed that:

> Two important issues that the investigation, therefore, needs to answer are: a) what clear conditions can the state set regarding the religious expression of religious communities so that the religious expressions at the same time do not violate democracy criteria, and (b) whether these democracy criteria are consistent with the limitation criteria in RF 2:21.[44]

The Act concerning faith communities is constructed in a seemingly neutral way but looking more closely at the wording of the Act some questions arise. The Act on Faith Communities stipulates that a religious community is defined as a religious body that performs worship. This has been criticized for being an ethnocentric prerequisite because it excludes other forms of faith communities that don't manifest religion with worship. In the relatively new state investigation concerning faith communities, this prerequisite has been suggested to be removed and replaced with a more neutral concept.

In several places in the report, the inquiry refers to "our fundamental values". This concept shall, in turn, form the basis of the democracy criteria. At the same time, the report underlines that the examination of the democracy criteria may not be a subject of the evaluation of the community's beliefs to society's values. This is important because, in the constitutional regulations concerning restrictions of the rights in the IoG, it is stipulated that it is prohibited to limit rights based on religion or other views, 2:21 IoG. Also, freedom of religion in 2:1p 6 in the IoG is absolute, which means that no limitations can be made. Shakman Hurd states that:

> The foreclosing on religion without beliefs shuts out dissenters, doubters, and those on the margins of or just outside those 'faith communities' celebrated by religious freedom advocates, whose voices are subsumed or submerged by the institutions and authorities presumed to speak in their name. It endows those authorities with the power to pronounce which beliefs deserve special protection or sanction of religious belief. Who decides what counts as a religious belief deserving of special protection and legal exemption rather than as some other form of belief?[45]

As Shakman Hurd notes that international freedom of religion participates in a market-based economy with regulated enactment of religious activities along particular lines. The "marketplace" offers certain ways to be religious while excluding others.[46] Closely related to this is the issue of religious independent schools in Sweden. The public system of municipal schools changed in 1992 when the possibility to start independent schools was introduced in Sweden. This possibility led to the establishment of several religious independent schools and now parents have the opportunity to choose the type of school their children attend. The existence or otherwise of independent schools is a matter of constant debate in Sweden, and religious independent schools in particular have been questioned by politicians. An inquiry was set up, SOU 2019:64, to investigate whether it was possible to introduce a ban on the establishment of independent schools. The Inquiry concluded that this is possible under certain conditions, not least of which is the need to take account of rights and freedoms.[47]

At present, there is no ban on the establishment of independent schools. However, several religious independent schools have recently been closed after an ownership and management review conducted by Skolinspektionen (the school inspectorate). The Education Act regulates how teaching and education should take place in schools and when denominational elements are permitted. Denominational elements are only permitted in education and must be voluntary. Teaching must be non-denominational.

From the interviews conducted by Westerlund, it is clear that views on the Swedish school and school system and the choice between municipal schools and independent schools vary. Those who favor independent schools seem to choose international independent schools in particular because of language and not because of religious beliefs.

Closing Remarks

This chapter deals with religion and law. From a legal perspective, it deals more specifically with the encounter with the Swedish public system for people who come to Sweden. In the law, i.e. the legislation concerning religion in the public sphere, there is no division between different religious communities apart from this special legislation for the Church of Sweden. All other religious communities are subject to the same rules. This means that no special consideration is given to different forms of manifestation that are typical of a specific religion or faith community.

In the IoG freedom of religion is absolute and cannot be limited. The core of freedom of religion in the IoG is, however, narrow and mainly includes the right to believe. More accurately, as stated in the preparatory works, every manifestation that falls within the other right shall be estimated according to the rules related to that specific right. In the ECHR freedom of religion is relative and can be limited. Article 9 includes a right to change one's religion or belief and freedom, either alone or in community with others and in public or private, to manifest one's religion or belief, in worship, teaching, practice and observance. Another right of interest in this context is freedom of association. This right stipulates a right to freedom of association: freedom to connect with others for general or individual purposes. If a faith community for some reason would choose to meet and organize as an association and not a faith community, the article and paragraph concerning freedom of association will be applicable.

There is no apparent economic gain with freedom of association compared to the freedom of religion. Associations can apply for funding according to different legislations depending on the aim of the association. The benefit of freedom of religion and the Act on Faith Communities is that it can serve as a platform or a channel between the state and the different faith communities. This channel can be positive, as the faith communities can play an active role in the democratic debate concerning topics that concern them. Another perspective, that can be both positive and negative, is that through the legislation the state can have an impact on both the organizational level and perhaps on the inner life of the faith communities.

Far from all Pentecostal congregations make use of the possibility to register as a faith community according to the Act on faith communities. This may have several explanations but one consequence of this is that there is a lack of transparency in the organization and belief systems and the adherents are in many ways isolated from the society. In the interviews conducted with members of the various parishes, it became clear that exclusion in society is common and that parishioners feel that they are met with suspicion and sometimes hostility in society. Whether this is due to ethnicity or religious affiliation or both is difficult to answer, but it highlights the issue and the importance of inclusion and the view of what is different or perceived as different. As it is not uncommon for the members of the congregation to move across national borders for various reasons, different expectations can also arise in the meeting with the majority society.

Sweden is in many ways a unique country in terms of its attitude towards religion as it is one of the most secular countries in the world where religion has not been a public issue until recently. In many other countries, especially in Europe, religion has a much more prominent role, which also means that these countries have a more positive attitude towards religion, for instance, in Italy and Spain. This is manifested not least by secular legislation that claims to be neutral and universal. The secular element is sometimes mistaken for neutrality, which can be questioned. Secularism can be argued to be another form of belief, as expressed in a European Court of Human Rights case. The case in question concerns religious symbols in the school environment in Italy. The case contains a dissenting opinion in which an in-depth discussion of secularism as a different type of belief is developed.[48] With the increased importance of rights in general and freedom of religion in particular, religion has re-entered the Swedish public sphere. Questions concerning religious freedom are becoming more frequent and it is clear that this is an issue on which there is no political or legal consensus.

The interviews conducted with parishioners in the various parishes revealed that the parishioners were overwhelmingly positive about the Swedish social order. It is difficult to interpret what this means. However, there seems to be an inherent conflict in the view of religion, especially the role of religion in society. This raises an old question about whether religion is a private matter or something that has a natural place in the public sphere. This distinction can lead to difficulties in talking about religion and it can complicate encounters in the public forum.

Another challenge is what we can call secular ambiguity. The state's secular support based on secular and neutral/objective rules can have an impact on faith and religious organizations. This could be called secular normativity.

Regarding the Pentecostal congregations presented in this book, it is clear that some of the members feel alienated and have little understanding of the surrounding society. The interviews revealed that one possible explanation for this alienation is that the faith deviates from what is perceived as typical Swedish, but it also shows that there is little understanding of different forms of religiosity in society as a whole.

The Pentecostal communities and their multifaceted organizational system are interesting from a constitutional point of view because they can be related to citizens and non-citizens who stay in Sweden and their relation to the government and state institutions. The theory that these people by principle are anti-institutional convey an important factor in the power relation between the state and the individual. In Sweden, institutions and governmental power are well established. This is a foundation for legitimacy, democracy, the rule of law, and to safeguard the rights of the individuals. In the legal requirements for obtaining state aid for religious communities, there are requirements for the organization of the community, which is interesting in this context, especially since the Pentecostal movement is described as an anti-institutional organization. The fluidity of the Pentecostal community may also have other implications than those expressed in Bäckströms article, not least legal consequences. To be able to fully function in the Swedish society knowledge about the Swedish legal system, or at least the public law system is required. A belief in the system is of great importance for the legitimacy of the system. A fundamental part of that system is human rights, both on an international, constitutional and public law level. The anti-institutional organization of the Pentecostal congregations is also important because as Westerlund notes in Chapter 4 of this volume, no religious practice takes place in a vacuum. Contexts shape both the position, understanding and scope of the lived religion. This can also be applied to law. No legislation takes place in a vacuum. Contexts shape the position, understanding and scope of law.

Victoria Enkvist is associate professor of constitutional law and senior lecturer in public law at the Faculty of Law at Uppsala University. Her research focuses mainly on rights and freedoms in different systems and how these rights are interpreted and applied in different situations. A main track in Enkvist's research is religious freedom and its legal framework. Enkvist is currently engaged in several different multidisciplinary research projects dealing with rights and subjects of rights.

Acknowledgement

This work was supported by the Swedish Research Council (no. VR 2018-01438).

Notes

1. Katarina Westerlund and Torbjörn Aronson, "City Church International i Stockholms stad", in Katarina Westerlund (ed.), *Internationell pentekostalism i Storstockholm Tre församlingar i ett förändrat religiöst landskap* (Uppsala: CRS-rapport no. 1, 2021), p. 72; Émir Mahieddin, "Évangéliques et Pentecôtistes face au sécularisme suédois: une perspective anthropologique", in David Koussens, Brigitte Basdevant and Guy Bucumi (eds), *Le paradoxe évangélique: Sécularisation et laïcisation face aux protestantismes évangéliques* (Montréal: Universitaires de Laval 2022), pp. 119–136. Within the framework of the project, interviews were conducted by the various researchers. In this chapter I refer both to the authors' analyses of these interviews and to the interviews conducted by other researchers in the project. In the section on schools, reference is made to the transcripts of the interviews conducted by Katarina Westerlund.
2. Mahieddin, "Évangéliques et Pentecôtistes face au sécularisme suédois", pp. 119–136.
3. Per-Erik Nilsson and Victoria Enkvist, "Techniques of Religion-Making in Sweden: The Case of the Missionary Church of Kopimism", *Critical Research on Religion* (2015), pp. 1–15. See also Per-Erik Nilsson and Victoria Enkvist, "The Hidden Return of Religion in Law and Law in Religion in Swedish Regulations on Faith Communities", in Anna-Sara Lind, Mia Lövheim and Ulf Zackariasson (eds), *Reconsidering Religion, Law, and Democracy: New Challenges for Society and Research* (Lund: Nordic Academic Press, 2017), pp. 93–106.
4. Magdalena Nordin, *Migration, religion och integration kunskapsöversikt 2023:2*, Delegationen för migrationsstudier JU 2013:17, pp. 13–14.
5. SOU 1994:42, p. 39. The report notes that religious pluralism has increased since the Second World War.
6. Anna-Sara Lind, "Freedom of Religion and Positive Duties of the State", in P. Slotte, Niels Henrik Gregersen and Helge Årsheim (eds), *Internationalization, and Reconfessionalization: Law and Religion in the Nordic Realm 1945-2017* (Odense: Syddansk Universitetsforlag, 2022), p. 420.
7. The project was funded by VR during the period 1 December 2018 to 31 December 2020.
8. The empirical research in the project focused on three different congregations in Stockholm, a Latin American community, an African community and an Arab community of Pentecostals. For more information about the methods and material in the project see Chapter 1, this volume.
9. See Chapters 1 and 8 for further discussions on migration and migration church.
10. ECRI General Policy Recommendation No. 5 (revised) on preventing and combating anti-Muslim racism and discrimination, adopted on 8 December 2021 Strasbourg, 1 March 2022, pp. 1–38.
11. David Thurfjell and Erika Willander, *Postmuslimer: Om sekularitet i ett mångreligiöst Sverige* [*Post-Muslims: On Secularity in a Multi-religious Sweden*] (Stockholm: Myndigheten för stöd till trossamfund, SST, 2023); Martin Berntson, Bertil Nilsson and Cecilia Wejryd, *Kyrka i Sverige: Introduktion till svensk kyrkohistoria* (Skellefteå: Artos & Norma bokförlag, 2012).

12 About the use of the word migrant see Chapter 1, this volume; see also Katarina Westerlund, "Att studera internationell pentekostalism", in Westerlund, *Internationell pentekostalism i Storstockholm Tre församlingar i ett förändrat religiöst landskap*, pp. 9–13.
13 The text is an edited version of the Professor Installation Lecture given by Magdalena Kmak on 24 March 2023 at the Åbo Akademi University, titled "What is Mobile Law?". For a more in-depth analysis about mobility of law see Magdalena Kmak, *Law, Migration and Human Mobility: Mobile Law* (Abingdon: Routledge, 2023).
14 See the Jewish community's statement regarding the concept of rituals in their response to the Swedish Board of Agriculture's report 1992:37, 15 January 1993. Also see SOU 1999:9, p. 2.
15 Nordin, *Migration, religion och integration kunskapsöversikt* 2023:2, s.13.
16 Ibid., pp. 13–14.
17 Winnifred Fallers Sullivan, Elisabeth Shakman Hurd, Saba Mahmood and Peter G. Danchin, "Introduction", in Winnifred Fallers Sullivan, Elisabeth Shakman Hurd, Saba Mahmood and Peter G. Danchin (eds), *Politics of Religious Freedom* (Chicago, IL: University of Chicago Press, 2015), p. 1.
18 NJA 2005 s.805 (Swedish Supreme Court).
19 Victoria Enkvist, *Religionsfrihetens rättsliga ramar* (Uppsala: Iustus förlag, 2013), pp. 96–97.
20 NJA 2005 s.805.(Swedish Supreme Court).
21 Émir Mahieddin's field notes from 2020.
22 Legislative measures are taken to address various problems where rights considerations are not always given a prominent role.
23 HFD 2013 ref. 72 (Supreme Administrative Court). See also HFD 2017 ref. 4 (Supreme Administrative Court).
24 SOU 2018:18.
25 Nilsson and Enkvist, "Techniques of Religion-Making in Sweden", pp. 1–15. Also see Nilsson and Enkvist, "The Hidden Return of Religion", pp. 93–106.
26 Enkvist, *Religionsfrihetens rättsliga ramar*, pp. 245–248.
27 Venice Commission of the Council of Europe, The Rule of Law Checklist, p. 14.
28 Ibid., p. 14.
29 Ibid., pp. 25–26.
30 Ibid., p. 26.
31 Raoul Wallenberg Institute, "Rule of Law and Access to Justice", retrieved 20 June 2025 from https://rwi.lu.se/fair-efficient-justice.
32 Mahieddin, "Évangéliques et Pentecôtistes face au sécularisme suédois", pp. 119–136.
33 Nilsson and Enkvist, "Techniques of Religion-Making in Sweden", pp. 1–15. Also see Nilsson and Enkvist, "The Hidden Return of Religion", pp. 93–106.
34 SOU 2019:35.
35 Referral from The Agency for Aid to Religious Communities, Ku2019/01318/CSM.
36 SOU 1972:36, p. 49.
37 Ibid.; SOU 1974:9, p. 147.
38 SOU 1972:36, p. 49.
39 Ibid., p. 49. For a more in-depth discussion see Enkvist, *Religionsfrihetens rättsliga ramar*, pp. 78–79.
40 SOU 1972:36, p. 48.
41 SOU 1970:2, p. 93.
42 Pamela Slotte, "Religion and Human Rights: Ambiguities and Ambivalences of Freedom", in Hedvig Bernitz and Victoria Enkvist (eds), *Freedom of Religion: An Ambiguous Right in the Contemporary Legal Order* (Oxford: Hart Publishing, 2020), p. 9.

43 Uppsala university referral, date 28 August 2018, Dnr UFV 2018/797.
44 Ibid., p. 4.
45 Elisabeth Shakman Hurd, "Believing in Religious Freedom in Politics of Religious Freedom", in Winnifred Fallers Sullivan, Elisabeth Shakman Hurd, Saba Mahmood and Peter G. Danchin (eds), *Politics of Religious Freedom* (Chicago, IL: University of Chicago Press, 2015), p. 51.
46 Ibid.
47 SOU 2019:64.
48 *Lautsi and others v. Italy*, Application no. 30814/06, 2011-03-18, Grand Chamber Judgement.

Bibliography

Berntson, Martin, Nilsson Bertil and Wejryd Cecilia. *Kyrka i Sverige: Introduktion till svensk kyrkohistoria*, Skellefteå: Artos & Norma bokförlag, 2012.
Enkvist, Victoria. *Religionsfrihetens rättsliga ramar*. Uppsala: Iustus förlag, 2013.
Hurd, Elisabeth Shakman. "Believing in Religious Freedom in Politics of Religious Freedom." In Winnifred Fallers Sullivan, Elisabeth Shakman Hurd, Saba Mahmood and Peter G. Danchin (eds), *Politics of Religious Freedom*. Chicago, IL: University of Chicago Press, 2015.
Kmak, Magdalena. *Law, Migration and Human Mobility: Mobile Law*. Abingdon: Routledge, 2023.
Lind, Anna-Sara. "Freedom of Religion and Positive Duties of the State." In P. Slotte, Niels Henrik Gregersen and Helge Årsheim (eds), *Internationalization, and Re-confessionalization: Law and Religion in the Nordic Realm 1945-2017*. Odense: Syddansk Universitetsforlag, 2022.
Mahieddin, Émir. "Évangéliques et Pentecôtistes face au sécularisme suédois: une perspective anthropologique." In D. Koussens, B. Basdevant and G. Bucumi (eds), *Le paradoxe évangélique: Sécularisation et laïcisation face aux protestantismes évangéliques*. Montréal: Presses Universitaires de Laval, 2022.
Nilsson, Per-Erik and Victoria Enkvist. "The Hidden Return of Religion in Law and Law in Religion in Swedish Regulations on Faith Communities." In Anna-Sara Lind, Mia Lövheim and Ulf Zackariasson (eds), *Reconsidering Religion, Law, and Democracy: New Challenges for Society and Research*. Lund: Nordic Academic Press, 2017.
Nilsson, Per-Erik and Victoria Enkvist. "Techniques of Religion-Making in Sweden: The Case of the Missionary Church of Kopimism." *Critical Research on Religion* (2015), pp. 1–15.
Nordin, Magdalena. *Migration, religion och integration kunskapsöversikt* 2023:2, Delegationen för migrationsstudier JU 2013:17, pp. 13–14.
Slotte, Pamela. "Religion and Human Rights: Ambiguities and Ambivalences of Freedom." In Hedvig Bernitz and Victoria Enkvist (eds), *Freedom of Religion: An Ambiguous Right in the Contemporary Legal Order*. Oxford: Hart Publishing, 2020.
Thurfjell, David and Erika Willander. *Postmuslimer. Om sekularitet i ett mångreligiöst Sverige* [*Post-Muslims: On Secularity in a Multi-religious Sweden*]. Stockholm: Myndigheten för stöd till trossamfund, SST, 2023.
Westerlund, Katarina and Aronson Torbjörn. "City Church International i Stockholms stad." In Katarina Westerlund (ed.), *Internationell pentekostalism i Storstockholm Tre församlingar i ett förändrat religiöst landskap*. Uppsala: CRS-rapport no. 1, 2021.

Reports, Inquiries, Referrals and Recommendations

SOU 2019:64. Nya regler för skolor med konfessionell inriktning
SOU 2019:35. Demokrativillkor för bidrag till civilsamhället
SOU 2018:18 Statens stöd till trossamfund i ett mångreligiöst Sverige
SOU 1999:9 Att slakta ett får i Guds namn – om religionsfrihet och demokrati
SOU 1994:42 Staten och trossamfunden
SOU 1974:9 Samhälle och trossamfund : sammanställning av remissyttranden över betänkanden av 1968 års beredning om stat och kyrka
SOU 1972:36 Samhälle och trossamfund slutbetänkande
SOU 1970:2 Om stat och kyrka: en sammanställning av remissyttrandena över Svenska kyrkan och staten

Chapter 7

International Pentecostals in Metropolitan Stockholm: Rethinking Relations between Voluntary and State Religion in Urban Sweden

Anders Bäckström

Introduction

The view that religion is disappearing in cities but persisting in rural areas endured until the end of the twentieth century; it was linked to the idea that the patterns of religion discovered in Europe were a global prototype rather than an exceptional case. Such ideas are increasingly challenged – a change brought about partly by the growing migration of people and ideas. This phenomenon has brought new kinds of religion to Sweden, opened up new international connections in relation to both the global economy and cultural dissemination, and created separate world views based on polycentric political connections. Thus, at one and the same time local communities that bridge borders also create global borders.

Today there are about 100 million people on the move within or between nations in the world. According to the University of Ryerson, two-thirds of the world's population will live in cities by 2050 and migration will be a significant driver of this growth.[1] These migration patterns transform metropolitan areas into hubs of new religions both private and public, of which international Pentecostals are an excellent example. One hypothesis embedded in the research project "Pentecostal Migrants in Secular Sweden: Impact and Challenges?"[2] can be summarized as follows: there is a relationship between the new religious patterns due to migration, new ideas and urban living, and a continued tension between individual choice and collective memories in urban localities, which results in uncertainty among public authorities about how to deal with these populations and welcome the grassroots advocates and diasporas that arrive in this way. This uncertainty is based on the tension between the transnational and voluntary character of new religious groups and the territorial embedding of the "organic" historical religions of Sweden and other European nations.

Disciplinary Perspectives

This book discusses the growing presence of international Pentecostals in multicultural Stockholm through both qualitative and quantitative empirical research as described in the introductory chapter. In this chapter the material will be framed by theoretical models drawn from the sociology of religion, complemented by data from investigations of migration patterns more generally and by results from additional studies of Pentecostal communities and populations. The underlying argument is that Pentecostals are good examples of the flow of people entering urban Sweden. As Torbjörn Aronson shows in chapter 3, the establishment of new Pentecostal communities peaked between 2014 and 2018, years with a monumental influx of refugees, family members and workers. These communities reflect the basic understanding of Pentecostals as international, fluid and unconnected to territory, but responding to this fluidity with a new emphasis on emotions, community life, traditional beliefs and family values. In addition, the chapter argues that there has been a turn to the social of religion, thus linking with Katarina Westerlund's notion in chapter 4 of religion as "lived theology". These developments are seen as a challenge to traditional forms of secularization offering instead a focus on individual life styles. They exist alongside innovative tendencies on the part of the neutral state to embrace and control religion. Finally, the international circulation of goods and ideas is captured by the notion of late modernity with its focus on individual choice and the growing idea of neo-nationalism expressed primarily by voluntary groups sometimes representing the political right.

The chapter will thus focus on four major areas which are based on the presence of Pentecostals in metropolitan Stockholm and the tensions and possibilities of integration that the welfare state of Sweden offers: first the use of definitions of religion in order to portray the kind of religion that neo-Pentecostals represent and the kinds of religion that public and legal authorities protect. The argument is that Pentecostals, like other communities, represents a wide variety of religiosities in a multicultural surrounding; second the ways in which the basic values of migrants are affected by the change of culture over time and how or if international Pentecostals adapt to the level of religiosity that exists in the receiving country. This includes a discussion on the identities of global religion in a cosmopolitan world order; third the ways in which the speed of change both in the culture as such, and among international Pentecostals, makes religious leadership an uncertain undertaking especially in relation to fragile Pentecostal communities; and fourth the manner in which the tensions and confusions between the understanding of the private and the public in secular societies are met by the state, and how religion has increasingly become a policy area beyond state and civil society. In this way, international Pentecostals are caught between sociologically defined theories of individual choice on the one hand and religiously based collective memories on the other. In accordance with these arguments the chapter will be structured into four sections followed by a short conclusion.

Religion and the Multicultural in a Swedish Context

In this section I will deal with two major concepts, religion and the multicultural, that often are defined differently. Zygmunt Bauman writes, for example, that religion "belongs to the family of curious, and often embarrassing concepts, which one perfectly understands until one wants to define them".[3] In many studies, religion functions as a provisory concept structuring the lives of the individual by giving deeds and actions meaning. Meaning, however, can be restricted to belief in God (narrow definition), related to everyday experiences connected to values of the society or to individual meaning of life (civil or lived religion) or concerned with the ultimate questions of life (broad definition). This ambiguity makes the borders between private-public uncertain and the transcendent-immanent binary unclear, infused as it is by individual emotions connected to rites of passage, nature or crises.

I have previously argued, that the way religion is understood in the twentieth century has been marked by the opposition between two minorities: the highly religious and the highly anti-religious.[4] The large in-between group with its vague and largely immanent philosophy of life encompassing the values of modern society is defined as private or secular. This relates to the Swedish historians Henrik Berggren's and Lars Trägårdh's argument that culture in Sweden should be perceived as "cool".[5] It manifests itself in a suspicion of "hot" culture expressions, especially the religiosity of (Muslim and Pentecostal) immigrant groups. Their argument is based on the idea that the Swedish contract between the welfare state and the individual will guarantee the independence of the individual. Thus, the proximity between the welfare state and the individual is central to the success of the twentieth century. In addition, it gave to Sweden a form of modernity that differs from a French, German or Anglo-Saxon, especially North American, form.[6]

Interestingly, the British sociologist David Martin describes Nordic culture as softly religious and secular at the same time.[7] He argues that the Nordic countries' historical integration between the state and a Lutheran Church has blurred the distinction between citizenship and membership of the folk churches. This is evident from the fact that Swedes in general consider regular worship to be superfluous as the individual, in accordance with Luther's doctrine of vocation, participates in society's professional life every day. It is common for researchers to miss the fact that the cultural background of Sweden is based on the Lutheran understanding of a God who works through both church and state.

This development has also been studied by the historian of religion David Thurfjell and sociologist Erika Willander. They use the term post-Christian and post-Muslim to reflect the above mentioned "cool" or "soft" religiosity.[8] The term refers to people who have grown up in a Christian (Swedish) or Muslim (e.g. Iranian) cultural context but in the survey consider themselves as secular. The authors argue, that being a good citizen can be interpreted as loyalty both to Lutheran doctrines and as an expression of a secular stance. From this follows the idea that the individual should be honest and responsible, celebrating the rites of the life cycle and the Christian year, but understanding these as part of secular rather than religious life. All this results in a blurred distinction between a secular self-image and a practised (or lived) religion.[9]

In an international perspective, trust in public authorities is considered strong in the Nordic countries. The link between the state and the individual, however, also includes the Nordic folk churches which are part of the national projects of the twentieth century. In the 1920s, the Social Democrats defined religion as private, but at the same time, they kept the state church as part of the Swedish *folkhemmet*. As the Swedish legal researcher Victoria Enkvist argues, religious freedom at this time was understood as part of an inclusive national church.[10] The culture of trust is, therefore, rooted in history and is one of the prerequisites for the freedom and security that are central to the rights of the individual today. As mentioned above this trust should not be seen as "hot" (that is, connected to traditional family values or exclusive faith communities). Rather it is "cool" (underpinned by the rule of law in the society as a whole). The values of democracy, human rights and human dignity that form a coherent society are seen as fundamental. Thus, the Swedish model of a "cool" trust in the welfare state is connected to a "cool" religiosity, which is part of a more general culture of trust.

Based on data from the World Values Survey (WVS) it is noted that groups with a "cool" and "soft" religiosity are distinctive or even exceptional in the global context, in contrast to groups with a "hot" religiosity which are closer to the global norm.[11] My argument is that Pentecostal migrants can be linked not only to a hot traditional and individually based religiosity (which is often assumed), but also to a cool liberal religiosity, or as David Martin put it, a soft social religiosity. My hypothesis goes, however, further arguing that there are, probably, "post-Pentecostals" in Sweden. This is a group which has grown up within a Pentecostal surrounding but regard themselves today as secular. Lundberg and Malmström's investigation of a group of immigrants from Nigeria shows that there are members of the community that are ready to regard themselves as secular when or if their financial and social situation is secured.[12] They might also consider membership in other churches like Hillsong or the Church of Sweden. Especially membership in Swedish churches might signal a wish to become integrated with Swedish culture. Religion can thus operate in different forms and Pentecostals, as other individuals and communities, exemplify all of these very varied possibilities in a multicultural society.

Sweden likes to be perceived as a modern, pluralistic and multicultural society. This became clear in the 1974 Constitution (Regeringsformen, RF) where democratic rights and freedoms, as well as gender equality, were given a prominent position. Chapter 1, §2, states that the public must work to ensure that the ideas of democracy become guiding principles in all areas of society. This argument should also be applied to the area of religion, a statement that became obvious in the investigation into *Statens stöd till trossamfund i ett mångreligiöst Sverige*, SOU 2018:18 [The Support of the State for Faith Communities in a Multi-Religious Sweden]. The 1974 Constitution stipulates that the power of the state should be exercised with respect for the equal value of all people. It also says that the freedom and dignity of the individual and opportunities for ethnic, linguistic and religious minorities should be encouraged in order that they may promote their own cultural and community life. This approach became even clearer in the 2010 amendment of the Constitution which stipulates that the opportunities for minorities to maintain and develop their own cultural and community life *should* be promoted.[13] In other words, assimilation as a political idea was largely abandoned in the 1970s to be replaced by the idea of mutual integration through recognized diversity. However, religious diversity has increased considerably since that time, with the effect that both assimilation and multiculturalism have become increasingly controversial.

The key question is the following: what kind of religion should the state protect? Both the 1948 United Nations Declaration of Human Rights and the 1950 European Convention on Human Rights speak of the freedom of people to practise their religion or beliefs in public. The Law on Religious Communities 1998:1593 evokes a community in which religious activities such as the organization of public worship is included. The task of the new Authority for the Support of Religious Communities established in 2017 is to give minorities the opportunity to maintain and develop their own cultural and social life. Thus, faith is not only something that concerns people's inner lives but something visible that exists in praxis, for example in (a) material objects (buildings, clothing, symbols), (b) rites and ritual regulations, and (c) moral and ethical norms, especially those regarding sexuality, family and the imagined community that we call a nation. The Swedish human rights expert Johan Modée argues that it is its external and public practice that makes religion controversial.[14] This kind of religion does not fit easily into the Swedish model of belief restricted to the private sphere.[15]

Migration and growing religious pluralism have triggered the need for careful legal study.[16] As Victoria Enkvist argues in chapter 6 it is clear that international Pentecostals need to become included in legal research. Interestingly the Swedish Professor Maarit Jänterä-Jareborg has observed that family law is generally seen as an area intimately linked to culture.[17] It follows that family law conflicts often arise when individuals move between countries with different legal traditions or when they have dual citizenship. The fact that the Swedish legal system has the power to determine the scope of other normative systems, both in the private and public realms, inevitably leads to conflicts between the public obligation to protect individual human rights on the one hand and the fundamental rights of minority groups, like the Pentecostals, on the other. Fellow lawyer Mosa Sayed argues further that people moving to Sweden should be allowed to retain their religious traditions while at the same time becoming Swedish citizens who comply with Swedish law.[18] Thus, citizenship becomes inclusive of all those who live within the society in question. This also applies to international Pentecostals who aim for Swedish citizenship as a human right

In sum this section indicates that a religiosity influenced by international Pentecostals can be defined in several ways in respect to the religious-secular-binary, and that the religious identities that the state advocates reflect a cool, soft or "post-religious" cultural understanding. This renders Pentecostal religiosity

– something that the state is supposed to protect – problematic as it cannot be restricted to the private sphere. Put differently, growing religious diversity as a result of migration renders the idea of multiculturalism politically controversial, given that human rights, according to the Constitution, are tied to the rights of the individual rather than the group. In such a situation, citizenship has become an attractive option for a variety of religious minorities such as international Pentecostals.

Global Religion and Value Shifts in Metropolitan Areas

As mentioned in the Introduction the image of increasing religion in metropolitan areas is the opposite of what secularization theorists anticipated. As the British sociologist Grace Davie argues, there are in fact two processes of religious change currently taking place in Europe: on the one hand the decline of historic churches and on the other the rise of migrant religiosity which often refers to Muslims, believers within Orthodox Churches and Pentecostals.[19]

In this chapter metropolitan areas are defined by population density. They include satellite cities, towns and intervening rural areas that are socioeconomically tied to the urban core, typically patterned by commuting. The city, however, is also a social, physical, economic and political construction. It is multiple with conflicting interests and values. People living in different areas of the city construct their realities differently. Like-minded people, like Pentecostals, tend to cluster in particular geographical areas and in particular groups or communities. Individuals commute to the centre not only for work, but also for shopping and worship.[20]

By using the term metropolitan, we draw attention to the fact that different forms of religion are accommodated in suburban areas with a steady flow of people between the centre and the periphery, and that religion is linked to international friends through global interconnectedness.[21] This argument is underpinned by a survey carried out in Britain by the theologians Paul Bickley and Nathan Mladin. They show that metropolitan London has become the most religious region in Britain, as 62 per cent of Londoners identify as religious, compared to 53 per cent in the rest of Britain.[22] In addition, London is the least Anglican place, with only 33 per cent of the population identifying as Anglicans. Religious adherents in London are young rather than old, and more churchgoing than the rest of Britain; a substantial number of them are women, many of them in leadership positions. Also important is David Goodhew's and Anthony-Paul Cooper's statement that poorer, working-class areas have become areas with high levels of churchgoing.[23] Decline is found among the white English middle-class. The investigation of secularity in a multireligious Sweden by Thurfjell and Willander indicates that there is a similar tendency in metropolitan areas, but the change is small and in need to become confirmed by further studies.[24] According to Statistics Sweden (SCB) it is clear, however, that 85 per cent of migrants born outside Europe live in, or close to, metropolitan areas. Jobs and close relationships are crucial factors.[25]

Interesting is also, that Bickley and Mladin observes a significant sense of religious discrimination among Londoners representing minority religions. They are of the opinion that governments have passed legislation which makes life more rather than less difficult. More generally, the approach of public authorities towards faith groups is regarded as reactive, crisis-driven and need-based. Faith groups are seen as levers (following austerity cuts) rather than partners. It is clear that poor religious literacy is a significant obstacle to more constructive engagement between faith communities and public bodies. These results can easily be applied to Swedish conditions, especially when it comes to the position of international Pentecostals. The anthropologist Jan-Åke Alvarsson believes that general poor religious literacy concerning religious minorities in Sweden leads to a general phobia directed towards religion, and that "pentephobia" is part of such an expression.[26]

An aspect that is often missing in general analyses of migration are the motives behind the travel of the individual. As the Respond-project has stated,[27] refugees should be viewed as "translators", not as passive actors who merely submit to policies. The project defines refugees as people who have been forced to find creative solutions to life in new and threatening situations and to deal with these new situations with both energy and newly-discovered knowledge. Such a view undermines the idea of "victims" entering a receiving country.[28]

This view is useful with respect to Pentecostal arrivals in Sweden, given that they are not only refugees but also international travellers who have goals of their own. One such objective is to bring fresh spirituality to a country which they think is in need of existential identity.[29] Sometimes this movement from the south to the north is called mission in reverse, a notion which is less fruitful in a global context. Behind this idea is the fact that proselytism is central to the social engagement of Pentecostals with the aim to evangelize secular Sweden.

Global Religion in a Cosmopolitan World Order

In his book *Pentecostalism: The World Their Parish*, David Martin confirms that one of the largest global shifts in the religious market since the 1970s is the growth of Pentecostalism and charismatic Christianity.[30] He argues, however, that neither Pentecostalism nor Evangelicalism makes much impact in Europe a situation explained by European exceptionalism. Estimates of religious change are however hindered by the tendency to limit the definition of religion to its "hot" and institutional forms.[31] On the contrary, urban areas are hubs of non-institutional religion which can indeed be based on Protestant private piety but can also relate to secular pilgrimages to cathedrals, sacred places, parks or forests – what I call a "cool" or soft cultural religion. Both forms of religiosity emphasize existential values of meaning and identity.[32]

In order to understand David Martin's thesis that for Pentecostals "the world is their parish" the notion of a cosmopolitan world order is helpful. This is the idea that all human beings are, or could be, members of a single community. Different views of what constitutes this community may include a focus on moral standards, economic practices, political structures and cultural forms. As an example, the philosopher K. A. Appiah suggests the possibility of a cosmopolitan community in which individuals from varying locations (physical, economic, cultural) enter into relationships of mutual respect despite their different beliefs (religious or political).[33] Cosmopolitanism can thus be defined as a form of global politics that, first, projects a sociality of common political engagement among human beings across the globe, and, second, suggests that this sociality should either be ethically or organizationally privileged over other forms of sociality.

As indicated above, Pentecostalism can be studied as part of metropolitan areas that houses different diasporic people. My claim is that this diasporic ethos can be understood both in terms of David Martin's phrase "Pentecostalism: the world their parish", and in relation to K.A. Appiah's idea that a global cosmopolitan community is composed of different religious and political beliefs that make up the "cosmos". This also means that the Pentecostal global parish includes different political (national) and ethical views which aim to build a privileged sociality of common world support and solidarity. International Pentecostals in the Stockholm area, are indeed part of such a community.[34]

From the work of the Swedish psychologist of religion Önver Cetrez, and sociologist of religion Magdalena Nordin, we know that Assyrian youth and Swedish-Chileans tend to adapt to the religious level discovered in the recipient country.[35] The same tendency is evident in the so-called Migrant World Values Survey (MWVS) where migrants' values are compared to both the country of origin and to the values of the recipient society, in this case Sweden. Such comparative data were published for the first time by Pippa Norris and Ronald Inglehart in a general study of *Muslim Integration into Western Cultures. Between Origins and Destinations*.[36] The results show that Muslim migrants place themselves at a mid-point with respect to the values that prevail in the country of origin and the recipient country in areas as diverse as democracy, gender equality, personal relationships (abortion, divorce, homosexuality) and religion.

In a similar study of 6516 non-European migrants in Sweden, Bi Puranen is able to show that migrants really do adapt to Swedish secular and liberal values, but that this does not include religious and family values in their entirety.[37] The decisive factor behind these changes of values is the amount of time spent in the country and the generation that the migrant belongs to. Bi Puranen emphasizes that the issue that is most confusing for migrants is the transition from cultures based on short-lives-stories with high birth rates and short lifespan to cultures, like the Swedish, with long-lives-stories, low birth rates and long-life-experiences. This represents a journey from traditional, authoritarian, collective decision-making cultures, based on religious values, to individualistic, non-authoritarian, freedom-based decision-making cultures based on secular values.

Bi Puranen summarizes the results in an interesting critical discussion on the major theoretical idea behind the WVS, namely that the change of values not only depends on the replacement of generations but can be part of the accommodation of the individual in a new cultural environment.[38] This means that values will change also after the formative years of life. A general growth of emancipative values increases, for example, women's self-esteem, self-confidence and self-sufficiency.[39] This shift of values follows certain patterns, as Ronald Inglehart and Christopher Weltzer have shown in what they call a sequential theory of modernization.[40] They argue that the rise of secular values precedes an increase in emancipative changes. This is because religion (in itself) is perceived to be patriarchal and to prevent women's emancipation in terms of sexuality and reproduction. It is important to note, however, that religion is measured by three questions only, which together make up the index of religiosity in the MWVS study. It is this index which is set against secular values in the so-called cultural map.[41]

These are the tensions in which international Pentecostals find themselves. They mainly come from parts of the global south where short-life-stories dominate. As a result, the adaptation to the logics of long-life-stories is demanding, noting in addition that this complex transition forms part of a liminal phase of life.[42] In such a situation, newly arrived migrants usually look back to the society and culture they have left. After approximately twelve years in the new country, the gaze is gradually turned forward with an increased belief in a future life in Sweden. Interestingly, Bi Puranen also stresses that trust in the Global South is normally directed inward towards one's own family or an extended family. In Sweden, however, trust is, for better or worse, primarily directed outwards towards the institutions of the welfare state.[43]

In this situation Pentecostal parishes function as a bridge between in-group-trust and a out-group-trust. On the one hand, they are local environments preserving languages and traditions with which members of the communities are familiar. On the other, they are helping new arrivals to navigate the jungle of authorities that exist in Sweden.[44] Bit by bit, it becomes clear that certain Swedish values are non-negotiable (democracy, gender equality, individual human rights and – most especially – children's rights) while other values are part of the ongoing negotiations between different voices in society, including the Pentecostals'.

In sum, this means that the response to the phrase "becoming Swedish-becoming secular" is both "yes" and "no". At one and the same time, international Pentecostals adapt to the emancipative values legitimized by the state while maintaining their religious outlook on life, in an attempt to combine both Swedish citizenship and an emphasis on family values.

Charismatic Leadership and the Privatization of Authority

In this section I will suggest that leadership among international Pentecostals should be analysed from the perspective of changes in the nature of authority. In fact, Pentecostal communities illustrate the multiplicity of authorities among religious leaders. It is often claimed that leadership within Pentecostal communities are based on charismatic authority which is given through prayer and laying on of hands, an authority that becomes visible through the powers of the Holy Spirit. There is also, however, a charismatic authority which is based on the interaction with members of the community and in the locality in question.

So, on the one hand authority is given by God which is illustrated by the charismatic powers of the leader. On the other hand, however, the pastors display an earned authority delegated by the members of the community and illustrated by the social relations that constitute the relevant interaction. This authority is also charismatic but it is clearly connected to the members of the community and the social surroundings in the society in question. This complex nature of authority is especially evident in the communities studied where the pastors are expected to represent the values of secular Sweden at the same time as they are expected to represent longstanding relations to the community through the exercise of spiritual powers in prayer or healing. The pastors interviewed in the three communities under review display, thus, a complex view of authority, which is illustrated in the strong influence of the pastor in the recruitment of members, in social issues of the community, in teaching, in healing practices and in mission activities directed towards the locality.

As the American sociologist Peter Berger has claimed, countries with strong state-church relationships, supported by a strong – but receding – social democracy, are some of the best places to investigate value shifts taking place on a macro level.[45] This involves not only an ongoing shift towards the privatization of religion but a more general shift towards the privatization of authority, which creates not only new hybridity's but multiple identities, which are important to identify.

Max Weber's theory of authority is helpful in understanding this change.[46] In Weber's view, authority is moving from traditional authority, via rational-legal authority, towards charismatic authority – the latter, moreover, is becoming a distinctive part of the twenty-first century. On the one hand, the theory indicates a link between a change in the nature of authority and an historical pathway towards the present situation with its emphasis on the individual and his or her gifts. But on the other, the theory also illustrates three competing ways of understanding authority both globally and locally. The basis for the theory is the growing speed of change and the difficulty in maintaining traditional views in a modern media-based society. As a result, individuals need to become increasingly flexible in their thinking, a shift that is illustrated in the following figure.

As Figure 7.1 suggests, the developments move primarily from rigidity to flexibility and from centralization (doing things in the right way) to de-centralization (doing the right things). As indicated, there are two different types of charismatic authority: one based in a religious authority which is given "from above" and manifested through spiritual gifts, and another based in an individually-developed authority. In this discourse, authority is something earned not given and is based on moral, cultural and religious maturity. According to the theory, members of the community in question delegate their power to the leader. This means that the power so delegated could be withdrawn by the group, especially if the authority becomes routinized.

Exactly that happened in a congregation in the south of Sweden, a process documented in an ethnographic study by Anders P. Lundberg.[47] The relationship between the pastor and the congregation reflected an unwritten but assumed

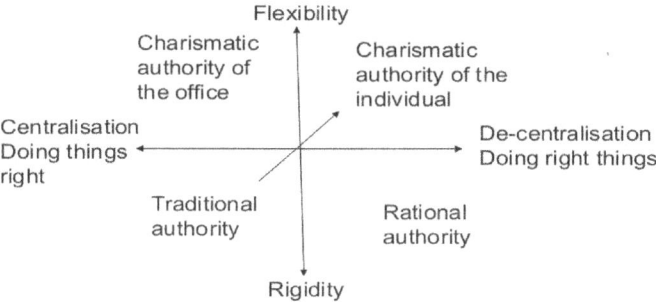

Figure 7.1. How flexibility between different types of authority might be exercised.

contract between pastor and congregation. According to this contract the pastor was expected to protect the congregants from illness and death. When a member of the community dies a crisis hits the congregation which breaks apart. In order to save the community, the pastor resorts to calling on the structures of plausibility, a notion developed by Peter Berger and Thomas Luckmann,[48] and implying that relationships in a community are upheld by a common world-view. This does not work, however, and the congregation disperses. As Émir Mahieddin describes in Chapter 5, neo-Pentecostal communities are fragile as they are kept together by a common cultural and religious background that crumbles over time. Hence the lack of clarity about what kind of authority is exercised by the religious leadership in international Pentecostal communities characterized by a high turnover of individuals. The theoretical understanding is complex in nature and it would benefit from further empirical investigation.

The Secular State and Religion as a Policy Area

I will begin this fourth section by clarifying the different definitions of the secular and their content in relation to the research on religious diversity, and the tendency of the secular state to establish religion as a new policy area, due to growing migration and the need to promote values connected to individual freedom, tolerance and democracy. This also applies to the late modern focus on the individual in places where the imagined stories of society have become fragmented and are taking on new and global forms.

The late modern idea of the freedom of the individual to construct his or her thoughts beyond traditional moral values elevates the importance of both the individual and the contextual. Put differently, a unified view of modern society has turned into what the sociologist Shmuel Eisenstadt calls multiple modernities, the thought that there is not only one modernity in the world, but several parallel modernities, not all of which need to be secular.[49]

The American sociologist Craig Calhoun reminds us that secularism is a political concept, the core of which is to separate religion from the public sphere.[50] As the sociologist of religion José Casanova argues, the historical process that we call secularization, which includes the transfer of authority from institutions to the individual, is often confused with the political idea or ideology of secularism.[51] For democracy to develop, it is the acceptance of pluralism rather than secularism that is required. Indeed, in a religiously and socially diverse society, secularism may become an obstacle that prevents religious communities from taking part in public life. Conversely, the German sociologist Hans Joas states that a plural society has the capacity to create the political freedom for religion to develop in different ways.[52]

Interestingly, this development of pluralism not only makes the choices of the individual fundamental, it also offers space for communities and networks to promote their values in a competitive market, as argued by the Swedish political scientist Marie Demker.[53] What we see today is that religion is given space in the public conversation, together with science, politics, law and culture, with the aim of creating a good society for all citizens. As I have argued previously the creation of a new ecology of conversation and cooperation is called for.[54] A challenge for the public authorities to accept is that international Pentecostals and their communities very often want to become full members of the receiving country without relinquishing their religious affiliation. This approach is of course possible, as Victoria Enkvist writes in her chapter, but the situation requires increased knowledge of the legal conditions for this acceptance to become realized (see also Mosa Sayed above).

Religion is today regarded as a policy area between the state and civil society. This becomes evident in the evaluation of two conflicting perspectives on social development as argued by the historian Lars Trägårdh.[55] The first is based on a neo-Tocquevillian understanding which represents the Anglo-American tradition. In this tradition, civil society is celebrated for community building and the provision of welfare and altruism; it follows that the individual is considered closely connected to the communities of civil society. The second perspective is rooted in a neo-Hegelian tradition which is firmly embedded in the Swedish social contract. Here, the state is understood to be the protector of common interests and individual autonomy as opposed to civil society which is seen as a site for particular interests and political action.

The deep mentalities associated with two very different social contracts explain why certain elements are celebrated while others are feared. In Sweden the state is regarded as a friend to the individual; it guaranties the freedom and liberties of the individual, protecting them from for example religious bonds. The tensions between these perspectives are particularly evident when the rights of children and religious schools are analysed, but it also occurs with reference to medical and social care. These discussions echo the underlying logics of the Swedish neo-Hegelian tradition and the values embedded in statist individualism. Here the alliance between the individual and the state is more important than the alliance between the individual and civil society as seen in the neo-Tocquevillian approach.

Linnea Lundgren has used Trägårdh's analysis of the two conflicting perspectives by looking at government commission reports on church-state and civil society-state relations during the years 1952–2019. She confirms that the discussion surrounding the visibility of minority religions is nothing new.[56] The discussion is shaped by the Swedish long-term and underlying political and moral logics of path dependency. This can be tracked over the whole period, but it quite clearly evolves, due to the constantly changing context, which informs two significant policy shifts. The first occurred in 1974, the point when minority religious communities were recognized through the new law on multiculturalism. During this period a strictly religious, indeed privatized, religion was preferred and welcomed by the state. The second shift occurs alongside the church-state reforms of 2000. This sparked a new interest in religion through the need for the neutral state to develop arguments concerning its involvement in religious matters. The idea of neutrality and of the multicultural became central to the rhetoric of the state, concepts which tend to disguise the real interests of the state in controlling religion. On the one hand, according to Lundgren, the state claims that minority religious communities should be supported in order to promote the idea of pluralism. But on the other, the communities in question must comply with the fundamental values of society, for example gender equality.[57] Such discrepancies make it difficult to discern the underlying motives of the state.

These developments introduce a crucial dilemma for the state: is religion a risk or a resource in society? The risk perspective is connected with the integrity of the individual while the resource perspective is connected with the needs of the state. It is exactly these tensions that pave the way for understanding religion as a crucial policy area. Religious minorities such as Pentecostals are a risk in so far as they represent an alleged example of hot religion; at the same time, however, they are welcomed by the state because of their ability to care for migrants and the most vulnerable in society.

In sum, I argue that this theoretical model is relevant to a study of Pentecostalism. Through their historical connection with the US, Pentecostals have become part of a global religious market with roots in American soil. This linked the development of Pentecostalism to the global expansion of American values of voluntarism and a free market during the twentieth century. The thesis put forward by two journalists from *The Economist*, John Micklethwait and Adrian Wooldridge, argues that a global Anglo-American-style religion appeared in the 1980s among Pentecostals in terms of expansion (mission), upward mobility from working-class to middle-class social identity (education), entrepreneurial spirit (economy) and political (conservative) values, which on the whole strengthen traditional family, sexual and community ideals.[58]

David Martin argues, further, that Pentecostals are indeed part of the global market of religion.[59] This does not mean, however, that they necessarily conform to the neo-liberal economic sphere. It is true that Pentecostalism began in the voluntary sector, where free competition for members was accepted as normal, but this does not make Pentecostals automatic partisans of a market free-for-all. Rather Pentecostals form strong communities lying between the state and the individual offering services that are not provided by the state. Such communities are not overly individualistic as the benefits they offer are dependent on a combination of personal and communal discipline. Pentecostals are thus free entrepreneurs in the religious market, using marketing devices and organizational forms, but it is wrong to see this simply as an example of a Protestant Ethic leading to disciplined economic endeavour.[60]

A second point follows from this: Pentecostal mega-churches are clearly a form of global religion which resembles international corporations. In the global south this religious sphere includes educational, medical and recreational provision, and even in some cases financial institutions. Thus, this religious model constitutes a principal form of voluntary organization, not just one voluntary organization among others.

As David Martin points out these forms of global religion are very different from the inherent model of religion in Europe. Typically, this kind of active voluntary sector is found in the US and in parts of Sub-Saharan Africa, Latin America and Asia, continents from which the members of the international Pentecostal communities in the Stockholm area have arrived. According to David Martin, this explains both why Pentecostalism develops strongly in societies which are organized according to the voluntary principle and why the Nordic model makes it harder for such a sector to develop.[61]

Conclusion

This chapter has discussed the growing presence of international Pentecostals in metropolitan Stockholm, using theoretical models drawn from the sociology of religion to frame the empirical results of the research project. The chapter departs from the idea that the urban not only mirrors modernity, pluralism and tolerance, but is in addition part of a global market containing new forms of spirituality detached from institutions and flexible in belief. The urban is also open to gender equality within all areas of commerce and culture. Thus, London and Paris are excellent examples of metropolitan cities, connected as they are by an urban elite. Stockholm is now approaching such a status.

The global character of these new forms of religion may be viewed as a counter-tendency to traditional secularization theory. Religion has always been of interest to the state, but the growing separation between state and church advocated during the twentieth century has been challenged by new questions, as religion becomes once again a policy area of growing significance. At the same time, increasing levels of migration prompt searching questions regarding value change, notably the ways in which this is or is not dependent on the replacement of generations.[62]

This brings us back to the introduction to this chapter where I argued that that the notion of Europe as an exceptional case has also been challenged. It is quite clear that Sweden is a social-democratic, state-controlled and neo-Hegelian society where certain values connected to democracy and equality are non-negotiable. But it is equally clear that since the 1980s Sweden has moved in a liberal direction when it comes to individual choice, freedom of expression and values related to the neo-liberal market. Thus, theories of a growing Anglo-American voluntaristic (neo-Tocquevillian) view of the society and of a neo-Hegelian path-dependency development in the European north both have explanatory value. The global market, new media connections, and new religious groups arriving in Sweden, encourage this development. What neither theory exhibits, however, are the current changes associated with increasing migration, and clarified by the MWVS study, which reveal that migrants themselves are affected by their time in Sweden – becoming increasingly private, emancipated, secular and sometimes becoming post-Pentecostals. This most certainly happens, but at the same time migrants are likely to retain religious and family values which are closer to the idea of a voluntary organization. As I have suggested, both these tendencies can be captured by the idea of citizenship as a cohesive factor in a Sweden which draws together both different individual authorities and different religious communities.

The number of international Pentecostal communities represent a multiculturality through their backgrounds in different continents with very varied languages and cultures. At the same time, they represent a lived religious experience which is captured in local neo-Pentecostal communities. Each community is at a different stage of integration and is thus at a specific point of cultural transformation between Swedish and African, Latin-American or Arab cultures, a transformation that also affects the leadership of the communities in question. It is clear that community leaders are caught between two expressions of a charismatic authority, first a charismatic authority given by God and made visible through the powers of the Holy Spirit, and second a charismatic authority delegated by the members of the community and made visible through the maturity of the individual. Both authorities are however an integral part of the speed of change in which the growth of the individual is a sign of an authentic leadership.

In what is undoubtedly a liminal state, the religious factor becomes identity-shaping. As migrants they alter between a form of trust which is directed towards the family where the logic of short-lives-stories dominate and a different form of trust which is directed towards public authorities within the logics of long-time-stories. In such a situation, religious identity makes sense beyond being Nigerian, Swedish and immigrant.

Pentecostal migrants in the Stockholm area are an excellent example of all these changes. Pentecostalism is a growing global phenomenon that creates links between host and home countries (through new communications), stimulates the economy in both host and home countries (through market competition), affects the landscape of host societies (through mission), but is also affected by the ethos of equality in secular Sweden (in order to become integrated). Thus, Pentecostalism can be studied as part of the evolution of metropolitan areas that house many diasporic people, who display both rigid and fluid connections, who are both traditional and liberal in mindset, and whose futures indicate a new transnational ethos that is beyond political control. Inevitable questions follow. Will this development result in the framing of new inter-cultural trajectories and new secular-religious negotiations based in metropolitan Stockholm, especially in suburbs where the native population and culture no longer has a majority position? And what role will international Pentecostals take in the negotiations between individual freedom and choice on the one hand and collective identities related to the voluntary sector on the other? The answers are for future research to discover.

Anders Bäckström is professor emeritus in the sociology of religion at the Faculty of Theology, Uppsala University. His research has focused on questions of the "new" visibility of religion in contemporary society and the role of religion in different welfare systems. He established the Linnaeus research programme at Uppsala University called "The Impact of Religion: Challenges for Society, Law and Democracy". One of his latest publications concerns "Research on Religion and Society: Experiences from the Emergence of a Centre of Excellence at Uppsala University 1997–2019" (*Studies in Religion & Society*, vol. 18, 2020).

Acknowledgement

This work was supported by the Swedish Research Council (no. VR 2018-01438).

Notes

1. See www.torontomu.ca/cerc-migration (accessed 9 February 2022).
2. See Chapter 1, this volume, for a description of the research project presented and the material analysed in this volume.
3. Zygmunt Bauman, "Morality in an Age of Contingency", in Paul Heelas, Scott Lash and Paul Morris, *Detraditionalization: Critical Reflections on Authority and Identity* (Oxford: Blackwell, 1996), pp. 49-58.
4. Anders Bäckström, "The WaVE project as a record of religious and social transformations in northern Europe", in Molokotos-Liederman, Lina with Anders Bäckström and Grace Davie (eds.) *Religion and Welfare in Europe: Gendered and Minority Perspectives* (Bristol: Policy Press, 2017), pp. 77–105.
5. The Swedish word "sval" is translated as "cool". It refers to an inclusive (mild) religiosity that is closely related to existential spirituality and cultural identity.
6. Henrik Berggren and Lars Trägårdh, *Är svensken människa? Gemenskap och oberoende i det moderna Sverige* [*Are Swedes Human? Community and Independence in Modern Sweden*] (Stockholm: Norstedts, 2015).
7. David Martin, "The Relevance of the European Model of Secularization in Latin America and Africa", in Hans Joas and Klaus Wiegandt (eds), *Secularization and the World Religions* (Liverpool: Liverpool University Press, 2009), pp. 278–295.
8. David Thurfjell and Erika Willander, *Postmuslimer: Om sekularitet i ett mångreligiöst Sverige* [*Post-Muslims: On Secularity in a Multi-religious Sweden*] (Stockholm: Myndigheten för stöd till trossamfund, SST, 2023).
9. Compare Nancy Ammerman, *Studying Lived Religion: Contexts and Practices* (New York: New York University Press, 2021).
10. Victoria Enkvist, *Religionsfrihetens rättsliga ramar* [*A Framework for Religious Freedom under Swedish Law*] (Uppsala: Iustus förlag), p. 80.
11. Thorleif Pettersson and Yilmaz Esmer, *Vilka är annorlunda? Om invandrares möte med svensk kultur* [*Who is Different? Immigrant Encounters with Swedish Culture*]. Integrationsverkets rapportserie (Stockholm: Stockholms stadsbibliotek, 2005).

12 Anders P. Lundberg and Nils Malmström, *Afrikanska pentekostaler på svensk mark* [*African Pentecostals in Sweden*] (Skellefteå: Artos and Norma Bokförlag 2021), p.222.
13 My italics. The Constitution, Chapter 2, § 2. The Law 2010: 1408.
14 Johan Modée, "Religion, tolerans och frihet" ["Religion, Tolerance and Freedom"], in Dan-Erik Andersson and Johan Modée (eds), *Mänskliga rättigheter och religion* [*Human Rights and Religion*] (Malmö: Liber, 2011), p. 20.
15 See Chapter 1, this volume, for a discussion of religion in the Swedish society.
16 Anders Bäckström and Grace Davie, *Uppsala University as a Hub for Multidisciplinary Research on Religion, Law and Society: A Tribute to Maarit Jänterä-Jareborg* (Uppsala: Iustus förlag), 2022.
17 Maarit Jänterä-Jareborg, "Transnationella familjer ur ett internationellt privaträttsligt perspektiv-särskilt avseende äktenskap" ["Transnational Families from an International Private Law Perspective – Especially with Regard to Marriage"], in A. Singer, M. Jänterä-Jareborg and A. Schlytter, *Familj, Religion, Rätt: En antologi om kulturella spänningar i familjen – med Sverige och Turkiet som exempel* (Uppsala: Iustus förlag, 2010), pp. 205–241.
18 Mosa Sayed, *Islam och arvsrätt i det mångkulturella Sverige. En internationellt privaträttslig och jämförande studie* [*Islam and Inheritance Law in Multicultural Sweden. A Study in Private International Law*] (Uppsala: Iustus förlag, 2009).
19 Grace Davie, "Revisiting Secularization in Light of Growing Diversity: The European Case", *Religions* 14: 1119, https://doi.org/10.3390/rel14091119 (accessed 19 November 2023).
20 See Chapter 5, this volume, where Émir Mahieddin argues that commuting is in itself a "place".
21 See Chapter 5 for a discussion of the meaning of suburban as place for believing.
22 Paul Bickley and Nathan Mladin, *Religious London: Faith in a Global City* (London: Theos, 2020), p. 11.
23 David Goodhew and Anthony-Paul Cooper (eds), *The Desecularisation of the City: London's Churches, 1980 to the Present* (London: Routledge, 2018), p. 8.
24 Thurfjell and Willander, *Postmuslimer*.
25 Bi Puranen, *Med migranternas röst II: Hur blir man värmlänning?* [*With the Voice of the Migrants II: How Do You Become a Member of the County of Värmland?*] (Stockholm: Institutet för framtidsstudier, 2021), p. 54.
26 Jan-Åke Alvarsson (ed.), *Pentecostalismen i Sverige på 2020-talet* [*Pentocostalism in Sweden in the 2020s*] (Skellefteå: Artos and Norma Bokförlag), p. 56. See also Chapter 4, this volume, where discrimination among international Pentecostals in Sweden is displayed.
27 See www.crs.uu.se/forskning/respond (accessed 14 May 2021). See also Soner Barthoma and Önver A. Cetrez, *Responding to Migration: A Holistic Perspective on Migration Governance* (Uppsala: Uppsala University Library, 2021).
28 This view, moreover, is underpinned by the Nobel Prize Laureate in Literature 2021, Dr Abdulrazak Gurnah, who emphasized, in an interview on Swedish national television (2 October 2021), that most migrants enter a new country with ambition, youth and resources.
29 See Chapter 5 of this volume for a more extended discussion of the missional objectives among the studied groups.
30 David Martin, *Pentecostalism: The World Their Parish* (Oxford: Blackwell, 2002), p. 167.
31 See also Chapter 1 of this volume for a discussion of the institutional form of religion in Sweden.

32 In Chapter 4 of this volume Katarina Westerlund discusses meaning and identity among international Pentecostals.
33 Kwame Anthony Appiah, *Cosmopolitanism: Ethics in a World of Strangers* (London: W. W. Norton, 2007). The former United Nations secretary-general Kofi Annan endorses this book as follows: "At its core, *Cosmopolitanism* is a reasoned appeal for mutual respect and understanding among the world's people. Anthony Appiah's belief in having conversations across boundaries, and in recognizing our obligations to other human beings, offers a welcome prescription for a world still plagued by fanaticism and intolerance. This volume's message is of enormous relevance to the work of the United Nations, and I hope it will be heard far and wide."
34 One problem is, however, that the existence of a Cosmopolitan world order is weakened by military conflicts in the world.
35 Önver A. Cetrez, *Meaning-Making Variations in Acculturation and Ritualization: A Multi-generational Study of Suroyo Migrants in Sweden* (Acta Universitatis Upsaliensis. Psychologia et Sociologia Religionum 17, 2005); Magdalena Nordin, *Religiositet bland migranter: Sverige-chilenares förhållande till religion och samfund* [*Religiosity among Migrants. Swedish-Chileans' Relation to Religion and Communions*] (Lund Studies in Sociology of Religion, Volume 5, 2004).
36 Pippa Norris and Ronald Inglehart, "Muslim Integration into Western Cultures: Between Origins and Destinations", *Political Studies* 60(2) (2012), pp. 228–251.
37 Bi Puranen, *Med migranternas röst I: Den subjektiva integrationen* [*With the Voice of the Migrants I: The Subjective Integration*] Forskningsrapport 2019/2 (Stockholm: Institutet för Framtidsstudier, 2019), p. 61; Puranen, *Med migranternas röst II*, p. 382. Bi Puranen is secretary general of the World Values Survey (WVS). The following countries of origin are included in the study: Syria (one-third of the material), Afghanistan, Eritrea, Iran, Iraq, Somalia, the Middle East and North Africa (MENA) region and Turkey. Of these, 40% arrived in Sweden in 2014 or earlier and the rest in 2015 or later.
38 Puranen, *Med migranternas röst II*, p. 74.
39 See also Chapter 4, this volume, which exemplifies women in the Pentecostal communities that appreciate equality and freedom in Sweden.
40 Ronald Inglehart and Christopher Weltzer, *Modernization, Cultural Change and Democracy: The Human Development Sequence* (New York: Cambridge University Press, 2005).
41 The questions in the WVS study that investigate religious commitment have changed over the years. Three were used in this material: (1) Indicate how important religion is in your life. (2) Whether you participate in religious ceremonies or not, would you say you are (a) a religious person, (b) not a religious person or (c) an atheist? (3) In addition to weddings and funerals, how often do you participate in religious ceremonies today? (a) More often than once a week, (b) once a week, (c) once a month, (d) only at especially holy celebrations or (e) about once a year. Puranen, *Med migranternas röst II*, p. 173.
42 See the anthropologist Victor Turner classic description of liminality: Victor Turner, *The Ritual Process: Structure and Anti-structure* (London: Routledge & Kegan Paul, 1969).
43 Puranen, *Med migranters röst I*, p. 208.
44 See Chapters 4 and 5, this volume, for more details about the struggles to navigate in the Swedish society.
45 Peter Berger (ed.), *The De-secularization of the World: Resurgent Religion and World Politics* (Grand Rapids, MI: William B. Eerdmans Publishing Company, 1999).
46 Max Weber, *Economy and Society: An Outline in Interpretive Sociology*, vol. 3 (Berkeley, CA: University of California Press, 1978), ch. XIV.

47 Anders P. Lundberg, "When all Comes Crumbling Down: A Nigerian Pastor and His Congregation in the Diaspora", *PentecoStudies* 19(1) (2020), pp. 62–80.
48 Peter Berger and Thomas Luckmann. *The Social Construction of Reality. A Treatise in the Sociology of Knowledge* (London: Penguin, 1967).
49 Shmuel Eisenstadt, "Multiple Modernities", *Daedalus: Journal of the American Academy of Arts and Sciences* (Winter 2000), pp. 1–29.
50 Craig Calhoun, "Secularism, Citizenship, and the Public Sphere", in Craig Calhoun, Mark Juergensmeyer and Jonathan van Antwerpen (eds), *Rethinking Secularism* (Oxford: Oxford University Press, 2011), pp. 75–91.
51 José Casanova, "The Secular, Secularization, Secularisms", in Craig Calhoun, Mark Juergensmeyer and Jonathan van Antwerpen (eds), *Rethinking Secularism* (Oxford: Oxford University Press, 2011), pp. 54–74.
52 Hans Joas, *Faith as an Option: Possible Futures for Christianity* (Stanford, CA: Stanford University Press, 2014).
53 Marie Demker, "Vilken plats vill kyrkan ha i den offentliga debatten?" ["Prospects for a Transformed Church in Public Debate?"], in Anders Bäckström and Anders Wejryd (eds), *Sedd men osedd: Om folkkyrkans paradoxala närvaro inför 2020-talet* [*Seen but Unseen: On the Paradoxical Presence of a Folk Church in the 2020s*] (Stockholm: Verbum, 2016), pp. 53–65.
54 Anders Bäckström, "The WaVE Project as a Record of Religious and Social Transformations in Northern Europe", in Lina Molokotos-Liederman with Anders Bäckström and Grace Davie, *Religion and Welfare in Europe: Gendered and Minority Perspectives* (Bristol: Policy Press, 2017), p. 96.
55 Lars Trägårdh, "Rethinking the Nordic Welfare State through a Neo-Hegelian Theory of State and Civil Society", *Journal of Political Ideologies* 15(3) (2010), pp. 227–230.
56 Linnea Lundgren, *A Risk or a Resource? A Study of the Swedish State's Shifting Perception and Handling of Minority Religious Communities between 1952-2019* (Stockholm: Ersta, Sköndal, Bräcke University College, 2021).
57 Ibid., p. 321.
58 John Micklethwait and Adrian Wooldridge, *God is Back: How the Global Rise of Faith is Changing the World* (London: Penguin, 2009), p. 220.
59 David Martin, "Voluntarism: Niche Markets Created by a Fissile Transnational Faith", in Robert W. Hefner, John Hutchinson, Sara Mels and Christiane Timmerman (eds), *Religions in Movement: The Local and the Global in Contemporary Faith Traditions* (New York: Routledge, 2013), pp. 180–195.
60 Donald E. Miller and Tetsunao Yamamori, *Global Pentecostalism: The New Face of Christian Social Engagement* (Berkeley, CA: University of California Press, 2007), p. 165. They write: "Hence the Pentecostal ethic is very similar to the Protestant ethic – namely, it produces people who are honest, disciplined, transparent in their business dealings, people who view their vocation, humble and elevated, as a calling by God that warrants commitment."
61 This discussion does not include civil society-organizations in Sweden which are part of the Folk movements and which about 50% of the population are related to.
62 Compare Pippa Norris and Ronald Inglehart, *Cultural Backlash: Trump, Brexit and Authoritarian Populism* (New York: Cambridge University Press, 2019).

Bibliography

Alvarsson, Jan-Åke (ed.). *Pentekostalismen i Sverige på 2020-talet* [*Pentecostalism in Sweden in the 2020s*]. Skellefteå: Artos & Norma Bokförlag, 2021.
Ammerman, Nancy T. *Studying Lived Religion: Contexts and Practices*. New York: New York University Press, 2021.
Anderson, Allan Heaton. *To the Ends of the World: Pentecostalism and the Transformation of World Christianity*. Oxford: Oxford University Press, 2013.
Appiah, Kwame Anthony. *Cosmopolitanism: Ethics in a World of Strangers*. London: W. W. Norton, 2007.
Barthoma, Soner and Önver A. Cetrez. *Responding to Migration: A Holistic Perspective on Migration Governance*. Uppsala: Uppsala University Library, 2021.
Bauman, Zygmunt. "Morality in an Age of Contingency." In Paul Heelas, Scott Lash and Paul Morris (eds), *Detraditionalization: Critical Reflections on Authority and Identity*. Oxford: Blackwell, 1996.
Berger, Peter (ed.) *The De-secularization of the World: Resurgent Religion and World Politics*. Grand Rapids, MI: William B. Eerdmans Publishing Company, 1999.
Berger, Peter and Thomas Luckmann. *The Social Construction of Reality: A Treatise in the Sociology of Knowledge*. London: Penguin, 1967.
Berggren, Henrik and Lars Trägårdh. *Är svensken människa? Gemenskap och oberoende i det moderna Sverige* [*Are Swedes Human? Community and Independence in Modern Sweden*]. Stockholm: Norstedts, 2015.
Bickley, Paul and Nathan Mladin. *Religious London: Faith in a Global City*. London: Theos, 2020. www.theosthinktank.co.uk/cmsfiles/Religious-London-FINAL-REPORT-24.06.2020.pdf
Bäckström, Anders. "The WaVE Project as a Record of Religious and Social Transformations in Northern Europe." in Molokotos-Liederman, Lina with Anders Bäckström and Grace Davie (eds.) *Religion and Welfare in Europe: Gendered and Minority Perspectives*. Bristol: Policy Press, 2017.
Bäckström, Anders. *Forskning om religion och samhälle. Erfarenheter av en centrumbildnings framväxt och etablering vid Uppsala universitet 1997-2019* [*Research on Religion and Society. Experiences from the Emergence of a Centre of Excellence at Uppsala University 1997-2019*]. Uppsala: Acta Universitatis Upsaliensis, 2020.
Bäckström, Anders and Grace Davie. "Uppsala University as a Hub for Multidisciplinary Research on Religion, Law and Society: A Tribute to Maarit Jänterä-Jareborg." In Marie Linton and Mosa Sayed (eds), *Festskrift till Maarit Jänterä-Jareborg*. Uppsala: Iustus förlag, 2022.
Calhoun, Craig. "Secularism, Citizenship, and the Public Sphere." In Craig Calhoun, Mark Juergensmeyer and Jonathan van Antwerpen (eds), *Rethinking Secularism*. Oxford: Oxford University Press, 2011.
Casanova, José. "The Secular, Secularization, Secularisms." In Craig Calhoun, Mark Juergensmeyer and Jonathan van Antwerpen (eds), *Rethinking Secularism*. Oxford: Oxford University Press, 2011.
Cetrez, Önver A. *Meaning-Making Variations in Acculturation and Ritualization: A Multi-generational Study of Suroyo Migrants in Sweden*. Dissertation, Acta Universitatis Upsaliensis, 2005.
Davie, Grace. "London's Churches. Sociological Perspectives." In David Goodhew and Anthony-Paul Cooper (eds), *The Desecularisation of the City: London's Churches, 1980 to the Present*. London: Routledge, 2018.

Davie, Grace. "Revisiting Secularization in Light of Growing Diversity: The European Case." *Religions* 14: 1119. https://doi.org/10.3390/rel14091119.
Demker, Marie. "Vilken plats vill kyrkan ha i den offentliga debatten?" ["Prospects for a transformed church in public debate?"]. In Anders Bäckström and Anders Wejryd (eds), *Sedd men osedd. Om folkkyrkans paradoxala närvaro inför 2020-talet* [*Seen but Unseen. On the Paradoxical Presence of a Folk Church in the 2020s*]. Stockholm: Verbum, 2016.
Eisenstadt, Shmuel. "Multiple Modernities." *Daedalus* (Winter 2000).
Enkvist, Victoria. *Religionsfrihetens rättsliga ramar* [*A Framework for Religious Freedom under Swedish Law*]. Uppsala: Iustus förlag, 2013.
Goodhew, David and Anthony-Paul Cooper (eds). *The Desecularisation of the City: London's Churches, 1980 to the Present*. London: Routledge, 2018.
Inglehart, Ronald and Christopher Weltzer. *Modernization, Cultural Change and Democracy: The Human Development Sequence*. New York: Cambridge University Press, 2005.
Joas, Hans. *Faith as an Option: Possible Futures for Christianity*. Stanford, CA: Stanford University Press, 2014.
Jänterä-Jareborg, Maarit. "Transnationella familjer ur ett internationellt privaträttsligt perspektiv-särskilt avseende äktenskap" ["Transnational Families from an International Private Law Perspective, with Special Attention to Marriage"]. In A. Singer, M. Jänterä-Jareborg and A. Schlytter (eds), *Familj, Religion, Rätt. En antologi om kulturella spänningar i familjen – med Sverige och Turkiet som exempel*. Uppsala: Iustus förlag, 2010.
Lundberg, Anders P. "When All Comes Crumbling Down: A Nigerian Pastor and His Congregation in the Diaspora." *PentecoStudies* 19(1) (2020), pp. 62–80.
Lundberg, Anders P. and Nils Malmström. "Afrikanska pentekostaler på svensk mark" ["African Pentecostals in Sweden"]. In Jan-Åke Alvarsson (ed.), *Pentekostalismen i Sverige på 2020-talet*. Skellefteå: Artos & Norma Bokförlag, 2021.
Lundgren. Linnea. *A Risk or a Resource? A Study of the Swedish State's Shifting Perception and Handling of Minority Religious Communities between 1952–2019*. Dissertation, Ersta, Sköndal, Bräcke University College, Stockholm, 2021.
Martin, David. *Pentecostalism: The World Their Parish*. Oxford: Blackwell, 2002.
Martin, David. "The Relevance of the European Model of Secularization in Latin America and Africa." In Hans Joas and Klaus Wiegandt (eds), *Secularization and the World Religions*. Liverpool: Liverpool University Press, 2009.
Martin, David. "Voluntarism: Niche Markets Created by a Fissile Transnational Faith." In Robert W. Hefner, John Hutchinson, Sara Mels and Christiane Timmerman (eds), *Religions in Movement: The Local and the Global in Contemporary Faith Traditions*. New York: Routledge, 2013.
Micklethwait, John and Adrian Wooldridge. *God is Back: How the Global Rise of Faith is Changing the World*. London: Penguin Books, 2009.
Miller, Donald E. and Tetsunao Yamamori. *Global Pentecostalism: The New Face of Christian Social Engagement*. Berkeley, CA: University of California Press, 2007.
Modée, Johan. "Religion, tolerans och frihet" ["Religion, Tolerance and Freedom"]. In Dan-Erik Andersson and Johan Modée (eds), *Mänskliga rättigheter och religion* [*Human Rights and Religion*]. Malmö: Liber, 2011.
Nordin, Magdalena. *Religiositet bland migranter: Sverige-chilenares förhållande till religion och samfund* [*Religiosity among Migrants: Swedish-Chileans' Relation to Religion and Communions*]. Lund: Lund Studies in Sociology of Religion, Vol. 5, 2004.
Norris, Pippa and Ronald Inglehart. "Muslim Integration into Western Cultures: Between Origins and Destinations." *Political Studies* 60(2) (2012).

Norris, Pippa and Ronald Inglehart. *Cultural Backlash: Trump, Brexit and Authoritarian Populism*. New York: Cambridge University Press, 2019.
Pettersson, Thorleif and Yilmaz Esmer. *Vilka är annorlunda? Om invandrares möte med svensk kultur* [*Who is Different? Immigrant Encounters with Swedish Culture*]. Integrationsverkets rapportserie. Stockholm: Stockholms stadsbibliotek, 2005.
Puranen, Bi. *Med migranternas röst I: Den subjektiva integrationen* [*With the Voice of the Migrants I: The Subjective Integration*]. Forskningsrapport 2019/2. Stockholm: Institutet för Framtidsstudier, 2019.
Puranen, Bi. *Med migranternas röst II: Hur blir man värmlänning?* [*With the Voice of the Migrants II: How Do You Become a Member of the County of Värmland?*]. Stockholm: Institutet för framtidsstudier, 2021.
Sayed, Mosa. *Islam och arvsrätt i det mångkulturella Sverige: En internationellt privaträttslig och jämförande studie* [*Islam and Inheritance Law in Multicultural Sweden: A Study in Private International Law*]. Uppsala: Iustus förlag, 2009.
Thurfjell, David and Erika Willander. *Postmuslimer: Om sekularitet i ett mångreligiöst Sverige* [*Post-Muslims: On Secularity in a Multi-religious Sweden*]. Stockholm: Myndigheten för stöd till trossamfund, SST, 2023.
Trägårdh, Lars. "Rethinking the Nordic Welfare State through a neo-Hegelian Theory of State and Civil Society." *Journal of Political Ideologies* 15(3) (2010).
Turner, Victor. *The Ritual Process: Structure and Anti-structure*. London: Routledge & Kegan Paul, 1969.
Weber, Max. *Economy and Society: An Outline in Interpretive Sociology*. Berkeley, CA. University of California Press, 1978.

Chapter 8

Broadening the Perspectives: An International Outlook

Allan H. Anderson, Simon Coleman, Kim Knibbe and Pamela Slotte Russo

Introduction

In this chapter internationally renowned scholars on Pentecostalism open up the results from the volume for a wider discussion. From various scholarly disciplines – mission and Pentecostal studies, anthropology, sociology, anthropology, and religion and law – the members of the international reference group of the research project "Pentecostal Migrants in Secular Sweden: Impact and Challenges?"[1] provide additional knowledge and insights on International Pentecostalism, and point towards blind spots and new research tracks.

Pentecostal "Migrant" Churches: Towards Definitions, Understanding Differences

Allan H. Anderson

The focus of this research project is on migration and how this has affected the religious demography of the population of greater Stockholm. It raises important questions relating to other issues, including the secularization/desecularization debate, religious freedom in a secular, democratic state, and what it means to be "Swedish" as Sweden becomes more culturally, linguistically, and religiously plural. In addition to observations on "migrant" or "international" Pentecostal churches (contested terms), here there is also information on the older churches (including the former "state church", the Church of Sweden), and religious groups that have increased in the Stockholm area in recent years. The data in this book suggests that in Stockholm, the influx of migrants whose first language is not Swedish has increased the religiosity of the city and its surroundings, and so we might speak of the "desecularization" of Stockholm while observing the continuing secularization of the rest of the country. Understanding how this process works is a prerequisite. The older churches, including ethnic Swedish Pentecostal churches, have experienced a rapid decline in recent years. The immigrants not only brought new churches and an increase in Christian observance in the city, but also a significant increase in Catholic and Orthodox adherents, and of course that of other religions, especially Islam. Here I will refer to "migrant" churches for want of a better term, even though the use of the term is contentious and suggests something "other" than an "ordinary" Swedish church. It is a term often used in the literature despite its inadequacies.

This response will focus on the Pentecostals, whose profile has been raised by the influx of the new churches, mainly led and populated by recent immigrants to Sweden whose first language is other than Swedish. It is important, however, to know the identity of these "Pentecostals", and whether the differences between "migrant" churches and "native" Swedish churches are cultural, religious, or both. With the proliferation of Pentecostalism worldwide, it is now increasingly difficult to divide Pentecostalism into types or groups.[2] Sweden may need to work out its definitions and categories because they will not be the same as those in the United States or even those in other European countries. One of the reasons given for the gulf between the migrant churches and the wider Swedish society is a lack of understanding on the part of the latter. This is why this project plays such a significant role. Pentecostalism has developed into a myriad of different forms, and so we should have some understanding of what the "family resemblances" are that enable us to call them "Pentecostal" in the first place. I have suggested that one way to understand this family resemblance is that they all emphasize an experience of the Holy Spirit and the exercise of spiritual gifts.[3] Any more precise definition will have too many exceptions to be useful. So, Pentecostalism refers to a wide variety of movements all emphasizing gifts of the Spirit (especially as listed in 1 Corinthians 12) and includes Pentecostal denominations emerging in the first quarter of the twentieth century, the charismatic movement in Catholic and Protestant churches, and the independent "neo-Charismatic" churches arising since the 1970s.

There are still considerable differences between various Pentecostal groups. Walter Hollenweger suggested that Pentecostalism has six common characteristics, which form the matrix out of which global forms of the movement have developed.[4] Although there will always be multiple exceptions, these characteristics are a starting point. Firstly, there is an oral liturgy that is often spontaneous and joyful and allows every member to participate and so be empowered. Secondly, Pentecostals have a narrative theology and witness, where preachers tell stories that connect with the everyday lives of their listeners, and members (especially women) give "testimonies" of their real-life experiences of God when formal leadership is often denied them. The third feature is possibly the most significant in this discussion: a reconciliatory and participant community, where everyone is treated as an equal without regard to gender, social status, or education. For "migrant" Pentecostals, their churches have many practical functions – such as obtaining a visa, receiving employment, dealing with racism, marginalization, and rejection, finding financial help, advice regarding marriage and family affairs, or healing from sickness and other afflictions. These churches are usually caring, therapeutic communities, refuges from the storms and difficulties of a new life in a strange country, and advice and comfort centres for every possible hurdle in an uncertain external environment. Many European churches, influenced by their individualistic and secular society, have largely lost this sense of therapeutic community and belongingness that is so much a central characteristic of Pentecostalism in the majority world.

The last three characteristics relate to Pentecostal liturgies. The fourth feature may not be as significant as it was in the past, but still is found in African churches: the inclusion of visions and dreams in personal and public worship. Fifthly, there is healing and deliverance by prayer. In all the discussion about Pentecostalism, it is often not appreciated just how important a place prayer is in Pentecostal rituals, particularly when there are physical, emotional, or psychological needs. Prayer is not simply a ritual or something that a pastor recites but is a cathartic and emotional release for sufferers of stress who are affected by the host of new challenges. Finally, there is the role of celebratory music and dance, where Pentecostals worship by participating together joyfully, and often in synch with their cultural and religious traditions. This too is an effective means of relieving anxiety.

Pentecostalism has an inherent ability to be culturally and religiously relevant, whether to native Swedes who have developed their distinctive form of Pentecostalism (particularly through their ecclesiological structures) or to recent immigrants looking for a place to feel at home in what is at first a strange and sometimes hostile environment. In Africa, the proliferation of new churches in the cities was partly the result of the rapid increase in urbanization, where people flocking to the new urban environment looked for more personable forms of religious groupings where they would feel welcome. African independent churches, including Pentecostal ones, provided for that. They were not only there to provide for religious needs, but also for social ones.

From the different authors in this study, the impression is given that the new Pentecostals in Sweden do not easily integrate with the native ones. Those that do, integrate because of the "radical ecclesiology" of Swedish Pentecostals, allowing for the strictly independent congregationalism advocated by the Swedish Pentecostal pioneer Lewi Pethrus. There is little integration on a social level because local churches maintain their independence and one would assume, also their distinctive character. The research interviews reveal some migrant church members feeling alienated and misunderstood. Their faith was not perceived as "typically Swedish". There are probably many barriers to be overcome before any movement toward real integration can occur, but both cultural and linguistic factors predominate. Because Pentecostalism is easily absorbed into a given culture, the greater the differences from a "host" culture (such as Swedish culture), the less likely that recent arrivals from another, very different culture are going to feel comfortable in Swedish Pentecostal churches. The language barrier is of course another factor.

The experience of African Caribbean people in Britain, among the first new immigrants after the Second World War, is a case in point. Although their first language is English, they found British churches often unwelcoming and "cold", even in the same denominations that they had belonged to in the Caribbean. Some perceived their reception as racist. The result was that they flocked to the

Pentecostal churches that maintained the religious culture of the Caribbean, where they were made to feel at home.[5] Today there is evidence that like many other denominations in Britain, the Caribbean churches have declined, and it is the younger people born and raised in Britain who have left. The same is beginning to happen in African-led churches in the UK, where the younger members are leaving churches that they consider to be "too African". This refers to language usage, musical genres, and worship styles. The children of immigrants born and educated in the host country have a very different context than that of their parents and do not feel the same affinity for the religious culture of their parents.[6] As this research demonstrates, with time, there is a high turnover of individual adherents in these churches.

Various authors have commented on the "reverse mission" of migrant Pentecostals, the "empire strikes back" at a secular Europe.[7] The frequently expressed belief among migrant churches is that Europe, which once sent many hundreds of missionaries to the majority world, now needs to be converted by the descendants of the missionaries' converts. Their new forms of Christianity are believed to be more vibrant and relevant than the older forms in their host country, indeed bringing "fresh spirituality" to Sweden. Over the years, however, the "conversion" of the host nation has proved extremely difficult, if not impossible to achieve. Britain has had migrant churches for over sixty years. Almost without exception, the migrant churches remain culturally and ethnically separate. Apart from a tiny number of individuals, the natives of the host country do not convert and the influence of the migrant churches on the broader society is miniscule. If Sweden can be an exception to this trend, the question will be what do the new and old Pentecostals have in common? Is it a common spirituality or experience that will determine this? We come back to the discussion above, for it is seldom on theological grounds that the very real differences lie. The rise in migrant religiosity does not mean that the increasing secularization in the wider society is reversed because the "rise" is proportionate with the increase in migrant numbers that are found all over western and central Europe. The research in this book bears witness to the link between increased migration and an increase in churches, but perhaps more significantly, an increase in religious plurality.

Europe is probably by far the most "secular" continent in the world today. Pentecostalism is indeed the exception to the decline in church attendance in some parts of secular Europe, the exception to the exception. Stockholm is an example of this. Although most of Europe has a very different and less developed Pentecostalism than the rest of the world, yet Sweden and some other European countries have significant Pentecostal populations. There is a reasonably strong Charismatic or renewal movement within European established churches, and in England, Charismatic Anglican churches are among the largest in the country. In some countries, Pentecostalism is continuing to grow and defy the assumption of Christian decline. Since the disintegration of Communism, there has been more freedom for Pentecostals in Central and Eastern Europe, but this has not been without challenges. In particular, new Pentecostal groups on a quest for mission have flooded former Communist countries with aggressive evangelistic techniques leading to opposition from dominant Orthodox churches and even from national governments. Some of the new churches have succeeded in attracting large crowds. But there have been other developments: the institutionalizing of Pentecostal denominations and the creation and expansion of Pentecostal theological colleges have resulted in more inward-looking Pentecostal movements in some European countries.

There is an enormous treasure of interdisciplinary research yet to be mined on Pentecostalism. This will be facilitated by a more meaningful interaction between theologians, scholars of religion, historians, and social scientists than there has been in the past. These studies cannot be carried out in isolation from other scholarly discourses. If religion is an inherent part of culture, then it is also a dynamic, ever-changing phenomenon. In today's world, global forces are changing the nature of Pentecostalism in all its variety of different forms worldwide. The pressure is often towards uniformity, and the easy accessibility of the media accelerates this process. But some forms of Pentecostalism remain stubbornly resistant to these pressures, especially when there is an attempt to preserve a distinct identity, as is sometimes the case with migrants. An area needing further reflection and more careful analysis is the extent to which globalization and migration in contemporary, multicultural Europe affect the character of Pentecostalism. The shapes of what has emerged because of the globalization process, how transnational and international networks both resemble and differ from the older networks of denominational Pentecostalism and the extent to which Pentecostalism has permeated and affected the beliefs, values, and practices of other Christians have yet to be analysed fully. This will be a task for future Swedish scholars to take this research further. Only when these investigations have taken place will we better understand the external forces that forge the religious identities of migrants and the increasingly important role of Pentecostalism as one expression of increasing religious pluralism in Sweden today.

Stockholm: A Pentecosmopolitan City?

Simon Coleman

Pentecostalism finds a home in both mobility and the city. As a "religion made to travel",[8] its restlessness adopts many forms – not only the kinesics of inspired worship but also the experiences of displacement that accompany mission, migration, and their mutual entanglements. And as an urban (rather than an urbane) phenomenon that highlights massed human bodies as sites of spiritual agency and transformation it draws on densities and scales of population that are readily available in city spaces. Given its affinities with two of the great social and economic processes of our time – globalization and urbanization – we should not be surprised to see Pentecostalism flourishing across many parts of the world. Yet this volume asks us to examine the fate of this movement within a country that appears to provide a uniquely challenging context for its capacity to thrive: "secular", "stable", "individualist" Sweden.[9]

While reflecting on these issues while reading the chapters of this book, I could not help juxtaposing the immediate present with the recent past. As a young anthropologist based in the UK, I first came to view Sweden as a potentially fertile site for the study of Pentecostalism when planning doctoral research during the mid-1980s. In ethnographic terms, I had been intrigued by the high profile of the Word of Life (*Livets Ord*), a newly formed, neo-Pentecostal ministry that appeared to be ruffling the feathers of numerous religious, political, and cultural interests in Sweden, and which was often branded by its opponents as a malign American influence rather than an invigorating spiritual revival.[10] In analytic terms, my interest had been piqued by a figure who appears at various points in this volume: the British sociologist (and Anglican priest) David Martin. What originally attracted me was not Martin's research on global Pentecostalism – *Tongues of Fire* did not appear until 1990, and *Pentecostalism: The World Their Parish* came out in 2001. Rather, I was struck by his magisterial *A General Theory of Secularization*, published in 1978. Martin's theory was "general" but not generic as he brilliantly identified inflections of processes of secularization across different historical trajectories of church-state relations, centre–periphery divides, elite and dissenting stances, in Europe and beyond. However, a feature of his analysis that gave me pause was his characterization of Sweden as *the* heartland of secular modernity. As many others have done, before and since, Martin placed the country at the end of a non-practising spectrum; yet he had relatively little to say about the size and cultural significance of the Swedish Pentecostal movement – which, with its nearly 100,000 or so members at the time, represented an anomalous achievement within the relatively homogenous ethnic and religious landscape of the country.

Much has happened since the publication of *A General Theory*. Sweden still has the reputation of being a secular and stable polity but has become a considerably more ethnically and religiously diverse society. In addition, two of its pillars of institutional stability have developed distinct cracks. The Social Democratic Party remains the country's largest political force but its specific vision of *Folkhemmet*, the "People's Home", has been challenged by an alternative version proposed most visibly (for the moment) in the rise of the conservative, populist, anti-migrant, "Sweden Democrats".[11] The Church of Sweden became disestablished in 2000 and has rapidly been losing affiliations so that only around half of the population are now members. Moreover, secularization does not occupy quite the same space in the social scientific imagination as it did nearly half a century ago – and as a theory it has begun to reflect some of the nuances and paradoxes identified by Martin some decades ago. It is frequently counterbalanced by references to the "post-secular" and complicated by widespread assumptions that religious and secular identities are not so much engaged in a zero-sum game as mutually constitutive.[12] Most notably for our purposes, Pentecostalism as both a transnational religious movement and analytical category has been transformed. Within my discipline, an entire subfield of the "anthropology of Christianity" has been catalysed since the turn of the century by acknowledging the importance of the spread of Pentecostal movements across the global South.[13] More broadly, appreciation of Pentecostalism's significance within global Christianity has increased. The parochiality of the Euro-centric view of it as a "minority" or "fringe" faith has been exposed by statistics indicating that it makes up one of the largest sub-divisions of the Christian world, surpassed by Catholicism in total numbers but not in speed of growth.[14]

Such developments highlight the analytical interest but also the timeliness of this book. Authors refer to new waves of Pentecostal migration to Sweden, but do not present a simple story of mobile incomers and static hosts: rather, both are being reconstituted – not only by each other but also by wider economic and cultural forces that relativize the boundaries of national territories and religious, cultural and social affiliation in new ways. The interdisciplinary character of this volume and the project from which it has emerged shows the benefits of evaluating the effects of such Pentecostal influxes through multiple indices: ecclesiology, demography, theology, law, and varieties of lived urban experience. In the following, I want briefly to explore two areas where I think authors point us to important dimensions of the new religious landscape that is being formed: the city as variegated context; and Pentecostalism as heterogeneous institutional form. Both of these themes will lead me to the question of the "cosmopolitan".

We start with the city. While Stockholm emerges as a major character in this volume, it contains many personalities and expressions in its role as context for varied forms of Pentecostal activity. For instance, Émir Mahieddin directs our attention less to city centres and more in the direction of suburbs – supposedly peripheral contexts where diasporic communities are more likely to be able to gather, but also ideal locations for young Pentecostals to reach out and exercise socio-spiritual ambitions as they strive to become "missionaries in the concrete" (*betongmissionärer*). In an imaginative move, he then juxtaposes suburbia with the subway, the latter a classic "non-place"[15] of transit that provides a fertile stage for Pentecostal performances of urban evangelization that can be directed at the anonymized city. Meanwhile, Katarina Westerlund refers to church services but also to spaces and activities that range from soup kitchens to coffee houses, media broadcasts to the intimacies of home groups. Importantly, she shows how the city enables economies of scale in the gathering of ethnic minorities: for instance, City Church International (CCI) caters to a broadly African congregational clientele – people from Ghana, Kenya, Ethiopia, Tanzania, Sierra Leone, though also some from Asia – with English as their common language. While both of these chapters depict broadly centripetal Pentecostal activities, oriented toward different parts of Stockholm itself, Anders Bäckström reminds us that the city may also act as backdrop for more centrifugal dispositions as its diasporic communities keep hold of links with distant homes. Migrants themselves therefore seek to establish identities within their new country at the same time as they consciously retain cultural, moral, and familial orientations elsewhere, mediated through transnational ties of kinship and/or denominational affiliation.

What Stockholm offers, then, is less a single location and more a range of urban affordances, diffused across and sometimes encouraging links between different settings and scales of operation. Although the point is not made explicitly in this volume, we can assume that such settings – ranging across intensities of close association and almost complete anonymity, as well as varieties of bridging and bonding – enable Pentecostal identities to be foregrounded or backgrounded according to context and activity. We might also wonder whether there are some occasions when downtown Stockholm is self-consciously occupied by believers – however temporarily – as its streets are made into strategic places of mission or stages for migrants to assert urban presence and spiritual influence in their Pentecostal guises. My analogy here is with David Garbin's account of how African Pentecostal churches in London usually gather at the margins of London, yet also gain visibility by participating in public events (such as parades) that bring them not only into civic culture but also into the city centre.[16]

My reference to central Stockholm as a place of potential mission and/or re-enchantment draws on the most common sociological trope in depicting Pentecostal activity: that of conversion. This theme is certainly developed at various points in the volume. Mahieddin, for instance, refers to imageries of spiritual mapping and warfare. It also lies at the heart of much of the anthropological depiction of Pentecostalism as a religion of "rupture" in relation to pre-existing moral frameworks in its mission fields. However, I want to highlight the occasions when authors present Pentecostalism in another territorial mode, which I refer to as "hosting". The Pentecostal migrants who come to settle in Sweden are not only encountering a country renowned for its secularity but also a national context where a strong Pentecostal presence has been present for a century or so. In his historical account, Torbjörn Aronson traces the twentieth-century crystallization of a movement that grew by combining a congregationalist ecclesiology with acknowledgment of the powerful leadership of Lewi Pethrus. It is worth remembering that Pethrus supported the foundation of a national Pentecostal newspaper (*Dagen*) in 1945, a banking and insurance company in 1952, and the Christian Democratic Party in 1964, while Pingströrelsen has also been responsible for running folk high schools, a TV company, a missionary research institute, and a university college.[17] In a sense, these represent the structural scaffolding of a movement ostensibly oriented around the idealization of anti-structure. While the comparison should not be asserted too strongly, we might see Pingströrelsen as displaying parallels with the Church of Sweden as it faces challenges to elements of a de facto ecclesiastical monopoly within its sphere of operation: after all, the movement did not run a parish system as such but did support the idea of "one church in one city". Aronson and others show how contemporary, incoming Pentecostalists are creating new assemblages of practice that may or may not be encompassed within the older movement but are interestingly not creating a major institutional panic as they broaden the spatial and cultural range of Pentecostalist practice. In the 1980s, *Livets Ord* had caused trepidation by raising the spectre of taking over the "classical" Pentecostal movement from within, or at least by poaching its members. In the present, Pentecostal migrants may embody degrees of ethnic or even ritual difference but they do not raise the threatening spectre of "re-missionizing the missionaries".

I turn finally to the question of my title: whether Stockholm might be viewed as a "Pentecosmopolitan" city. The neologism comes from Obvious Katsaura and is inspired by his work on Lagos, a city brimming with churches and congregations.[18] For Katsaura, cosmopolitanism entails an openness to a world of difference and contrasts, enabled by extensive mobility, an "ability to interpret images of various others", and a capacity to culturally and geographically map one's location to a wider world.[19] As an eclectic, trans-local, polynucleated, movement, and one that – in theory – is in a constant state of becoming, Pentecostalism has the potential to "reverberate" (ibid.) cosmopolitanism as it takes numerous forms – and indeed Katsaura observes that Lagos's "pentecostal ecology" reflects a "paradoxical accommodation of denominational dominionism and denominational coexistence".[20]

Lagos is the epitome of a "Pentecostalite" city[21] in direct contrast to Stockholm, and the legal, cultural, and demographic profiles of the two could hardly be more different. Nonetheless, I think it is worthwhile juxtaposing Stockholm as religious context not only with London and Paris, as we see in this volume, but also with its West African counterpart. After all, in doing so, we are following the orientations of many diasporic Pentecostalists who find themselves based in Stockholm but imaginatively inhabiting at least two urban realms.[22] As this book shows, we need to comprehend Stockholm not only as the capital of a secular nation but also as a complex, variegated religious landscape, offering spiritual centres and peripheries, places of missionary publicness and anonymity, and opportunities for congregational boundary building as well as boundary traversing. In turn, we see Pentecostalism adopt many forms and orientations across this landscape: world-accommodating as well as world-conquering, hosting as well as missionizing, gaining stability through Pingströrelsen yet also fluidly diffusing into other forms – and arguably blowing both "hot" and "cold" in Anders Bäckström's vocabulary. It would be interesting to learn more about how different manifestations of such Pentecostalism(s) respond to the growing presence of Catholic and Orthodox Christians in the city. For the time being, we might profitably place Stockholm and Lagos on the same analytical map for a project dedicated to comparative Pentecosmopolitanisms. I believe that in doing so, we would also be working in the spirit of David Martin – making ourselves alert to varieties of religious expression across patterned but shifting temporal and cultural frameworks, and always aware of the complexities of not only of the secularization but also the Pentecostalization of the world.

Globalization, Place and the Religious-Secular Problem Space in Studying International Pentecostalism

Kim Knibbe

It is an honour to be asked to reflect on the findings presented in this edited volume. The combination of angles from which the phenomenon of international Pentecostalism in Sweden is approached is a unique strength of this volume. In the following, I will highlight several key themes, link them to the international literature on these themes, and discuss how the Swedish case, and the combination of perspectives in this book, throw new light on this.

The first of these themes is globalization and its relation to spatial practices such as mapping and place-making. As scholars have noted long ago, Pentecostalism and globalization have a strong "elective affinity" with each other.[23] It is embedded within its theology, as it were, but also within the practices developed within Pentecostalism, from the smallest prayer group where an outpouring of the spirit is experienced in the form of charismatic gifts, to the largest mega-church with slick church planting programmes and a (digital) media ministry (e.g. Hillsong).[24] As a postdoctoral researcher starting to research Nigerian-initiated Pentecostalism in Europe in 2007, this was immediately brought home to me by the incredibly strong drive evidenced by all the leaders I met to (re) Christianize Europe. A major focus of my research was the Redeemed Christian church of God, a Nigerian-initiated mega-church that has parishes all over the world. What struck me, in particular, was the ways this church mapped the world in order to develop a deliberate strategy, mobilizing people and resources to move across the world. Flying around the world was literally seen as an important mark of success[25]: during an all-night prayer meeting that I attended on the redemption camp near Lagos, with around half a million people present, the general overseer invited everyone to claim their wealth with an anecdote about his first second-hand car and how people asked him how his car was doing today. The story ended with his proclamation that "next year, people will be asking you 'how is your jet doing today?'!

Interestingly there is also the link between this globalizing outlook and prosperity teachings evident in this story, a link that has been examined deeply by many scholars who pioneered and established the field of Global Pentecostalism studies. However, I chose to focus on an aspect that at the time was much less a focus of research but happily is a strong focus in this edited volume: the ways such churches connected with local contexts. This led to a joint special issue titled "Spaces and Places in the Christian African Diaspora in the Netherlands" collecting the work of a group of ethnographers.[26] In this special issue, we focused on placemaking mapping and other spatial practices to examine the interactions between African-initiated Pentecostal churches and the cityscapes in which they established themselves.

The research project in this volume has taken this question to the Swedish context but has also taken this question a step further by including the "homegrown" churches in their analyses, as well as the sociological and legal contexts in which international churches have to find their way. By combining different disciplinary perspectives and expertise, we receive multidimensional insights that do not only inquire into the "other", the newcomers but also examine in detail how the existing religious landscape has been shaped historically. Striking here is the influence of national legal contexts, as is evident in Chapter 6 (by Victoria Enkvist), and the influence of church policies of denominations with a longer history in Sweden, as is evident in the chapter by Anders Backstrom. Chapter 5 (by Émir Mahieddin) in particular brings this kind of research further by tracing and interpreting the place-making practices of Pentecostals in Stockholm, showing in telling detail how they reimagine the urban landscape as the backdrop of their lives and mission as Pentecostals. As we found, and as he highlights as well, a focus on spatial practices highlights power differentials in quite unexpected ways, where a move to the margins is reimagined as a place from which Pentecostal power may build and spread.

Another theme that has often been discussed is the fate and relevance of the secularization thesis in light of the dynamic growth of Pentecostalism, as well as other religions worldwide, putting to shame those sociologists who predicted a decline of religion worldwide. This is discussed for Sweden in Chapter 2 (by Magdalena Nordin and Torbjörn Aronson) with admirable clarity. The findings there are in line with trends worldwide: secularization takes place among the major denominations, while other religious groups grow as well. From a global perspective, this is explained by the demographic advantage of religious people (they have more children).[27] However, there is another consequence of the simultaneous presence of both processes that I would like to highlight here because it has important consequences for the underlying concepts with which we work in studying phenomena such as that discussed in this book.

I would argue that the presence and vibrancy of international Pentecostal churches, as well as other religious denominations not discussed here, requires sociologists to question the methodological nationalism of their concepts and theories, and situate the contexts they wish to discuss more firmly as part of a postcolonial landscapes. This also implies a troubling distinction of native and immigrant that is still often wielded in sociological research. As Spronk and I argued recently "The concept of the secular brings into view how not only the religious 'other' is of interest, but also, or even more so, the cultural specificity of those cultural and institutional arrangements which are considered to be 'native', having passed through a process of secularization."[28] In addition, the simultaneous presence of both religious dynamism and secularization processes necessitates the deployment of perspectives that examine secularism and secularity as political, social, and cultural formations that shape the contexts in which this religious dynamism plays out. This has been elaborated extensively by the "multiple secularities" project led by Prof. Monika Wohlrab Sahr, for example.[29] As Asad pointed out many years ago, religion and the secular co-constitute each other.[30] This creates a "religious-secular problem space" as Agrama calls it,[31] in which what is religious and what is secular continuously has to be determined to find out how the religious should be contained, managed, or given rights and freedom. Such a conceptual shift also throws new light on questions of religious freedom.[32] Generally, intersections between religion and the secular become visible around specific themes, such as sexuality, as we have explored in the Netherlands, and issues to do with gender.[33] But also, again, when taking a spatial lens to the issue, as became visible in the process of urban renewal described by one of the articles of the special issue mentioned above: because of laws against financing churches, new facilities for churches could not be financed through municipal funds.[34]

Therefore, I would plead that this rich, multidimensional project represented in this book will be followed up with more focused "lived religion" and "lived secularity" research exploring the cultural encounters between international Pentecostal churches with not only Christian but also secular Swedish organizations and fields of practice.

Governing Religion – Encountering Law

Pamela Slotte Russo

One of the focuses of the research project in this volume has been the encounter between the Swedish justice system and the kind of religiosity that the Pentecostal movement embodies. The goal has been to find out if the legal protection of religious minorities and individuals is adequate, and if not, what the challenges are. The hypothesis has been that the encounter is not frictionless.

What kind of an encounter are we here talking about, and where does the encounter de facto take place? Apart from the many levels of law that regulate persons "on the move", religious minorities and their followers in Sweden live in a society "ruled by law". Not only "religion" is regulated, but also common life in many different respects, family life, work life, student life, etcetera. And also, religious life, which the project has wished to focus on: How does Swedish law order, constrain and shape religious life – and lived religion?

The project aimed to study a two-way process and how not least migrating Pentecostals both challenge and are influenced by Swedish "secular" society. When it comes to this two-way process, as it pertains to the legal dimensions of the project, the empirical material in terms of ethnographic material served as a point of departure. The law discussion is inspired by some reflections in the informants' narratives but is conducted on a more general level.[35] The analysis is largely based on an analysis of laws and their preparatory works, together with related inquiries (*utredningar*) and legal literature, and to a certain extent also relevant case law. It is thus more about "law on the books" than about "law in action", as well as about what we may to a high degree want to call the perspective of the Swedish state, public authorities, and majority society.

This analysis of the existing legal frames for the encounter (which to a certain extent includes a historical outlook) is, in turn, framed by a story about secularized Sweden. Swedish law of the land, influenced by international and European discussions and legal transplants, is understood to give expression to a kind of secular modernity that characterizes the national context. That all inhabitants enjoy freedom of religion also forms part of the narrative, and the secular is equated with neutrality and equal treatment etcetera.

As other research has shown, perceptions of the "secular" and the "religious" are interconnected.[36] Various chapters in this volume also together demonstrate how the way Swedish law approaches and regulates religion has a prehistory that still today affects the legal gaze.[37]

The idea is that the religiosity encountered in the studied Pentecostal congregations takes shapes that do not (entirely) tie in with "traditional Swedish" patterns. The way of practising religion can even conflict with the law of the land in different respects. To the extent that informants speak up in this volume, they also attest that how they want to live out their faith in everyday life appears partly foreign to Swedish society.

When it comes to the legal framework, the informants' posture comes across as ambivalent. Whereas freedom of religion as such is welcomed, state governance is not perceived as something undividedly positive. This is a well-known quandary also internationally.[38] Like other minority communities, Pentecostal congregations can apply for registration as a faith community. Among other things, this may bring with it financial advantages. However, simultaneously they will then come to have standing under Swedish law and in principle must conform to legislation applying to registered communities. This includes embracing and promoting certain "fundamental values of society". According to Enkvist, this raises the question if faith communities hereby are pressurized and expected to revise their creed and core activities in a way that is at odds with freedom of religion as this freedom is usually interpreted.

The question of why law has/takes on the role it does, and why the above-mentioned encounter is experienced in the way it is, has several dimensions. Things that are touched upon in this volume are the fundamental question of trust (in public authorities), inadequate communication on part of public authorities, but also insufficient insight into the Swedish legal system not least among those who have newly arrived in the country, for example, due to linguistic barriers. This makes it hard to demand and realize one's rights, to know how one is allowed to live out one's religion in Sweden in a meaningful and simultaneously, so to speak, legal manner. It can make it difficult to seize (all) the positive opportunities that the Swedish legal framework provides as regards freedom of religion and religious practice. Insufficient insight may also make it harder to critically address the need for legal reforms in certain respects.

In Chapter 6, Enkvist also underlines that Swedish legislation on religion – and this is also noticeable internationally – leaves great room for interpretation, not least since religion in itself is an open concept. This makes it hard to foresee what is required when it comes to following the law.

Simultaneously, Swedish legislation on religion has in another sense sooner a narrow rather than a broad focus. And this volume problematizes the categories with which law elaborates concerning religion, how the regulation itself is characterized, and the nature and purpose of state governance understood. Not least from a minority perspective, it is important to see the governance for what it is and to expose the consequences and how well – or poorly – law manages to pay regard to, acknowledge, and protect different religious positionings. For example, the gaze is directed towards the distinction between the private and the public that national and international freedom of religion legislation operates with, and which has also otherwise been thoroughly problematized in recent years.[39]

For sure, the forms that religious practice takes may fall within the scope of protection offered by other fundamental and human rights, like freedom of expression and freedom of association. However, additional theoretical perspectives could have deepened the analysis further and connected with a broader, including international, discussion. For example, Enkvist mentions that arguments focusing on tradition and culture are strongly in favour of majority religion. In the literature, this is today discussed in terms of culturalization, "the process by which practices, symbols, and groups that have previously been considered religious become classified as cultural or part of heritage".[40] Expressions of the "traditional", and "historical" religion of a land become spoken of in terms of "culture" and "heritage". What takes place is a kind of neutralization of (majority) religion, which legitimizes its continual presence in different (public) spaces, and which the authors of this volume also uncover and problematize in other ways.

An aspect of this culturalization of majority religion is that it may go hand in hand with a "religification" of minority positions, where religion becomes a primary marker of identity at the expense of other categories. This is maybe something that could have been explored even more in this volume, an intersectional perspective, although it is touched upon here and there in the chapters.

In future research it would be interesting to know even more about the encounter with the legal framework from the perspective of the examined groups and persons within them, and how they localize, describe, and evaluate the encounter and assess the adequacy of the legal framework. This would include learning more about their awareness of human rights protection of religious freedom and religious minority positions, and which concrete legal strategies they employ as a result of their awareness or lack of awareness (and self-definition as migrant community or not), including how such awareness of the international and national framework on religious freedom affect the choices they make about, for example, family matters like marriage, divorce, and inheritance. How do they navigate the challenges they encounter? Simply by "privatizing" religion, or are there openings for resistance and advocacy? In which sense is law a/the decisive factor and in which sense not when it comes to structuring how life and "religion" is lived?

Allan H. Anderson is an Emeritus Professor of Mission and Pentecostal Studies at, the Department of Theology and Religion, University of Birmingham, UK. Most recent monographs: *To the Ends of the Earth: Pentecostalism and the Transformation of World Christianity* (2013), *An Introduction to Pentecostalism* (2014), and *Spirit-Filled World: Religious Dis/Continuity in African Pentecostalism (2018).*

Simon Coleman is Chancellor Jackman Professor at the Department for the Study of Religion, University of Toronto. His research interests include the globalization of Pentecostalism, the Prosperity Gospel, and pilgrimage. He has conducted fieldwork in Sweden, Nigeria, and the United Kingdom. Among his books are *The Globalisation of Charismatic Christianity* (2000), *The Anthropology of Global Pentecostalism and Evangelicalism* (2015, edited with Rosalind Hackett), and *Powers of Pilgrimage: Religion in a World of Movement* (2022). Simon is co-editor of the journal *Religion and Society* and of the book series Routledge Studies in Pilgrimage, Religious Travel and Tourism.

Kim Knibbe is an Associate Professor of Sociology and Anthropology of Religion at the University of Groningen. She has conducted research and published on Pentecostalism, contemporary spirituality, and Catholicism. Recent publications include a special issue on Theorizing sexuality, religion, and secularity in postcolonial Europe, co-edited with Rachel Spronk. Findings from her recent research project have also informed the free online course "Religion and Sexual Wellbeing. Pleasure, Piety and Reproductive rights".

Pamela Slotte Russo is a Professor of religion and law at the Åbo Akademi University and Vice-director of the Centre of Excellence in Law, Identity, and the European Narratives at the University of Helsinki, Finland. She is also a McDonald Distinguished Senior Fellow of Law and Religion at Emory Law School, Atlanta, United States. Among her recent publications are the co-edited volumes *Christianity and International Law: an Introduction* (Cambridge University Press, 2021) and *Internationalization and Re-Confessionalization: Law and Religion in the Nordic Realm 1945-2017* (University Press of Southern Denmark, 2022).

Notes

1 The project is located at the Center for Multidisciplinary Research on Religion and Society at Uppsala University (CRS). Associate professor in Church History Torbjörn Aronson, professor emeritus in Ecclesiology Sven-Erik Brodd, professor emeritus in Sociology of Religion Anders Bäckström, associate professor in Public Law Victoria Enkvist, fil. dr. in anthropology Emir Mahieddin, professor in Sociology of Religion Magdalena Nordin, and professor in practical theology Katarina Westerlund participated in the research project. https://crs.uu.se/forskning/pentecostal--migrants-in-secular-sweden. This volume presents results from the research project.
2 Allan Heaton Anderson, *To the Ends of the Earth: Pentecostalism and the Transformation of World Christianity* (Oxford: Oxford University Press, 2013), ch. 4; Allan H. Anderson, *An Introduction to Pentecostalism: Global Charismatic Christianity*, 2nd edition (Cambridge: Cambridge University Press, 2014), ch. 2.
3 Anderson, *To the Ends of the Earth*, ch. 8; Anderson, *An Introduction to Pentecostalism*, ch. 6.
4 Walter J. Hollenweger, *Pentecostalism: Origins and Developments Worldwide* (Peabody, MA: Hendrickson, 1997), pp. 18–19.
5 Malcolm J. C. Calley, *God's People: West Indian Pentecostal Sects in England* (Oxford: Oxford University Press, 1965).
6 Caleb Opoku Nyanni, The Spirits, and Transition: The Second Generation and the Church of Pentecost-UK, PhD, University of Birmingham, 2018.
7 Afeosemime U. Adogame, *The African Christian Diaspora: New Currents and Emerging Trends in World Christianity* (London: Bloomsbury, 2013), pp. 169–189.
8 M. Dempster, D. Byron and Douglas Petersen, *The Globalization of Pentecostalism: A Religion Made to Travel* (Eugene, OR: Wipf and Stock Publisher, 2011). We might also think of the title of Pentecostal studies scholar Allan Heaton Anderson's 2013 book, *To the Ends of the Earth: Pentecostalism and the Transformation of World Christianity* - a text that emphasizes the significance of Pentecostalism as "a missionary, polycentric, transnational religion" (p. 1).
9 On individualism and collectivism in the "Swedish Model" see Å. Daun, "Individualism and Collectivity among Swedes", *Ethnos* 56(3–4) (1991), pp. 165–172.

10. Simon Coleman, *The Globalisation of Charismatic Christianity: Spreading the Gospel of Prosperity* (Cambridge: Cambridge University Press, 2000).
11. See e.g. https://sd.se/vad-vi-vill for information on policies of the Sweden Democrats.
12. H. Agrama, *Questioning Secularism: Islam, Sovereignty, and the Rule of Law in Modern Egypt* (Chicago, IL: University of Chicago Press, 2012).
13. J. Robbins, "The Anthropology of Christianity: Unity, Diversity, New Directions", *Current Anthropology* 55(S10) (2014), pp. 157–171.
14. For figures, see for instance www.pewresearch.org/religion/2011/12/19/global-christianity-exec.
15. N. Augé, *Non-Places: An Introduction to Supermodernity* (London: Verso, 1995).
16. D. Garbin, "Marching for God in the Global City: Public Space, Religion and Diasporic Identities in a Transnational African Church", *Culture and Religion* 13(4) (2012), pp. 425–447.
17. J.-Å. Alvarsson, "Research on Pentecostalism in Sweden", *Approaching Religion* 5(1) (2015), pp. 16–30.
18. O. Katsaura, "Pentecosmopolis: On the Pentecostal Cosmopolitanism of Lagos", *Religion* 50(4) (2020), pp. 504–528.
19. Ibid., p. 505.
20. Ibid., p. 506.
21. B. Meyer, "'Praise the Lord': Popular Cinema and Pentecostalite Style in Ghana's New Public Sphere", *American Ethnologist* 31 (2004).
22. S. Coleman and K. Maier, "Redeeming the City: Creating and Traversing 'London-Lagos'", *Religion* 43(3) (2013), pp. 353–364.
23. David Martin, *Pentecostalism: The World Their Parish* (Wiley-Blackwell, 2002); Allan Anderson et al., *Studying Global Pentecostalism: Theories and Methods* (Berkeley, CA: University of California Press, 2010).
24. Miranda Klaver, "Mediatized Christianity", in Miranda Klaver (ed.), *Hillsong Church: Expansive Pentecostalism, Media, and the Global City* (Cham: Springer International Publishing, 2021), https://doi.org/10.1007/978-3-030-74299-7_8, pp. 211–225.
25. Kim Knibbe, "'We Did Not Come Here as Tenants, but as Landlords': Nigerian Pentecostals and the Power of Maps", *African Diaspora* 2(2) (2009), pp. 133–158.
26. Kim Knibbe and Marten van der Meulen, "The Role of Spatial Practices and Locality in the Constituting of the Christian African Diaspora", *African Diaspora* 2 (September 2009), pp. 125–130, https://doi.org/10.1163/187254509X12477244375012.
27. Pew Forum on Religion and Public Life, *The Future of World Religions: Population Growth Projections, 2010-2050* (Pew Research Center, 2 April 2015), www.pewforum.org/2015/04/02/religious-projections-2010-2050; Pippa Norris and Ronald Inglehart, *Sacred and Secular: Religion and Politics Worldwide* (Cambridge: Cambridge University Press, 2004).
28. Kim Knibbe and Rachel Spronk, "Theorizing Sexuality, Religion, and Secularity in Postcolonial Europe", *New Diversities* 24(2) (2022), https://doi.org/10.58002/8mrz-2v55, pp. 2–12.
29. Monika Wohlrab-Sahr and Marian Burchardt, "Multiple Secularities: Toward a Cultural Sociology of Secular Modernities", *Comparative Sociology* 11(6) (2012), https://doi.org/10.1163/15691330-12341249, pp. 875–909.
30. Talal Asad, *Formations of the Secular: Christianity, Islam, Modernity* (Stanford, CA: Stanford University Press, 2003).
31. Hussein Ali Agrama, "Reflections on Secularism, Democracy, and Politics in Egypt", *American Ethnologist* 39(1) (February 2012), https://doi.org/10.1111/j.1548-1425.2011.01342.x, pp. 26–31.

32 Pamela E. Klassen, "Contraception and the Coming of Secularism. Reconsidering Reproductive Freedom as Religious Freedom", in Birgitte Schepelern Johansen Scheer and Nadia Fadil (eds), *Secular Bodies, Affects and Emotions: European Configurations* (London: Bloomsbury Publishing, 2019).
33 Joan Wallach Scott, *Sex and Secularism* (Princeton, NJ: Princeton University Press, 2017); Kim Knibbe, "Secularist Understandings of Pentecostal Healing Practices in Amsterdam: Developing an Intersectional and Post-Secularist Sociology of Religion", *Social Compass* 65(5) (2018), https://doi.org/10.1177/0037768618800418, pp. 650–666.
34 Marten van der Meulen, "The Continuing Importance of the Local. African Churches and the Search for Worship Space in Amsterdam", *African Diaspora* 2(2) (2009), pp. 159–181.
35 In addition, this volume offers an account of organizational changes within the Pentecostal movement in Sweden adjacent to changes in Swedish legislation concerning religious communities and the Church of Sweden. See Chapter 3 in this volume.
36 See e.g. Asad, *Formations of the Secular*.
37 To what extent this prehistory is specifically *Swedish* remains unsaid.
38 See e.g. Jeroen Temperman, "Recognition, Registration, and Autonomy of Religious Groups: European Approaches and their Human Rights Implications", in David Kirkham (ed.), *State Responses to Religious Minorities* (Aldershot: Ashgate, 2013), pp. 151–165.
39 See e.g. Peter G. Danchin, "The Tangled Law and Politics of Religious Freedom", *Santa Clara Journal of International Law* 10 (2012), pp. 73–91; Pamela Slotte, "The Religious and the Secular in European Human Rights Discourse", *Finnish Yearbook of International Law* 21 (2012), pp. 231–286.
40 Teemu Taira and Lori Beaman, "Majoritarian Religion, Cultural Justification and Nonreligion: Finland in the International Context", *Temenos - Nordic Journal of Comparative Religion* 58(2) (2022), p. 194. See also e.g. Avi Astor and Damon Mayrl, "Culturalized Religion: A Synthetic Review and Agenda for Research", *Journal for the Scientific Study of Religion* 59(2) (2020), pp. 209–226.

Bibliography

Adogame, Afeosemime U. *The African Christian Diaspora: New Currents and Emerging Trends in World Christianity*. London: Bloomsbury, 2013.
Agrama, H. *Questioning Secularism: Islam, Sovereignty, and the Rule of Law in Modern Egypt*. Chicago, IL: University of Chicago Press, 2012.
Agrama, Hussein Ali. "Reflections on Secularism, Democracy, and Politics in Egypt." *American Ethnologist* 39(1) (2012), pp. 26–31. https://doi.org/10.1111/j.1548-1425.2011.01342.x.
Alvarsson, J-Å. "Research on Pentecostalism in Sweden." *Approaching Religion* 5(1) (2015), pp. 16–30.
Anderson, Allan Heaton. *An Introduction to Pentecostalism: Global Charismatic Christianity*, 2nd edition. Cambridge: Cambridge University Press, 2014.
Anderson, Allan Heaton. *To the Ends of the Earth: Pentecostalism and the Transformation of World Christianity*. Oxford: Oxford University Press, 2013.
Anderson, Allan, Michael Bergunder, Andre F. Droogers and Cornelis van der Laan. *Studying Global Pentecostalism: Theories and Methods*. Berkeley, CA: University of California Press, 2010.
Asad, Talal. *Formations of the Secular: Christianity, Islam, Modernity*. Stanford, CA: Stanford University Press, 2003.

Astor, Avi and Damon Mayrl. "Culturalized Religion: A Synthetic Review and Agenda for Research." *Journal for the Scientific Study of Religion* 59(2) (2020).
Augé, N. *Non-Places: An Introduction to Supermodernity*. London: Verso, 1995.
Calley, Malcolm J. C. *God's People: West Indian Pentecostal Sects in England*. Oxford: Oxford University Press, 1965.
Coleman, Simon. *The Globalisation of Charismatic Christianity: Spreading the Gospel of Prosperity*. Cambridge: Cambridge University Press, 2000.
Coleman, S. and K. Maier. "Redeeming the City: Creating and Traversing 'London-Lagos'." *Religion* 43(3) (2013), pp. 353–364.
Danchin, Peter G. "The Tangled Law and Politics of Religious Freedom." *Santa Clara Journal of International Law* 10 (2012), pp, 73–91.
Daun, Å. "Individualism and Collectivity among Swedes." *Ethnos* 56(3–4) (1991), pp. 165–172.
Dempster, M., D. Byron and Douglas Petersen. *The Globalization of Pentecostalism: A Religion Made to Travel*. Eugene, OR: Wipf & Stock, 2011.
Garbin, D. "Marching for God in the Global City: Public Space, Religion and Diasporic Identities in a Transnational African Church." *Culture and Religion* 13(4) (2012), pp. 425–447.
Hollenweger, Walter J. *Pentecostalism: Origins and Developments Worldwide*. Peabody, MA: Hendrickson, 1997.
Katsaura, O. "Pentecosmopolis: On the Pentecostal Cosmopolitanism of Lagos." *Religion* 50(4) (2020), pp. 504–528.
Klassen, Pamela E. "Contraception and the Coming of Secularism: Reconsidering Reproductive Freedom as Religious Freedom." In Birgitte Schepelern Johansen Scheer and Nadia Fadil (eds), *Secular Bodies, Affects and Emotions. European Configurations*. London: Bloomsbury Publishing, 2019.
Klaver, Miranda. "Mediatized Christianity." In Miranda Klaver (ed.), *Hillsong Church: Expansive Pentecostalism, Media, and the Global City*, 211–225. Palgrave Studies in Lived Religion and Societal Challenges. Cham: Springer International Publishing, 2021. https://doi.org/10.1007/978-3-030-74299-7_8.
Knibbe, Kim. "Secularist Understandings of Pentecostal Healing Practices in Amsterdam: Developing an Intersectional and Post-Secularist Sociology of Religion." *Social Compass* 65(5) (2018), pp. 650–666. https://doi.org/10.1177/0037768618800418.
Knibbe, Kim. "'We Did Not Come Here as Tenants, but as Landlords': Nigerian Pentecostals and the Power of Maps." *African Diaspora* 2(2) (2009), pp. 133–158.
Knibbe, Kim and Marten van der Meulen. "The Role of Spatial Practices and Locality in the Constituting of the Christian African Diaspora." *African Diaspora* 2 (September 2009), pp. 125–130. https://doi.org/10.1163/187254509X12477244375012.
Knibbe, Kim and Rachel Spronk. "Theorizing Sexuality, Religion, and Secularity in Postcolonial Europe." *New Diversities* 24(2) (2022), pp. 2–12. https://doi.org/10.58002/8mrz-2v55.
Martin, David. *Pentecostalism: The World Their Parish*. Wiley-Blackwell, 2002.
Martin, David. *A General Theory of Secularization*. New York: Harper & Row, 1978.
Martin, David. *Tongues of Fire: The Explosion of Protestantism in Latin America*. Oxford: Wiley-Blackwell, 1990.
Martin, David. *Pentecostalism: The World Their Parish*. Oxford: Wiley Blackwell, 2001.
Meulen, Marten van der. "The Continuing Importance of the Local. African Churches and the Search for Worship Space in Amsterdam." *African Diaspora* 2(2) (2009), pp. 159–181.

Norris, Pippa and Ronald Inglehart. *Sacred and Secular: Religion and Politics Worldwide*. Cambridge: Cambridge University Press, 2004.

Meyer, B. ""Praise the Lord": Popular Cinema and Pentecostalite Style in Ghana's New Public Sphere", *American Ethnologist* 31(1) (2004), pp. 92–110.

Nyanni, Caleb Opoku. The Spirits and Transition: The Second Generation and the Church of Pentecost-UK. PhD, University of Birmingham, 2018.

Pew Forum on Religion and Public Life. *The Future of World Religions: Population Growth Projections, 2010-2050*. Pew Research Center, 2 April 2015. www.pewforum.org/2015/04/02/religious-projections-2010-2050.

Robbins, J. "The Anthropology of Christianity: Unity, Diversity, New Directions." *Current Anthropology* 55(S10) (2014), pp. 157–171.

Scott, Joan Wallach. *Sex and Secularism*. Princeton, NJ: Princeton University Press, 2017.

Slotte, Pamela. "The Religious and the Secular in European Human Rights Discourse." *Finnish Yearbook of International Law* 21 (2012), pp. 231–286.

Taira, Teemu and Lori Beaman. "Majoritarian Religion, Cultural Justification and Nonreligion: Finland in the International Context." *Temenos - Nordic Journal of Comparative Religion* 58(2) (2022), pp. 193–216.

Temperman, Jeroen. "Recognition, Registration, and Autonomy of Religious Groups: European Approaches and their Human Rights Implications." In David Kirkham (ed.), *State Responses to Religious Minorities*. Aldershot: Ashgate, 2013.

Wohlrab-Sahr, Monika and Marian Burchardt. "Multiple Secularities: Toward a Cultural Sociology of Secular Modernities." *Comparative Sociology* 11(6) (2012), pp. 875–909. https://doi.org/10.1163/15691330-12341249.

Index

Arab/Arabic viii, 3, 47, 62–63, 65–68, 70, 78, 81–83, 85, 87–88, 99, 131
assimilation 39, 42, 48, 98, 121

Catholic 1, 7, 11, 16, 19, 21–22, 26–29
church plants/church planting 41–42, 44–47
civil society 106, 118, 128
congregationalism 7, 44–45, 47, 48, 52, 141,
constitution 6, 97, 100–101, 103, 109, 112, 121–122
cosmopolitan 9, 10, 78, 90, 118, 123–124, 145–147
counter-places 8, 79, 81, 97

democracy viii, 5, 100, 102–104, 109, 112, 120, 124–129
denomination 15, 21–25, 28, 37, 40, 42–44, 46–47, 51, 107, 110, 140–143, 145, 147, 149
desecularization 7, 15–18, 30, 44
discrimination 38, 64–65, 67, 69, 72, 123

ecclesiology 7, 9, 37, 39, 40, 42–45, 48–49, 51–52, 141, 145–146
European Convention on Human Rights 97, 101–102, 121
existential 123

family 4, 50, 65–68, 70–72, 118–121, 124, 129, 131, 140, 150, 152
free church 2, 7, 21–24, 26–29, 37, 44, 46–47, 86
freedom of expression 6, 8, 97, 101–102, 152
freedom of religion 6, 7, 11, 96–97, 100–103, 105, 108–111, 150–151

gender 4, 16–17, 67, 120, 124–125, 129–130, 140, 149

identity 1, 6, 9–10, 29, 66–70, 72, 89, 98, 123, 129, 131, 140, 143, 152
immigrant 7–8, 17, 19, 24–29, 38–39, 47–49, 51–53, 78, 81–82, 84, 87, 119, 120, 131, 139–142, 149
immigration viii, 7, 10, 16–17, 23, 26, 29–30, 38–40, 49, 50, 52, 85
institutionalized 5, 11, 60–61
integration viii, 2, 7, 27, 30, 38–39, 41, 42, 44, 48–49, 52, 72, 84, 98, 102, 105, 118–119, 121, 124, 131, 141
intolerance 64–65
Islam 18, 81–83, 85, 98–99, 140

Kingdom of God 71–72

late modernity 118
lived religion 8–9, 61–64, 68–72, 150, 119–120, 150
Lutheran 5, 15, 23, 44, 60, 85, 121

mega-churches 24, 130
migrant world values survey 124
minority groups 39, 97, 99, 102, 106, 121
mission/missionaries 8, 9, 23, 25, 30, 37, 43–44, 47, 63, 68–69, 70–71, 79–82, 84, 87–90, 123, 126, 129, 131, 139, 142–143, 145–147, 149
mobility 4, 10–11, 69, 89–90, 97–99, 129, 143, 147
multicultural 118–120, 129, 143
Muslim 1, 3, 15, 37, 80–83, 85, 97–98, 119, 122, 124

neutrality 97, 105–108, 129, 150
neo-Charismatic 1, 40, 50, 140
neo-nationalism 118
Nordic viii, 4, 119–120, 130
norms 10–11, 63, 67, 121

Orthodox 1, 7, 11, 15, 19, 21–22, 26–29, 122, 139, 143, 147

Pentephobia 123
practical theology 3, 61, 69
prejudice 64–65, 69–70

racism 11, 140
refugees 25, 38, 48–49, 84, 86, 118, 123
Roma 38, 48, 51
rule of law 103–104, 112, 120

Sami 38, 52
secularization vii, ix, 4–7, 9, 17–18, 30, 60, 118, 122, 127, 130, 139, 142, 144, 147, 149
segregation 38, 39, 72
spirituality 6, 8, 39, 42, 45, 62–63, 70–71, 123, 130, 142
stereotyping 4, 65

tolerance 4, 127, 130,
transdenominational 42
transnational 42, 46–47, 52, 98, 117, 131, 143, 144–145

World Values Survey 4, 120, 124

xenophobia 86

www.ingramcontent.com/pod-product-compliance
Lightning Source LLC
Chambersburg PA
CBHW061245230426
43662CB00020B/2431